Land's

O'Groats

The Great British Bike Adventure

by Phil Horsley

An Essential Guide for the Touring Cyclist

ISBN 1 871890 08 X

British Library Cataloguing in Publication Data
A catalogue record for this book is available from the British Library

Both the author and publisher have made great efforts in the compilation of this guide book. However, as it is the work of human beings and the routes can change, errors and discrepancies cannot be ruled out. Therefore, no guarantee can be given for the accuracy of every piece of information. No legal liability is accepted for any accidents or damages sustained for whatever reason.

All trade enquiries to:
CORDEE, 3a De Montfort Street, Leicester LE1 7HD

Cover photographs by: Tim Hughes (Cyclographic)

This book is available from specialist equipment shops and major booksellers. It can, along with a large selection of cycling guides and maps be obtained direct from the publishers. Please write for a copy of our comprehensive stocklist of outdoor recreation/sports, travel books and maps.

CONTENTS

MAP KEY

Recommended Route – 'A' Roads

Recommended Route – Other Roads

Recommended Route – Cycle Tracks

Pub or Hotel

Café

S Shop

Camping Site

Tourist Information Centre

YHA or SYHA Hostel

Railway Station

Church

Castle

Place of Interest

INTRODUCTION

As you float into the bar of the John O'Groats House Hotel, or the State House Hotel at Lands End, and receive the congratulations, the sense of achievement is terrific. You've done it, the 'End to End', 'Cornwall to Caithness', 'the Great British Bike Ride'[1], Lands End to John O'Groats, the ultimate road ride in Britain, and the dream of cyclists since the invention of the Penny-farthing. For many riders the achievement is satisfaction enough, as they combine speed and endurance to cover the distance in seven days or less. For others the sense of achievement is complemented by exploration. If your dream includes discovering the romance and the rainbows, the nooks and the crannies which are part of today's Britain, as you follow the wheelmarks of a century of 'End to Enders', then this book is for you.

My childhood memories are of newspaper reports of a road littered with men in tutus pushing prams, cyclists with broken-winged seagulls on handlebar cages, and Jimmy Savile. The reality is not so different. Mike Day and Michael Areb rode it on unicycles in l4 days [l986]; Arvind Pandya ran it backwards in 26 days [1990]; a McDonnell F-4K Phantom jet did it in 46 minutes 44 seconds in 1988. The men's bicycle record is held by Andy Wilkinson, 1 day 21 hours, 2 minutes [1990], and the women's by Pauline Strong (2 days:6:49).

Most 'feat' riders use the main roads [A30, A38, A6, A7, A9]. These are fast and direct. They are also smelly, noisy and dangerous, and the routes chosen for this book avoid them wherever possible. Instead this Guide takes you along 'B' roads, quiet roads and cycle paths, along valleys heady with the aromas of summer, and exuberant with birdsong, alongside lochs turning golden with the sunset, the home of seal, eagle and deer, and dotted, at frequent intervals, with cafes and pubs bursting with locals eager to share the thrills of the day.

THE 'JAZZ ROUTE'

Soon after the development of the Ordinary, or Penny-farthing, bicycle in the early 1870's, the push was on for 'trying the experiment of a bicycle ride from the Lands End to John O'Groats House' [2]. The first men credited with the run were H. Blackwell and C.A. Harman, taking thirteen days in July 1880. It is worth noting that the first officially recognised run by a woman, Lilian Dredge, was not until 1938 [3].

In these early days cyclists had to contend with roads which had been neglected due to the popularity of the railways. They were rough, often dusty or mucky and covered in dung. Many Victorians, too, saw the bicycle as a menace, it being the fastest thing on the roads, and quiet compared to the horse. Ion Keith-Falconer, sarcastically, referred to his ride in 1882 as a 'walking tour' so frequently did he have to push his machine [4]. Even in 1929 the main danger on the roads seems to have been posed by rabbits, and it wasn't until the 1950's that delays caused by traffic became a problem for End-to-End record breakers.

The record for a solo cycle was down to 6 days, 16 hours, 7 minutes in 1885 [James Lennox of Dumfries], under 4 days by 1905, under 3 days in 1908 and under 2 days for the first time in 1965 [Dick Poole]. Record attempts became increasingly sophisticated, and, in 1937 Sid Ferris was followed by a lorry-borne bed, of which he is reported to have made occasional use [5].

The account of his own ride by W.B. Dawson in 1933 makes an interesting comparison with today, for the ride was only possible due to his enforced idleness in the Depression. He carried few maps, finding directions by asking the 'natives', a task made difficult by the large number of fellow travellers on the roads, looking for work, begging or tramps. He, of course, met lots of cyclists, as was the norm in those days, and was particularly impressed by tradesmen's boys who could 'plunge on the pedals like steam hammers', and not at all impressed by record-breakers. 'It is not right that this great road should be a race-course, a kind of jazz route. Surely a highway that stretches the length of England and Scotland must be full of interest'. Scotland scared him stiff with its' strangeness, and 'I ran into Wick with the feeling that everyone knew where I was going'. [6]

Each summer hardly a day goes by without cyclists riding into either of the respective 'Ends' with a heightened sense of achievement and discovery, many also raise considerable sums for charity, though few cyclists these days attempt to go for the record.

DREAM TO REALITY

It's a long way. Some record breakers reduced the total distance to 861 miles, though Ion Keith-Falconer rode 994 miles. The route in this book is 977 miles long. On the other hand there are no rules to say you must average 50 or 100 miles a day, or even do the trip in one go. There is no official route. Indeed it is part of the fun to lay out the maps on a dark winter's night and dream about the journey.

Each cyclist has their own constraints; the time available, their bank balance, aunts in Weston-super-Mare they promised to drop in on, their fitness and their bike. There is no point in including here details of an essential 40-piece tool kit if your method of mending a puncture begins with flagging down a passing motorist. These notes are intended to help you turn the dream to reality.

YOUR BIKE

Aim for comfort and efficiency. Most of the cycling will be on roads or good quality cycle tracks, so you don't need off-road tyres or an off-road frame. Dropped handlebars and a well-balanced touring frame allow a variety of riding positions and distribute the body weight over the bike more efficiently, improving stability and riding position. Padded foam sleeves on the handlebars or padded cycling mitts reduce strain on the hands. A comfortable saddle is a must, but not easy to find, especially for women. Leather or plastic covered with leather are usually recommended because they are cooler and can mould to your shape. Toe clips help to keep your feet on the pedals, and mudguards are essential to avoid the 'black stripe' up your back. Distribute your gear on front and rear panniers.

The three most common mechanical problems are punctures, worn brakes and broken spokes. Avoid punctures by using high-pressure tyres inflated hard, but roadside repairs are easier if you carry a spare inner tube. Don't forget the pump. Keep an eye on wear on the brake blocks and regularly adjust appropriately.

Carrying a load increases the danger of broken spokes. Even if you don't know how to replace one, or are reluctant to carry the tools to remove the freewheel sprockets, it is a good idea to carry a spoke key to get you to the next bike shop, and a couple of spare spokes of the correct sizes [taped to your frame] for them to use if they are out of your size. Your tool kit should also include allen keys and spanners to fit your bike, a puncture repair kit, tyre levers, a spare bowden cable to replace a broken gear or brake cable, and a lubricant (WD40 or equivalent) for regular use on bearings and chain.

YOUR BODY

You don't have to be super-fit. Your fitness will improve as the days go by, but Cornwall and Devon are hilly, so keep in perspective your expectations at the beginning.

Look after your body as you would your bike. Contrary to popular opinion, chocolates and sweets do not provide the energy you need. You are much better off with carbohydrates. More muesli, porridge and beans on toast and less sugar and grease. Snack on nuts, raisins, dried fruit, bananas, flapjacks etc. Carry water and keep your liquid level up before you become thirsty. In hot weather excessive sweating may lead to a shortage of salt, which will need replacing.

YOUR GEAR

Lists of gear are easy to make. What is not so easy is crossing off your list things you will regret bringing half way up a hill on a hot afternoon. You don't really need to saw your toothbrush in half, but question every item. For example, although I usually camp I rarely carry a stove, fuel and cooking utensils, preferring to eat 'cold', or go to the pub for a meal. Having said that, here are some thoughts about gear.

Shoes How about those dual purpose cycling/walking shoes/trainers, with a firm sole.

Clothes Clothes need to be comfortable and keep you warm, and be able to dry easily if they become wet. Custom-designed cycling gear doesn't look great off a bike but is very comfortable on it. Shirts and jackets need to be long at the back to avoid those draughty waistline gaps.

Helmet The best helmets have a hard outer shell and adjustable inner padding, and are well ventilated. There is plenty of pressure these days to wear them, but the choice is still yours.

Raingear The choice is a personal one, between cape, ordinary waterproofs and expensive Goretex or equivalent. Don't forget the waterproof overshoes. Keep those pinkies dry and warm.

And also If you are camping don't forget the insulating mat, and 'space blankets' (survival blankets) are amazingly warm and light. Do you need wax earplugs, a Sam Browne reflective belt, a bungee cord, a lock for your bike? When you reach the Scottish border, midge repellent is handy.

CYCLING UP OR DOWN?

Don't let anyone tell you that if you start at Lands End, it is uphill all the way. Most cyclists travel south to north and a whole catalogue of reasons have been put forward to justify this. Two of these have some merit. Inclement weather does come from the south-west rather more often than it comes from any other direction, at least in England, and Land's End in the summer is a good place to leave and not one to aim for. A lot of tosh is talked about Scottish weather being better in August than May; about the grouse-shooting season; and about the mountainous ascents in Scotland. The pleasure is just as great riding End-to-End in reverse. Nevertheless, this Guide is written south-north, though it can, of course, be used backwards.

HOW LONG WILL IT TAKE?

This depends not only on your fitness and the weight you carry, but also whether you prioritise the feat or the fun of the trip. If you want to do it in seven days you probably would not choose this route, and you will be going like the clappers, all day, everyday. Most cyclists will spend two or three weeks on the trip, but if you have the time and the inclination, why rush it? After all, how many times in your life will you cycle from Lands End to John O'Groats?

ACCOMMODATION : THE 'SAVOY' OR THE 'SURVIVAL BAG'

Bed and breakfast accommodation lists are obtainable from the Ramblers Association, the CTC, some of the long-distance walking Path Associations, and from Tourist Boards. Please consult the appendix to this book. Local Tourist Information Centres will have up-to-the-minute information on vacant accommodation, and many operate a 'book-a-bed-ahead' scheme.

Youth hostels of the YHA and SYHA on or adjacent to this route are listed, as are independent hostels and camping barns. The telephone numbers are given. The location of camp sites is shown on the route maps. Rough camping in Scotland is much easier than south of the border.

TRAVELLING TO AND FROM THE 'ENDS'

For those who have a partner or friend willing to drive to both ends to collect you and your bike, read no further. The only realistic option, apart from cycling home, is the train.

For the next few years the future operation of the railways is unclear, and such aspects as the carriage of cycles on trains are not high on the priorities of prospective train operators. All you can do is to check the situation with British Rail, private operators or your travel agent prior to setting out.

Railway lines run to Penzance in Cornwall, with connections to most large cities in Britain, and to Wick and Thurso in Caithness. From both the line runs to Inverness to connect with trains to Glasgow and Edinburgh. On most trains the number of cycles able to be carried is limited, so it makes sense to book in advance, if you can, the carriage of your bike. A fee of £3 a day is payable. Most train 'guards' are as accomodating as they are able to be. This Guide gives route directions from Penzance to Lands End, and from John O'Groats to Wick and Thurso.

SUPPORTING ORGANISATIONS

The CTC [Cyclists' Touring Club] is Britain's largest cycling association with around forty thousand members. Three 'Lands End to John O'Groats' route itineraries are available free of charge to members, a Main Road route, a Youth Hostel route on minor roads, and a B and B route, again on minor roads, all three around a thousand miles in length. Also available on completion of the ride are a Certificate and cloth badge.

The CTC exists to promote cycling as a means of transport and travel, and to protect cyclists' interests. A whole package of information and services is available to members: including touring information, technical advice, a mail-order service for maps, books and clothing, cycle and travel insurance and a local group network. Contact the CTC at Cotterell House, 69 Meadrow, Godalming, Surrey, GU7 3HS, Tel (01483) 417217, Fax (01483) 426994.

The Land's End – John O'Groats Association is open to anyone who has completed the journey from End to End by any means of transport. With four hundred plus members, the Association exists to help organise attempts in aid of charity, and for social purposes. The Secretary is Mrs Carol Webb, 25 Langdon Way, Coringham, Stanford-le-Hope, Essex, SS17 9DS, Tel (01375) 679036, and the two route advisers are Colin Jones, 33 Constance Road, Northwick, Worcester, WR3 7NF and Colin Jordan, Rosemary Cottage, 34 Churchill Lane, Powick, Worcester, WR2 4QS.

HAZARDS

Rain Even in Scotland rain rarely lasts as long as twenty-four hours. Remember, being warm and wet is infinitely preferable to being cold and wet, and, most of all, make good use of plastic dustbin liners in your panniers to keep things dry. The Strathclyde police have been known to wear them under their uniforms, so they must work.

Sun Don't forget the sunblock for your nose and a lightweight cap for your head. Take a tip from the Tour de France riders.

Wildlife Panicking deer have been known to leap out in front of cyclists, and I have known a puncture from running over an (already dead) hedgehog. Cows instinctively mistrust bicycles, so if you meet a herd of milkers, pull over and let them by, and look for the cow with a perfect map of the world on its hide. That leaves only dogs and midges.

The sight of a pack of German Shepherds or Collies, fangs bared, jaws drooling, making all speed towards you, can be unnerving. I'm told the answer is not to panic, but to cruise slowly by uttering soothing expressions of canine affection, or even to dismount and push. Somehow, with me, this gets lost in translation, and usually my voice does an impression of Attila the Hun as a Drill Sergeant and my legs turn to water. There are anti-dog sprays you can buy and I'm told a squeeze of your water bottle between the eyes works wonders.

Even the most rabid Rottweiler is nought compared to the midge, which breeds in profusion as soon as the Scottish border is crossed. Fortunately they are not keen on too much sun or wind, but love those mellow evenings with the sun setting in the west, and the sky aflame. If you don't chain smoke and haven't got smoke from a camp fire into which to stick your head, then the only answer is strong chemicals such as 'Bug Off' or 'Jungle Formula'.

GETTING LOST

With luck, if you follow this Guide you will not get lost, but we are all fallible. Do not panic! Britain has a superb network of finger-posts (do not underestimate the ability of small boys to mischievously swivel them round) and a fair scattering of helpful inhabitants just waiting to help you out, (again beware of small boys with short trousers). Simply reconnect with the route at the next town or village. Pubs are frequently mentioned in this Guide for no other reason than as direction finders.

Most cyclists will feel a need to carry a good road map, there is none better than the Ordnance Survey 'Travelmaster' series, at a scale of 1:250 000 (1 inch to 4 miles) six sheets cover the route.

LOOKING AFTER YOURSELF

You are the engine of your machine. Find a rhythm which suits you. There is no point in 'plunging on the pedals like a steam hammer' just 'because it is there'. Carry a drink and a snack at all times. How about keeping a diary or a journal, to allow time for reflection later.

USING THIS GUIDE

This Guide is intended to help you complete the route. It does not try to be definitive. In particular the support given to Sustrans by the Millennium Fund may significantly improve the provision for cyclists over some of this route in the next few years. Taunton, the Wye Valley, parts of Lancashire, the A74 between Carlisle and Gretna, and the A82 alongside Loch Linnhe and in the Great Glen could all benefit from better cycle path provision.

I wish you a safe, comfortable and joyous ride.

REFERENCES

1. John Potter of 'Bike Events'
2. Memorials of the Hon. Ion Keith-Falconer, MA
   by Rev. Robert Sinker
   Deighton, Bell & Co, Cambridge 1888
3. Cycling : Lands End to John O'Groats
   Alan J. Ray
   Pelham Books, London 1971
4. Sinker Ibid
5. Ray Ibid
6. Land's End to John O'Groats
   WB Dawson
   Cunliffe Brothers, Todmorden 1934

THE SOUTH-WEST

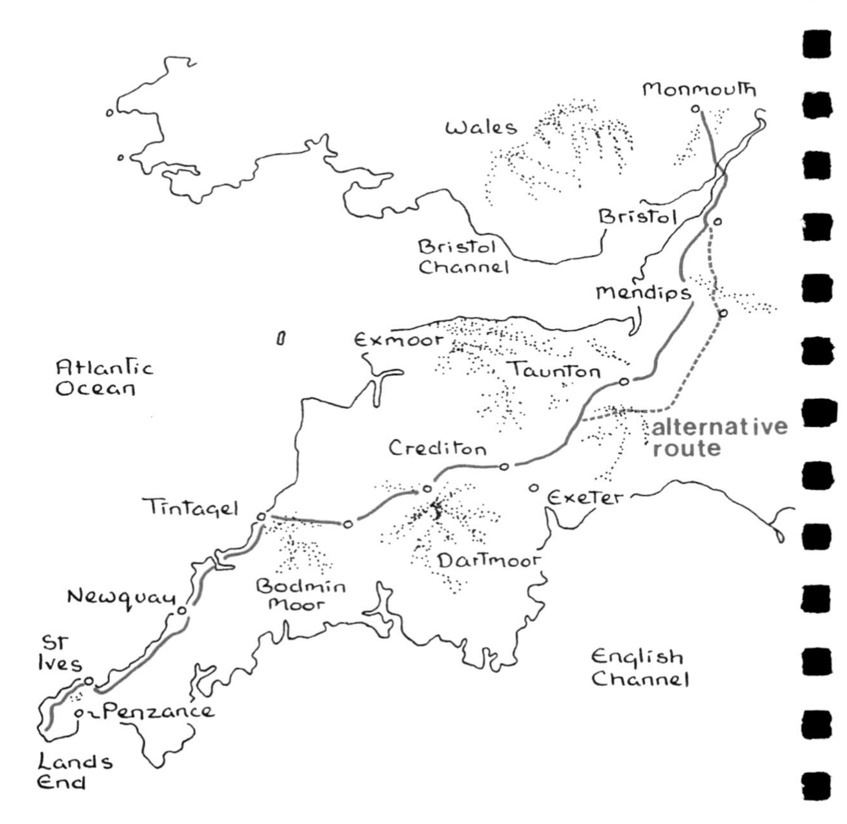

THE SOUTH-WEST

For the old timers the route in Cornwall was easy, the A30 leading straight up the middle from Land's End. Todays discerning cyclist will avoid this road like the plague. No amount of protection is sufficient on this fast busy road. This Guide takes the northern coast, more rugged but more direct than the southern. The major problems for the cyclist are the valleys descending to the sea, involving short, sharp climbs, particularly between Newquay and Padstow. The advice is not to rush and let the legs acclimatise slowly. Life does not become much easier in Devon, a county with more steep hills than any other in Britain, though most are short. After this, Somerset is a joy, but just in case you are missing the hills, an alternative is provided over the Blackdown Hills and the Mendips.

Cornwall held out as an independent Celtic Kingdom against the Saxons until AD926. It had its own language, but it was fast dying out in the l6th century. The last fluent speaker was Dolly Pentreath, who lived near Land's End until 1777. In Cornish the Lords Prayer begins "Agan Tas, neb us yn nef, bydhens uchellys dhe hanow". Many of the place names, and the local surnames, are the only remaining link with the language.
Cornish tin-mining is one of the most ancient industries in Britain, and with such a spectacular coastline, fishing too has been of immense importance. One local speciality is Stargazy Pie, made of whole pilchards with their heads poking out through the crust. Both these occupations are well into decline, replaced by tourism.

Devon. Tourism is also Devon's main industry, followed by farming. Devon has had centuries of peace, allowing the wool industry to prosper, first under the monasteries, and when they were dissolved by King Henry the Eighth in 1536, the favoured gentry took over. Devon remains a prosperous, comfortable county.
This route avoids both the moors and the coasts, home of the famous sea captains (Raleigh in East Devon, Drake in South Devon). Instead it cuts east-west across a swathe of thinly populated land with a scattering of farms and villages.

Somerset. "Cornwalls as ugly as can be: Devonshires better certainly; But Somersetshire is the best of the three, And Somersetshire is the county for me". So says a local rhyme recorded by Robert Southey in 1807.
Medieval wealth has left us several marvels; Wells Cathedral; Glastonbury Abbey; and a host of wonderful church towers, Ilminster and Huish Episcopi among them.
Whereas the Cornish villages are of grey granite, Devon's are of cob (muck, straw and horsehair), and Somersets are mellow limestone and sandstones. For the cyclist there is always something around the corner, from the Moors and Levels to the Mendip hills and the wonderful villages in South Somerset.

Penzance - Lands End

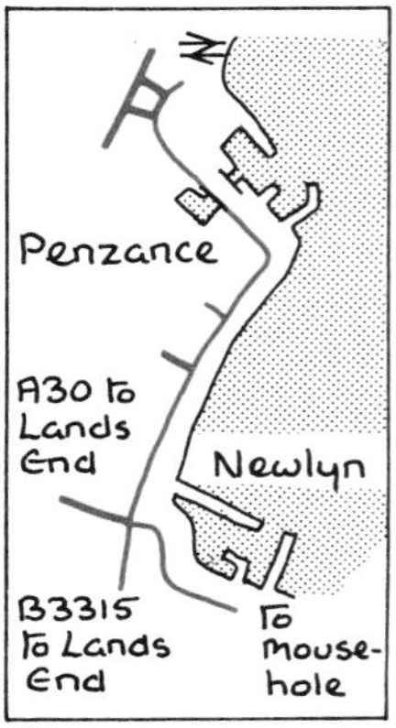

Penzance
A30 to Lands End
Newlyn
B3315 to Lands End
To Mousehole

Penzance

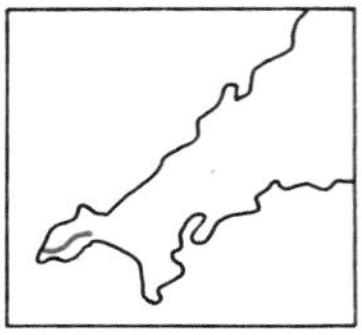

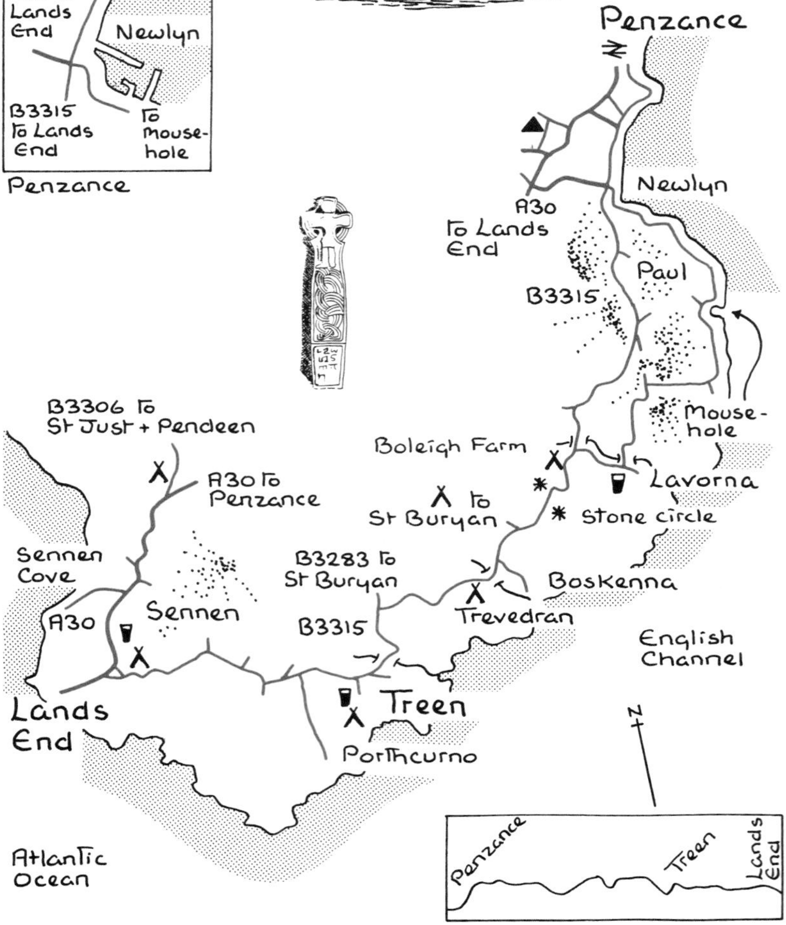

Penzance
Newlyn
A30 to Lands End
Paul
B3315
Mousehole
Boleigh Farm
Lavorna
St Buryan
Stone circle
B3306 to St Just + Pendeen
A30 to Penzance
Sennen Cove
B3283 to St Buryan
Boskenna
Sennen
Trevedran
A30
B3315
English Channel
Lands End
Treen
Porthcurno
N
Atlantic Ocean

Penzance
Treen
Lands End

PENZANCE – LANDS END 12.5 miles

This pre-route section is included for cyclists travelling to Penzance by train. Avoid the heavy traffic on the A30, but be warned, this lush windswept corner of Britain is well visited and nowhere is it car-free. Any cyclist in Cornwall must learn to love those pesky steep pulls out of the valley dips.

Penzance **S** Burnt to the ground, along with Mousehole, Paul and Newlyn, by a party of two hundred Spaniards in 1595, and again badly treated, in revenge, by the Roundheads in the Civil War fifty years later, Penzance rose from the ashes to become a regency resort. The balmy climate is reflected by the exotic Morrab Gardens and the Egyptian House. Today it is a lively, stimulating holiday and harbour town, housing the Trinity House National Lifeboat Centre.

Mousehole **S** A jumble of much painted, tiny streets tumbling down to the harbour.

Boscawen-un. A roadside burial chamber, ancient crosses, the Nine Maidens, a Bronze Age stone circle, and a standing stone. It is said that each stone represents a girl who danced on the Sabbath to a tune played by the nearby stone, the piper.

Porthcurno. Here landed the first trans-atlantic cable to America.

Land's End A commercial complex owned by Peter de Savary. Visible are the Longships lighthouse, built 1797, and the Wolf lighthouse eight miles beyond. Between here and the Scilly Isles lies the lost village of Lyonesse, drowned with all its inhabitants in an awful natural catastrophe untold years ago.

TIC Penzance (01736) 62207
YHA Penzance (01736) 62666
Land's End (Boscaven) (01736) 7884375
Cycle Centre, Penzance (01736) 51671
Geoff's Bikes, Penzance (01736) 63665

Lands End - St Ives

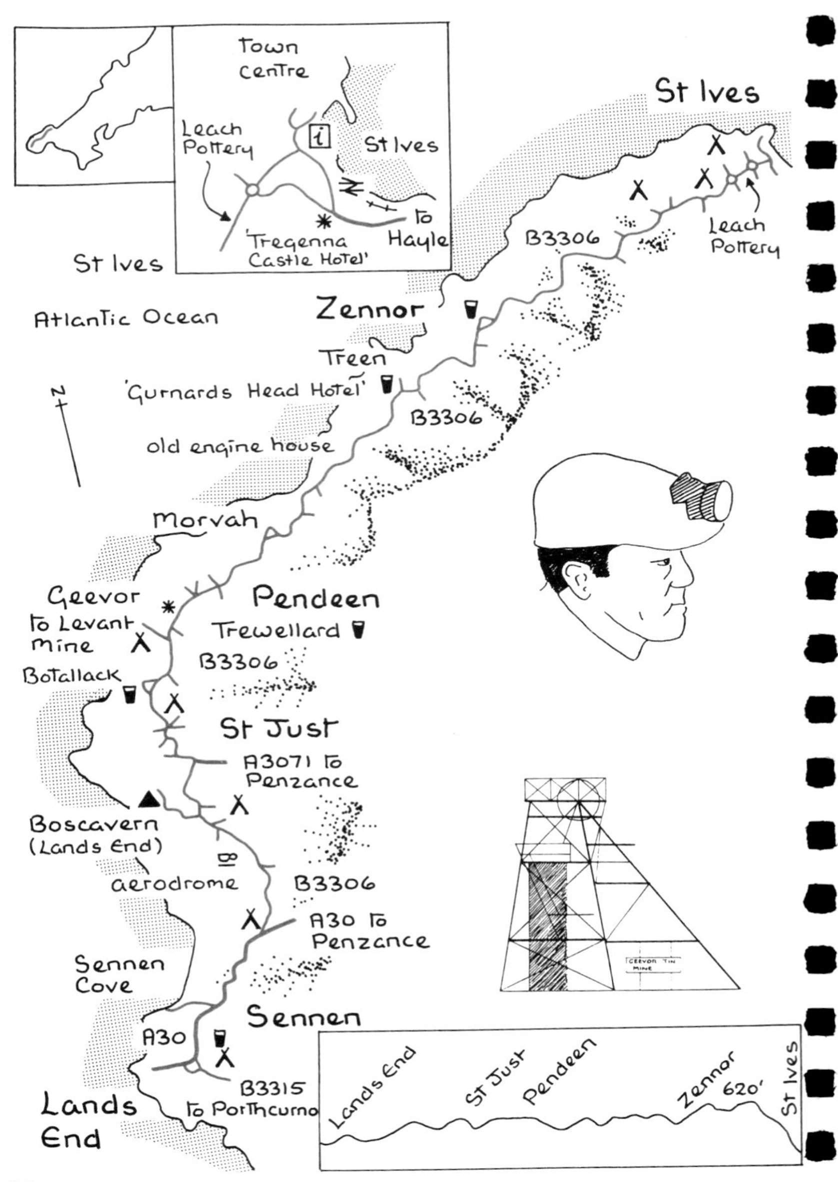

LAND'S END – ST IVES 17.5 miles

A lovely warm-up section, through this old-fashioned, rocky landscape humming with visitors, and oozing with farmhouse cream teas. The route follows an old line of cliffs, formed when the sea was four hundred feet higher than at present. The hills inland are groaning with ancient burial chambers, cromlechs, dolmen, hill forts and fogous.

Sennen S Englands most Westerly village. The tiny church is dedicated to the 6c Irish saint, St.Senan. It is said that when being carried to his burial, he sat up in his bier, and directed that his festival be celebrated on the eigth of March, not the first, but declined to say why.

St.Just S The 19c capital of Cornish tin mining. The name is from St. Justus, sent to England by Pope Gregory the First in the late 6c. to help convert the Saxons to Christianity. He became Archbishop of Canterbury in 604. The church has restored 14c wall paintings. Bank Square has a Plan-an-Guare ('place of plays' in Cornish), used as an amphitheatre from 16c.

Pendeen S The Geevor Mine Museum is in the mine closed as recently as 1991. The Levant Beam Engine is the oldest working beam engine in Cornwall, recently restored to steam power.

Zennor A compact, grey, windswept, village, the home for a while of D.H. Lawrence, and the Mermaid of Zennor, reputed to have lured many a local lad to his doom. Note the Wayside Museum.

Tin Mining. Tin mining in Cornwall is the earliest British industry of which we have any record, dating back to 1700BC. The expiry of Watt's patent for the steam engine in 1800 saw the rapid development of pumping engines, especially by Trevithick of Camborne, and the manufacturers, Harveys of Hayle. The landscape was covered with engine houses, of which only a few remain, and industrial villages developed with gaunt methodist chapels. The average age of a miner on his death was twenty seven.

TIC Penzance (01736) 62207
St.Ives (01736) 796297
YHA Land's End (Boscaven) (01736) 7884375

St Ives - St Agnes

St Ives
Hayle
Portreath
Porthtowan
398'
St Agnes

St Agnes
St Agnes Head
B3277 to Truro
Goonvrea
Chapel Porth
Towan Cross
'Victoria Inn'
Porthtowan
Cambrose
RAF
B3300
B3300 to Redruth
Portreath
to Illogan
to Pool
B3301
Magor Farm 2mls
Godrevy Point
'Sandsifter Hotel'
Gwithian
B3301
The Towans
A30
St Ives
Carbis Bay
Hayle
A3074
Leach Pottery
Lelant
A30
A30

Lelant and Hayle
B3301 to Portreath
A30
A30
Phillack
Hayle
Lelant Station
'Badger Inn'
A3014 to St Ives
The Saltings
'Old Quay House Inn'
A30 to Penzance

ST IVES – ST AGNES 21 miles

A typically Cornish run, with a thoroughly varied coastline of sand dunes and wave-lashed cliffs, grey settlements and plenty of people.

St Ives S Fascinating but incredibly busy, a wonderfully situated picturesque granite town. The harbour was a prime fishing port, especially for pilchard. Famous for its painters (exhibitions in the Old Mariner's Church, Barbara Hepworth, the sculptor (museum); and Bernard Leach, the modern world's greatest potter.

Hayle S Miles of sand dunes, or 'towans' have swallowed up acres of farmland, and the palace of King Theodore who tried to resist, unsuccessfully, the stream of Irish saints in 6c, whose names are strewn around this end of Cornwall. Hayle was a working town with foundries, coalyards, smelting works, dynamite works, breweries, and, a rarity on this coast, a good harbour.

Portreath S Once a coal port, now a resort for the people of Camborne and Redruth.

Camborne – Pool – Redruth. A mile or two to the east of this route, these settlements flourished with copper mining, particularly 1820-70. Trevithick, born here in 1771, is best remembered for the invention of the railway engine. School of Mines Geological Museum, Camborne; Holmans Engineering Museum, Camborne; Tolgus Tin, an 18c and 19c mill, Redruth, now a 'gold' centre; East Pool mine, Cornish engines; Agar mine, Pool, an early rotative beam engine. The hill behind, Carn Brea, has a vast Iron Age fort.

TIC St Ives (01736) 796297

Hayle Cycles (01736) 753825
Rotary Spokes, Hayle (01736) 756973
Bike-chain, Redruth (01209) 215270
Aldridge Cycles, Camborne (01209) 714970
Cycle Dynamics, Camborne (01209) 612647

St Agnes - Mawgan Porth

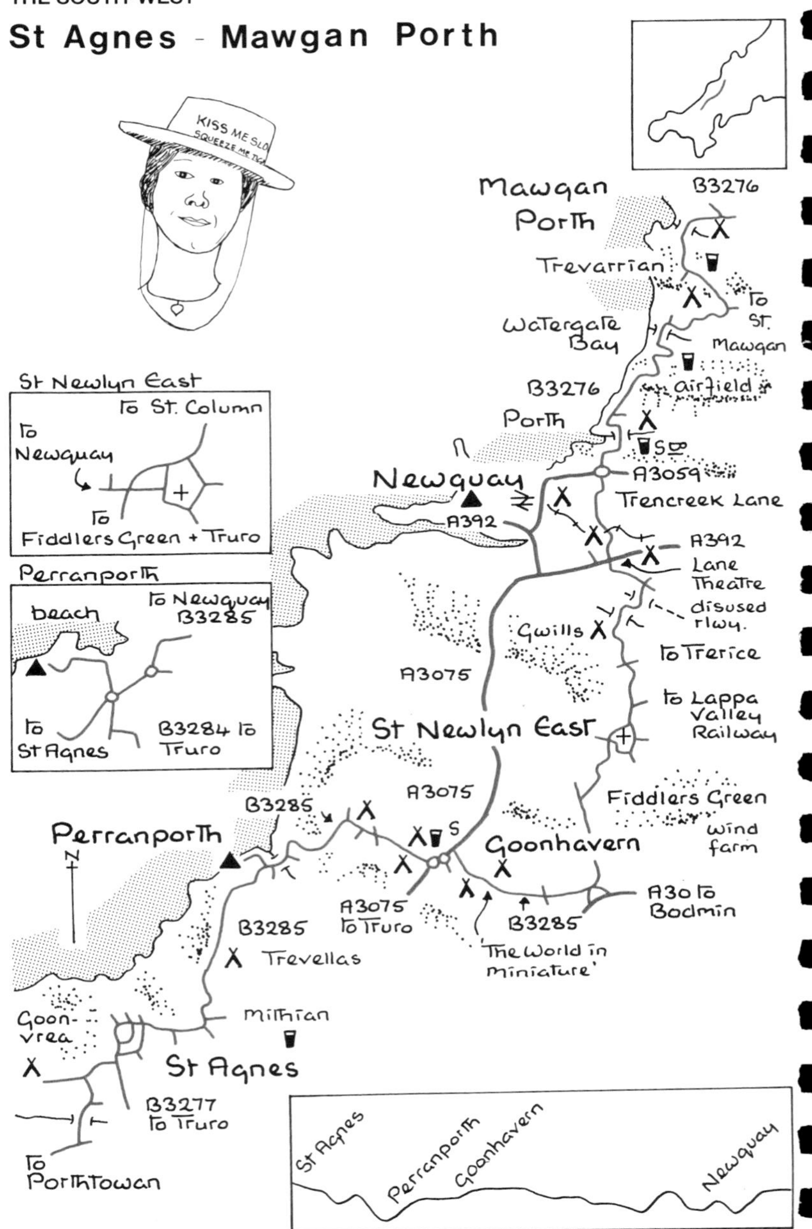

ST AGNES – MAWGAN PORTH 19 miles

On the one hand, the coast is magnificent, big Atlantic breakers crashing onto sandy beaches; on the other hand, your legs are beginning to feel the ups and downs, and nowhere is untouched by visitors, from a fingerprint to a punch.

St Agnes **S** A former mining town, it now has shops for surfers. It is known for its giant, Bolster, who obtained a new wife each year, killing the old one by throwing stones at her. He made his mistake by pestering St Agnes herself, who tricked him into draining his blood away to sea.

Perranporth **S** A busy holiday centre with those towans again.

St Newlyn East **S** Away from the holidaymakers, this used to be a Victorian mining village.

Trerice. A fine Elizabethan house with a lawn mower museum.

Newquay **S** The best beaches and most ugly town in Cornwall.

Mawgan Porth **S** Little remains of the St Column Canal, a horseshoe shaped canal, begun in 1773 and designed to distribute sea sand around the farms for fertiliser. At each end was an inclined plane from the cliff top to the shore.

TIC Newquay (01637) 871345
YHA Perranporth (01872) 573812
Newquay (01637) 876381
Cycle Revolution, Newquay (01637) 872364
Newquay Cycle Centre (01637) 871067

Mawgan Porth - St Endellion

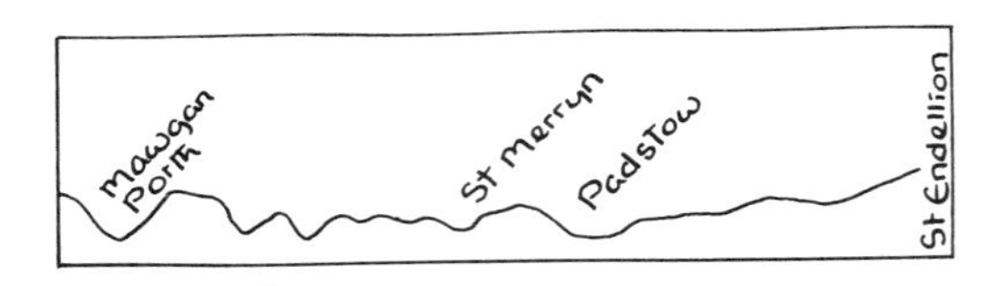

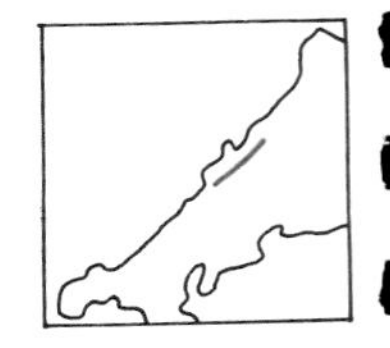

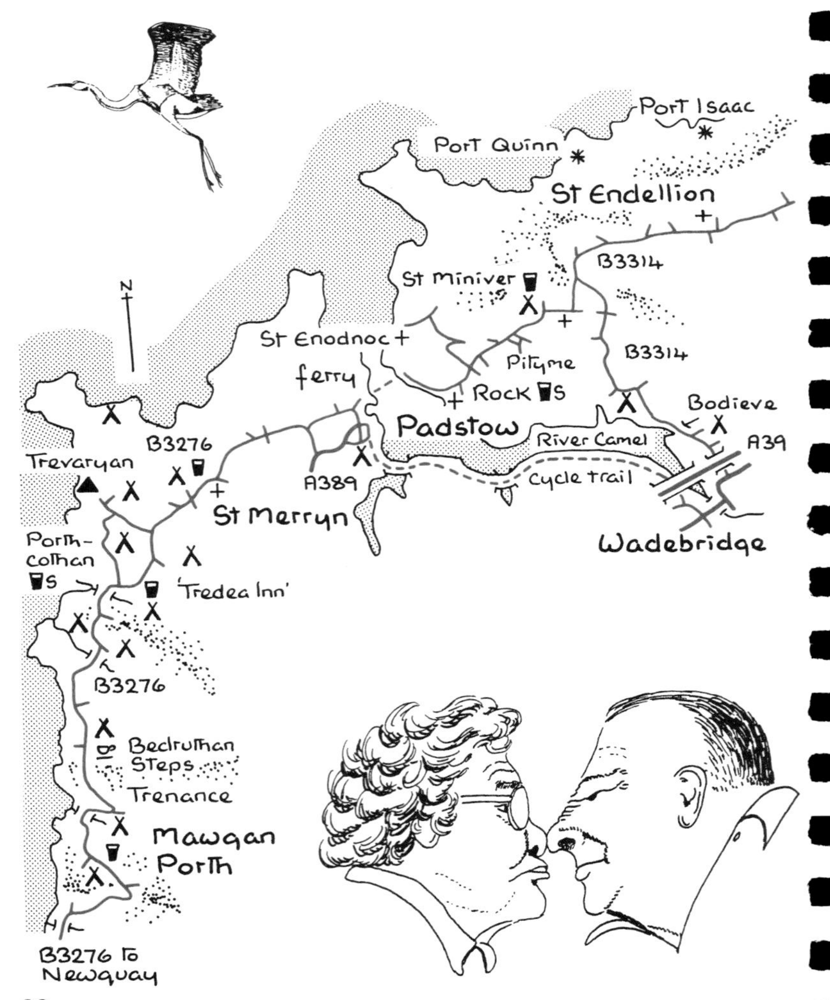

MAWGAN PORTH – ST ENDELLION 14 miles

Roller coaster ride along a coast more popular with surfers than cyclists. Feel those leg muscles! At Padstow there is a choice of route; across the estuary on the Padstow-Rock ferry (cycles £1.20 in 1995), or along the superb Camel Trail cycle path.

Bedruthan Steps Three hundred feet, sheer cliffs.

St Merryn S This is affluent 'cottage-in-Cornwall' country. The l5c church of St Marina has an unusual tower and a beautiful 14c font carved from catacleuse, a local blue slate.

Padstow S Very busy and attractive small port, famed for the May Day pagan fertility rite involving a Hobby Horse. Prideaux Place was built about the time of the Spanish Armada, and was a haven for King Charles following defeat in the Civil War. The Court House, on South Quay, was the 16c home of Sir Walter Raleigh. The harbour was also used by Sir John Hawkins, Drake and Frobisher.

Padstow – Wadebridge (the Camel Trail). This line was the farthest fling of the London and South Western Railway. In its heyday the 'Atlantic Coast Express' steamed along here, headed by a 'Battle of Britain' or 'West Country' class loco., but the battle for supremacy in Cornwall was lost to the Great Western Railway. It makes a wonderful cycle path.

The Ferry. For six centuries a ferryboat called 'Blacktor' has plied this channel. The Camel Estuary is guarded by the Doom Bar, on which hundreds of seamen have perished.

St Enodnoc's Church, Rock. In 1863 this was dug out of the sand, having been buried for years. It is mostly Norman, and surrounded by tamarisk. There is a coffin rest at the lych-gate. The church bell was once the ship's bell of the 'Immacolata', an Italian ship wrecked in 1875. Sir John Betjemen is buried here.

St Minver. The church has a huge spire and 1717 'vinegar' Bible. This is an old manorial village with stocks used less than a hundred years ago by two boys caught stealing apples.

TIC Padstow (01841) 533449
YHA Treyarnon Bay (01841) 520322
Bridge Cycles, Wadebridge (01208) 814545
Cycle Revolution,Wadebridge (01208) 812021
Babes and Bikes, Wadebridge (01208) 815262

St Endellion – Davidstow

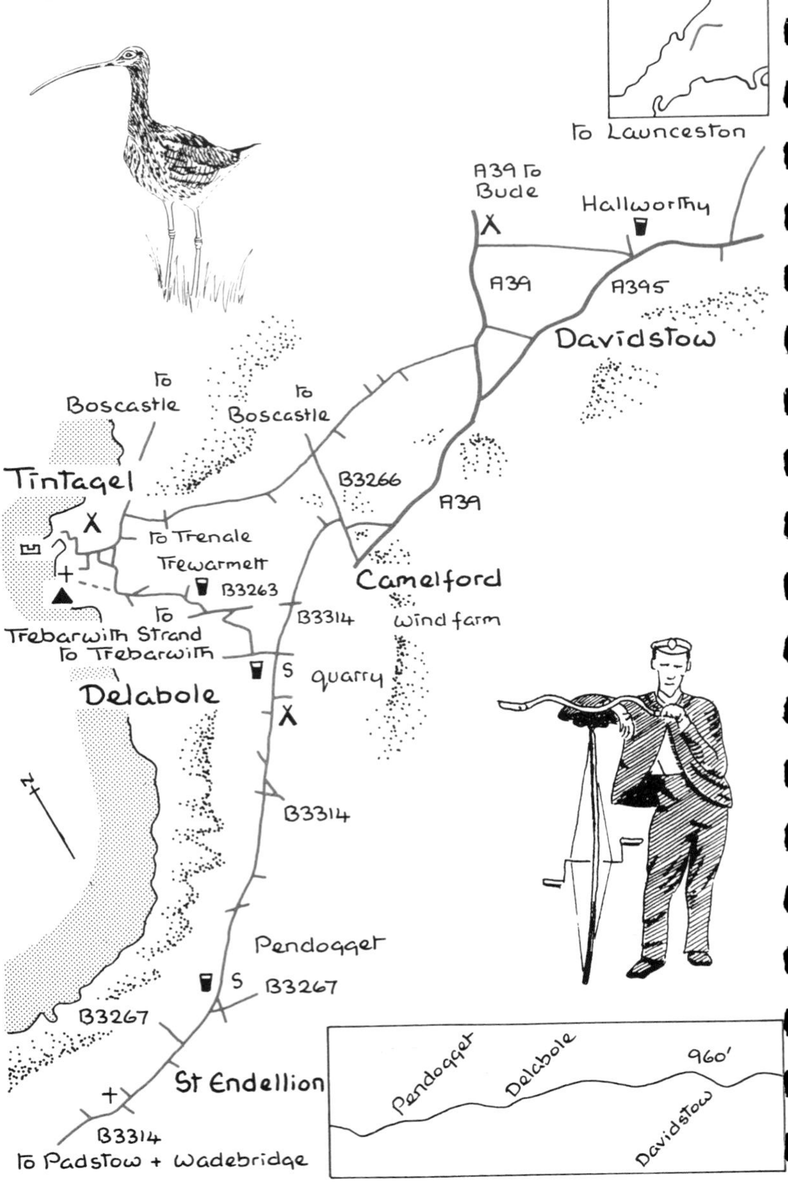

To Launceston
A39 To Bude
Hallworthy
A39
A395
Davidstow
To Boscastle
To Boscastle
Tintagel
B3266
A39
To Trenale
Trewarmett
B3263
Camelford
To Trebarwith Strand
B3314
Wind farm
To Trebarwith
S
quarry
Delabole
B3314
Pendogget
S
B3267
B3267
St Endellion
B3314
To Padstow + Wadebridge

Pendogget
Delabole
960'
Davidstow

ST ENDELLION – DAVIDSTOW 13.5 miles

Breeze along to Delabole, then, possibly with a detour to Tintagel, pull up on to the edge of Bodmin Moor (924 ft) with your head in the wind, the open skies above and the flute-like call of the curlew.

St Endellion. St Endelienta was a virgin saint, the daughter of a 6c Welsh King, who lived as a hermit feeding on nothing but the milk of her cow.

Delabole **S** Quarrying began four hundred and fifty years ago, with production peaking at the turn of the century, when five or six hundred men were employed. The hole is five hundred feet deep and covers six acres. There is a museum.

Tintagel **S** Unless you catch Tintagel early in the morning, you will be sharing it with lots of tourists. The legend is that Gorlois, Duke of Cornwall, withdrew his wife, Igerne, to his Cornish stronghold at Tintagel, to keep her away from Uther Pendragon, the King of England, who had fallen for her. Uther, in pursuit, killed Gorlois, and gained admission to Igerne. The result was Arthur. Those who doubt the existence of King Arthur do so in the face of a vast amount of tradition. What is certain is that the present ruins are not Arthur's, but were built by the Earl of Cornwall, Henry the First's son, six hundred years after Arthur is thought to have died. They were subsequently occupied by Edward, the Black Prince, then used as a prison before falling into disrepair in the 15c.
The hideous King Arthurs Hall was built 1928-33 to commemorate the acts of chivalry. The old post office was originally a 14c manor house. The herringbone walls hereabouts are thought to have a Cretan influence.
Offshore is the island of Lundy. "If you can see Lundy, its going to rain, if you can't, its raining already". Lundy is Norse for Puffin Island.

Camelford. The North Cornwall Museum and Gallery is here. Also, one mile north on the Boscastle Road, at the Old Station, is the museum of Historic Cycling.

Davidstow. Locally sometimes called Dewstow, Dewi being the Welsh form of the name David.

TIC Camelford (01840) 212954
YHA Tintagel (01840) 770334
Cycle Hire and Sales, Tintagel (01840) 770060

Launceston

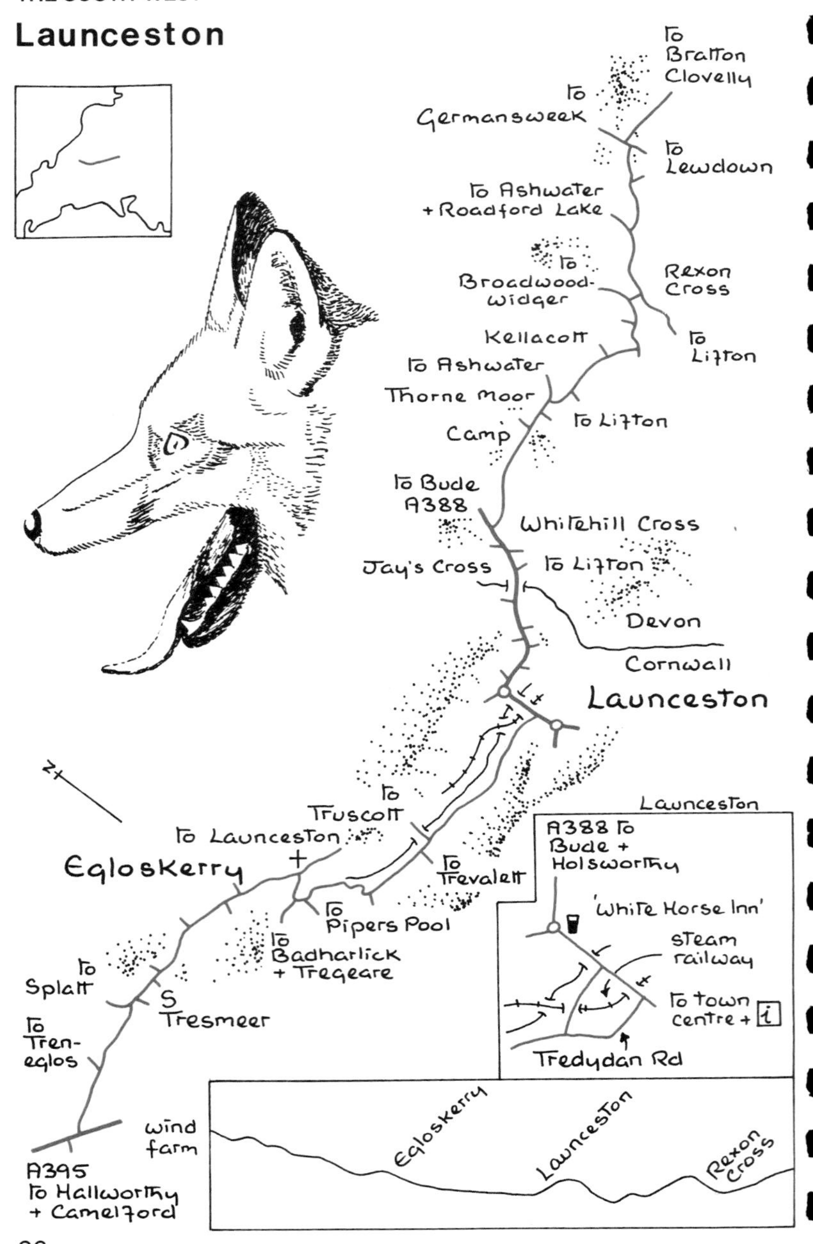
To Bratton Clovelly
To Germansweek
To Lewdown
To Ashwater + Roadford Lake
To Broadwood-widger
Rexon Cross
To Lifton
Kellacott
To Ashwater
Thorne Moor
To Lifton
Camp
To Bude A388
Whitehill Cross
To Lifton
Jay's Cross
Devon
Cornwall
Launceston
To Truscott
To Launceston
Egloskerry
To Trevalett
To Pipers Pool
To Badharlick + Tregeare
To Splatt
S
Tresmeer
To Tren-eglos
wind farm
A395 To Hallworthy + Camelford
Launceston
A388 To Bude + Holsworthy
'White Horse Inn'
steam railway
To town centre + i
Tredydan Rd
Egloskerry
Launceston
Rexon Cross

LAUNCESTON 22 miles

When you lie back and think of England, there's a fair chance its like this; rolling green country, clotted cream, lush hedgerows, butterflies, badgers, traces of old railway lines, deceased grey tractors turning to rust.

Egloskerry. Sir Keri's church is Norman and contains the alabaster effigy of Sir Guy de Blanchminister, inexpertly restored with his crude nose and the pompons from his slippers attached to his breast.

Launceston **S** This former capital of the Duchy of Cornwall occupies a once strategic site on the main Devon – Cornwall road. The original motte and bailey castle, built in 1067, was the heart of Robert, Count of Mortain's lordship, which embraced the whole of Cornwall. The unique double-shell keep was added in the 12c. The Domesday Prison, a ruined gate-house, once housed Quaker George Fox, arrested in 1656 for distributing 'dangerous' religious pamphlets in St Ives, and imprisoned for eighteen months for refusing to remove his hat before a county judge. The town hall was built by Henry the Third. Lawrence House contains a local museum. The Parish church of St Mary Magdalene has excellent ornamental carving in the granite exterior. A local railway line runs regular steam services to nowhere in a delightfully relaxed manner.

TIC Launceston (01566) 772321/772333
John Towl Cycles, Launceston (01566) 774220
South West Cycle Centre, Launceston (01566) 772706

Okehampton

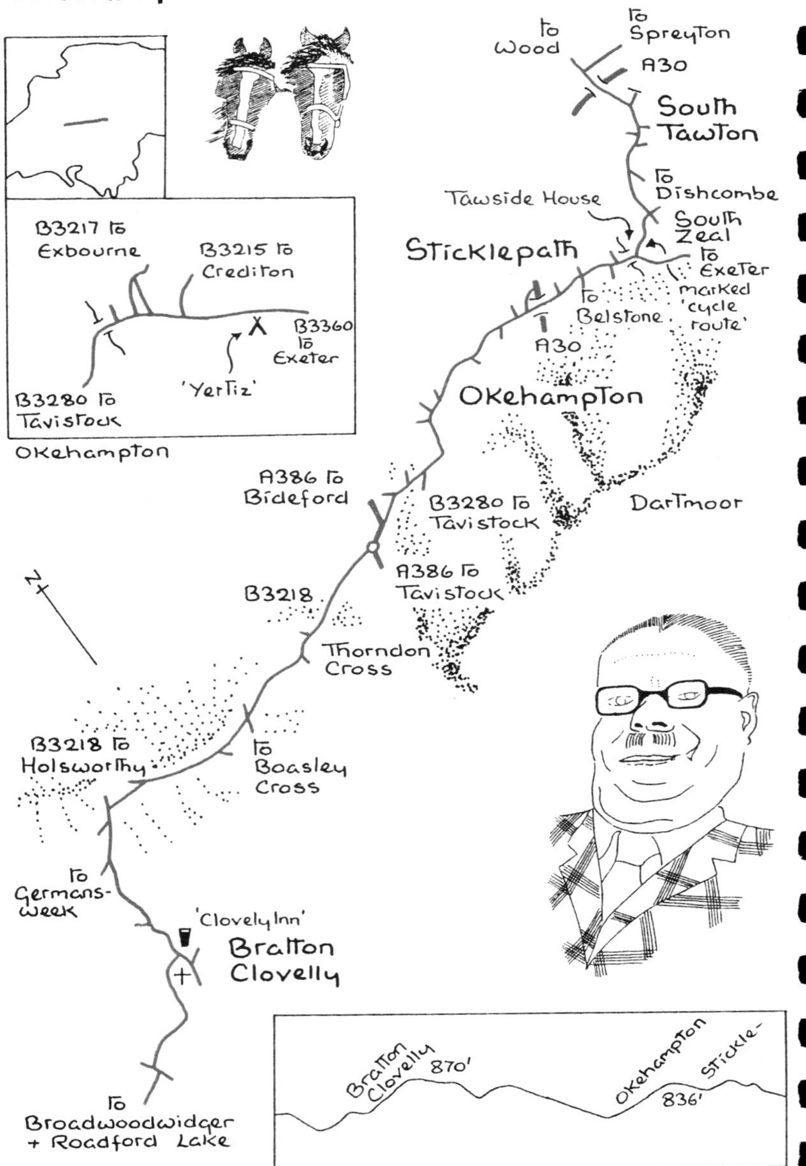

To Wood
To Spreyton
A30
South Tawton
To Dishcombe
Tawside House
South Zeal
Sticklepath
To Exeter
marked 'cycle route'
To Belstone
A30
Okehampton
B3217 To Exbourne
B3215 To Crediton
B3360 To Exeter
'YerTiz'
B3280 To Tavistock
Okehampton
A386 To Bideford
B3280 To Tavistock
Dartmoor
A386 To Tavistock
B3218
Thorndon Cross
B3218 To Holsworthy
To Boasley Cross
To Germansweek
'Clovely Inn'
Bratton Clovelly
To Broadwoodwidger + Roadford Lake
Bratton Clovelly
870'
Okehampton
836'
Stickle-

OKEHAMPTON 18.5 miles

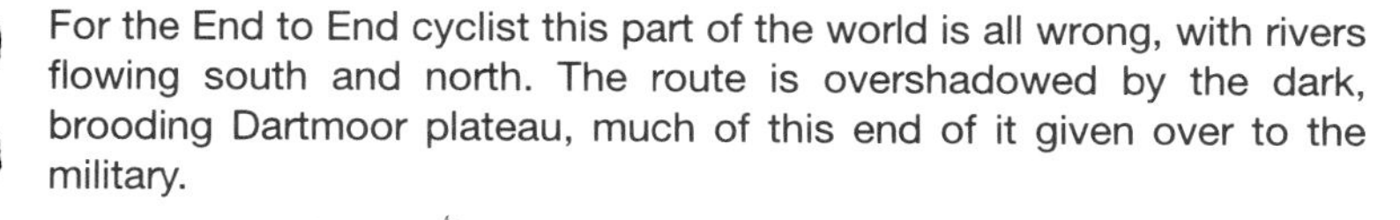

For the End to End cyclist this part of the world is all wrong, with rivers flowing south and north. The route is overshadowed by the dark, brooding Dartmoor plateau, much of this end of it given over to the military.

Okehampton S The barony of Okehampton was one of the many grants made by William the Conqueror, this to Baldwin de Brionis. The castle dates from this time. It is said to be haunted by Lady Howard, who murdered at least two of her four husbands. She is said to travel nightly to Tavistock in a coach made from one of her husband's bones, there to pick a blade of grass from the castle mound. Not until the mound is bare will she be allowed to rest. See also the 17c Town Hall, the Charter Hall and the Old Mill (the Museum of Dartmoor Life).

Sticklepath S The Finch Foundry was originally a corn mill and cloth mill, then converted to an edge-tool factory to make agricultural implements. It was run from 1814 to 1960 by the Finch family. Now a working museum, it includes three waterwheels, one operating a large sandstone grinding wheel whose operation gave rise to the saying "keep your nose to the grindstone".

South Zeal. A lively ex-copper mining village with a splendid 16c manor house turned pub.

South Tawton There is an excellent 15c granite church framed by thatched cottages.

Dartmoor has been called the last major wilderness in southern England. The mostly trackless, wild, granite moorland is bleak and treeless. Few settlements exist, yet it was long the home of early man. Ancient stone trackways, avenues of standing stones, stone circles, barrows and hut circles all tell of early occupation.
Today it is a heavily used environment, by farmers, mining companies, walkers and water companies. A hundred years ago the Armed Services acquired much of the moor and it remains an ideal training ground with live ammunition.

TIC Okehampton (01837) 53020
Bostock Cycle Centre, Okehampton (01837) 53248

Crediton

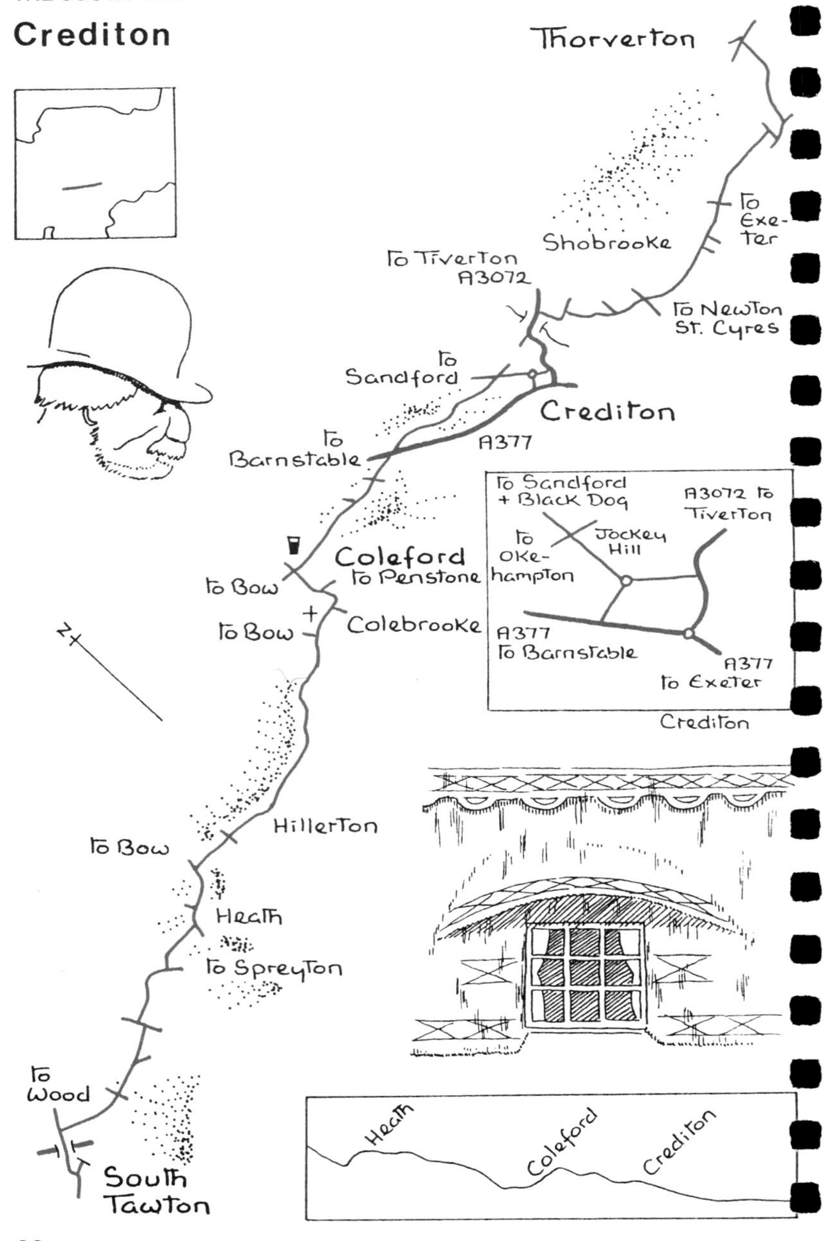
Thorverton
To Exe-ter
Shobrooke
To Tiverton A3072
To Newton St. Cyres
To Sandford
Crediton
To Barnstable
A377
Coleford
To Penstone
To Bow
Colebrooke
To Bow
To Sandford + Black Dog
A3072 To Tiverton
To Oke-hampton
Jockey Hill
A377 To Barnstable
A377 To Exeter
Crediton
N
Hillerton
To Bow
Heath
To Spreyton
To Wood
South Tawton
Heath
Coleford
Crediton

CREDITON **14.5 miles**

Another 'ducking and diving' day, seeking the line of least resistance as the valleys drain to both north and south. Country cruising, for the most part peacefully, save for the groan of a tractor or the yap of a dog. Towards Crediton the farms are larger, the soil redder and the fields more arable. Crediton is a working farmers town; South Tawton and Coleford exquisite thatched villages.

Crediton **S** The main town in this area of amazingly red soil, it was in the 15c a very prosperous wool town. Until 1050 it was head of the Exeter diocese and the birthplace of St Boniface, but long-forgotten fires have swept away much of the old Crediton. The large church of the Holy Cross is of sandstone and Thorverton stone, and very colourful, red, orange, pink and purple.

TIC Crediton (01363) 772006

The Cycle Shop, 100 High St, Credition

Cullompton

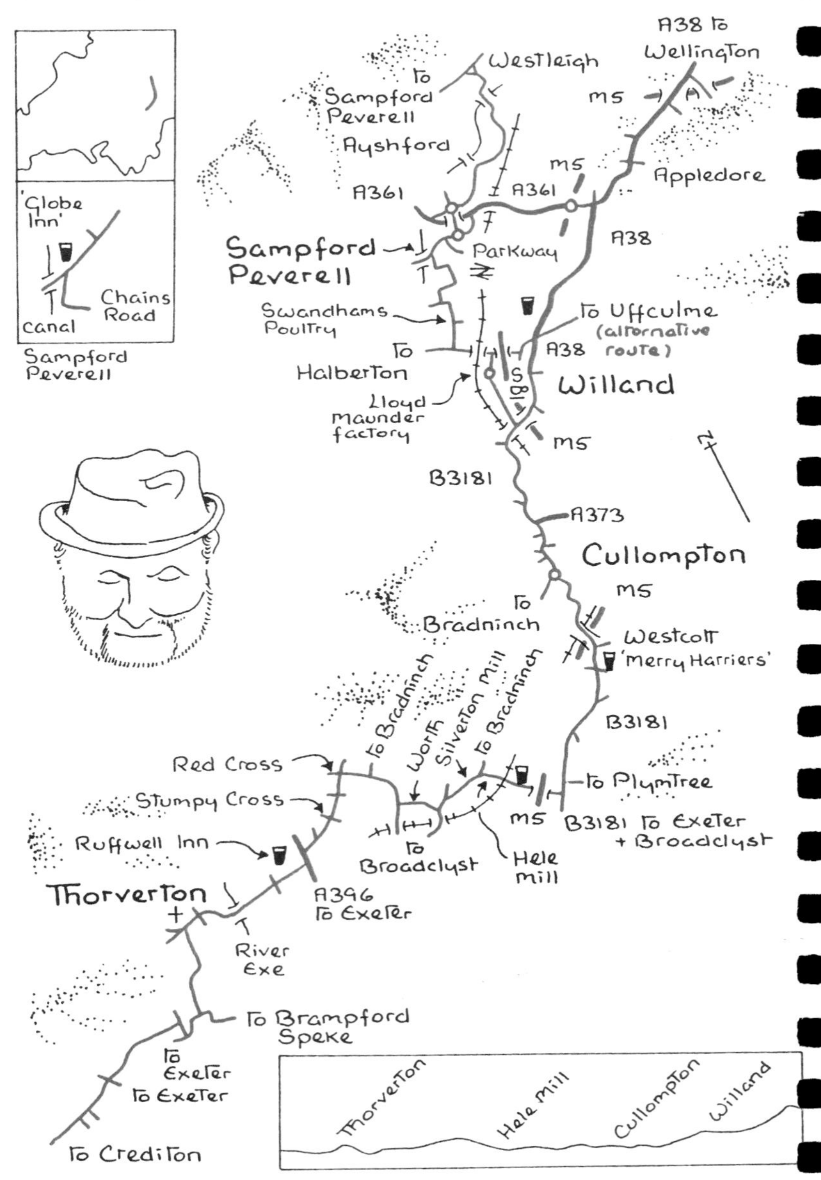
'Globe
Inn'
Chains
Road
Canal
Sampford
Peverell
A38 To
Wellington
Westleigh
To
Sampford
Peverell
Aysford
M5
Appledore
A361
A361
A38
Sampford
Peverell
Parkway
Swandhams
Poultry
To Uffculme
(alternative
route)
To
Halberton
A38
Willand
B3181
Lloyd
Maunder
factory
M5
B3181
A373
Cullompton
M5
To
Bradninch
Westcott
'Merry Harriers'
To Bradninch
Worth
Silverton Mill
To Bradninch
B3181
Red Cross
Stumpy Cross
To Plymtree
Ruffwell Inn
M5
B3181 To Exeter
+ Broadclyst
To
Broadclyst
Hele
Mill
Thorverton
A396
To Exeter
River
Exe
To Brampford
Speke
To
Exeter
To Exeter
To Crediton
Thorverton
Hele Mill
Cullompton
Willand

CULLOMPTON 11 miles

A comfortable, round, untroubled land inhabited by relaxed, round, friendly people. A fast, low-gradient mile-eating section along the Culm Valley to Willand, then the choice is between continuing along the A38 to Wellington, by this time more hilly and busier with traffic; taking the minor roads through Sampford Peverell, a wee hilly section of awkward lanes; and the major alternative through Uffculme and over the Black Down Hills.

Thorveton A large, attractive village with cob and thatch and an 18c colonnaded butchers shop.

Cullompton S A prosperous woollen town in 16c & 17c, it suffered a terrible fire in 1839. The chuch of St Andrew has a rare richness of roofing.

Sampford Peverell S Reknown in the 19c for the Sampford ghost, which, for three years, kept up a stream of violent knocking accompanied by flying swords, candlesticks and books.

The Tiverton Canal. The 19c saw several attempts to put a canal across the peninsula and thereby link the English and Bristol Channels. The Grand Western Canal was proposed from Exeter (linking there with the Exeter Ship Canal) to Taunton (connecting via the Bridgwater and Taunton Canal, and the River Parrott, to the sea). The Taunton – Tiverton section was opened in 1838, with seven vertical lifts and an inclined plane. The canal was never completed to Exeter. It was a financial disaster and closed in 1869, but remains in water today from Tiverton to near Holcombe Rogus.

TIC Tiverton Services (M5) (01884) 821242

Wellington - Taunton

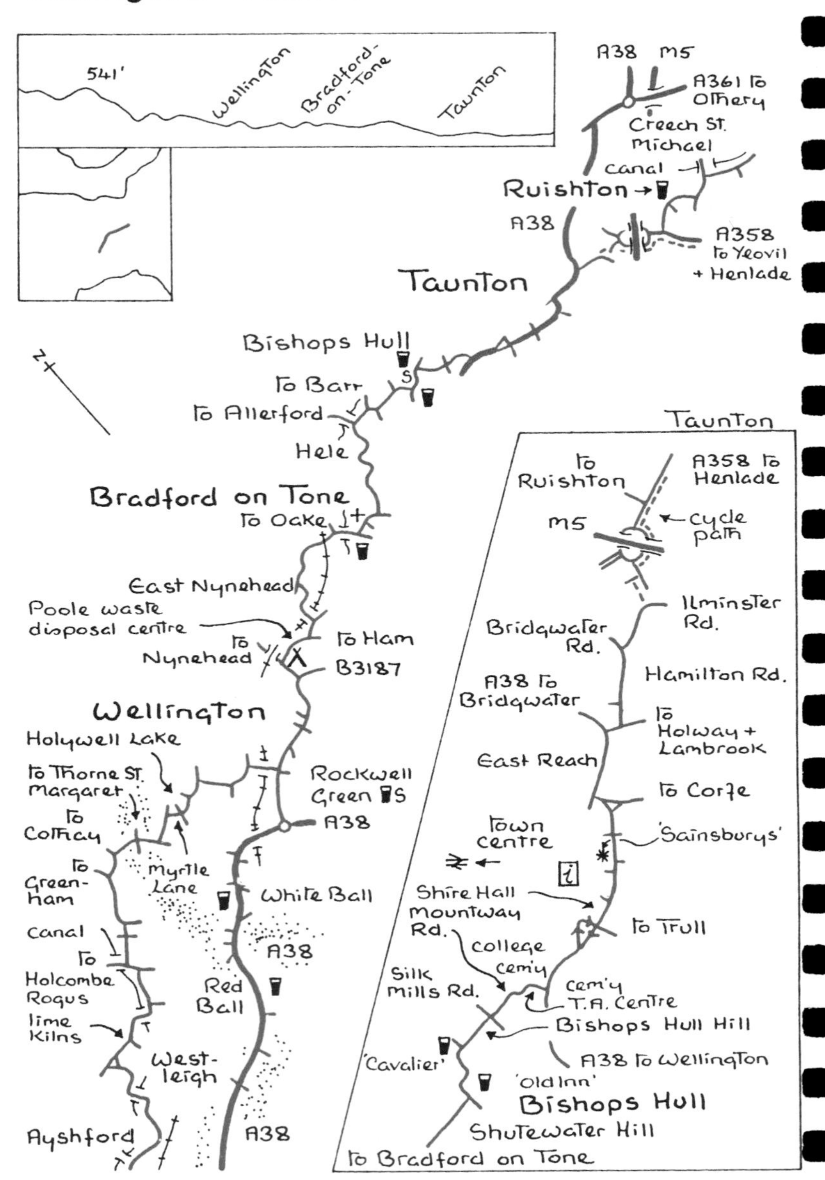

WELLINGTON - TAUNTON 11 miles

The ride crosses the north-south watershed either on the busy A38 or on the jumpy, awkward Devon lanes. The country is lush, heavy and heaving like Sheba's breasts, with discreet lanes, hidden corners and high hedges. Taunton has made an attempt to accomodate cyclists, but some brushes with traffic are inevitable.

Holcombe Rogus. The Bluett family owns probably the finest Tudor house in the county.

Wellington **S** Built on cloth, Wellington is better known nowadays for aerosols, beds and bricks. In 1808 the town gave a title to Sir Arthur Wellesley, who became the first Duke of Wellington.

Bradford on Tone A cider museum and a 15c bridge.

Taunton **S** The manor of Taunton Deane, one of the largest in England, was centred on Taunton. A castle was built and a market established, still one of the largest in the West of England. For centuries this was a cloth town. The castle 'saw action' in the Wars of the Roses, the rebellion of the pretender Perkin Warbeck in 1497, and sieges during the Civil War. An Assize Court was held until 1857, including Judge Jeffreys 'Bloody Assizes' of 1685 following the Battle of Sedgemoor.
Cider making in the area can be traced back to the 9c, mostly on farms and distributed to labourers as part of their wages. The Somerset County museum is in Weir Lodge.
Taunton has a potentially exciting cycle route network, at present in its infancy.

Ham. The place name derives from 'Old English', often denoting a flat, low-lying pasture near a river, but it can simply mean 'enclosure'.

TIC Taunton (01823) 274785

Kings Cycles, Wellington (01823) 662260
LJ Shepherd Cycle & Pram Centre, Wellington 662443
Bob Maslen Cycles, Taunton (01823) 282077
Burton Cycles, Taunton (01823) 283631
Newmans Cycles, Taunton (01823) 332762
Ralph Colman Cycles, Taunton (01823) 275822/277799

Taunton - Westhay (Somerset Levels)

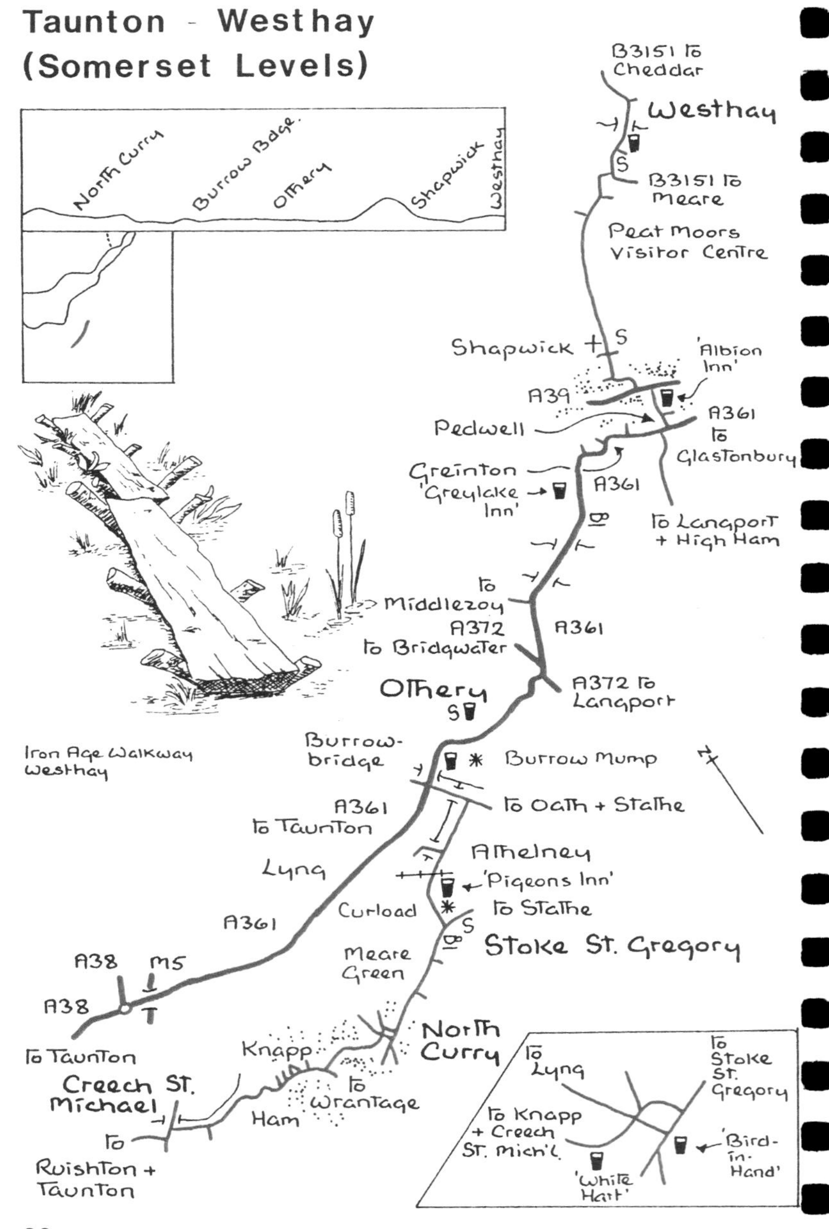

TAUNTON – WESTHAY
(Somerset Levels and Moors) 21.5 miles

Fine cycling through verdant, watery, eclectic country with the bit around Athelney an unmissable section of rural England in all its quirky glory.

Curload The centre of English basketmaking, with the strange sight hereabouts of fields of withies and willows.

Athelney Of the great Abbey nothing much remains except an 1801 monument to King Alfred. The Viking menace to England began in the late 8c with an attack on Lindisfarne. In 878 the Danes made a surprise attack on Wessex and obtained a good foothold. In retreat King Alfred chose Athelney because of the security offered by the marshes and here he stayed for 7 weeks while he regrouped his forces, eventually marching to save Wessex from the Vikings. We shall meet the Vikings again much further north. While at Athelney King Alfred burnt the cakes.

Burrow Mump. Part castle, part church, dating from 15c, now a war memorial.

The Battle of Sedgemoor. In opposition to the Catholic James II, the Duke of Monmouth in 1685 landed in Dorsetshire and assumed the title of 'King' at Taunton, before suffering defeat at Sedgemoor. This was the last battle on English (but not Scottish!) soil.
Monmouth was taken and hanged, as were many of the rebels, without trial. A body of soldiers under Colonel Kirke ravaged the countryside hereabouts, killing all the 'insurgents' they could find. Even these excesses were surpassed by the due process of law, for Judge Jeffreys by bullying witnesses and intimidating juries, obtained many more convictions, 300 of whom were executed, the rest mutilated, imprisoned or exiled. "At every spot where two roads met, on every market place, on the green of every large village which had furnished Monmouth with soldiers, ironed corpses clattering in the wind, or heads and quarters on poles, poisoned the air and made the traveller sick with horror." As a reward for his services in the "Bloody Assize", Jeffreys was raised to the peerage, and afterwards made Lord Chancellor.

TIC Bridgwater (01278) 427652
St John Street Cycles, Bridgwater (01278) 423632
The Bicycle Chain, Bridgwater (01278) 423640

Westhay - Congresbury (the Somerset Moors)

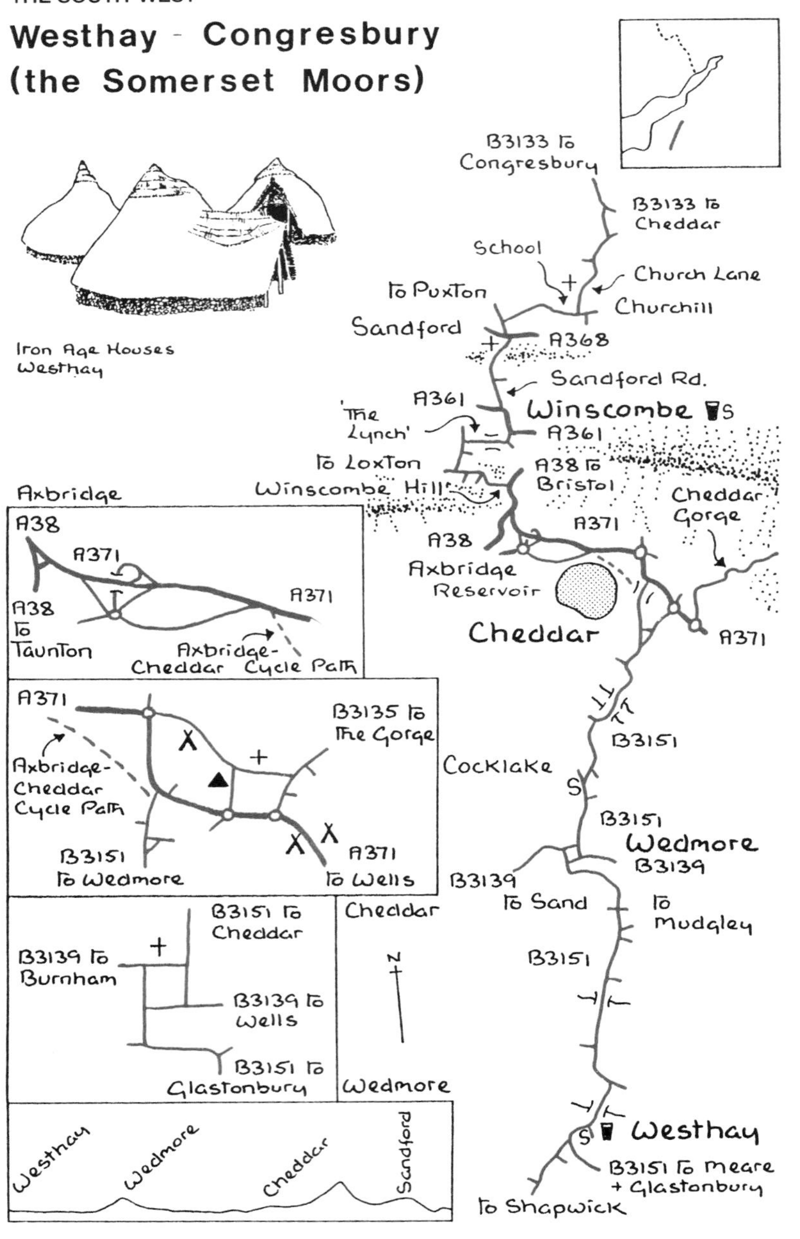

WESTHAY – CONGRESBURY
(The Somerset Moors) 17.5 miles

A most relaxed ride across the Levels, with its multi-layers of historical habitation. The Peat Moors Visitor Centre is well worth a visit, though its future is uncertain. Cheddar means tourists, and beyond lies bonny country with overblown villages.

Shapwick S The church, 1331, houses a collection of modern hassocks.

Wedmore S St Mary Magdalene is an impressively light, powerful church.

Cheddar S Known for its Gorge, cheese and long queues for the working rural theme village. The commercialised Gorge has two main caves (Cox's and Gough's) containing limestone features, the bones of prehistoric man, and Roman coins. Should you wish to cycle up the Gorge, link in with the alternative route on page 50. At the top is Pavey's Lookout Tower, built 90 years ago by Ronald Pavey, a man convinced that he could fly.

Axbridge S A delightful village in strawberry country, with a timber-framed Merchants House and 15c church.

Webbington. On the Loxton road, at Webbington, is the Wheelwrights Working Museum and Gypsy Folklore Collection, including gypsy caravans available for bed and breakfast.

The Somerset Moors. These peat moors have been worked since medieval times, though the horticultural use of peat has mushroomed in recent years. Modern extraction is mainly to the West of Westhay. Many areas of past extraction are being conserved for wildlife with wet meadow and water plants, and wetland birds and dragonflies. Before the banks, sea defences, ditches and rhynes were built, the area used to flood regularly and settlements such as the 'Isle of Wedmore' cut off.

The Levels. An area, in the past, of freshwater swamp negotiated by rafts, dugouts and on long wooden causeways. The 'islands' were often occupied by those seeking a contemplative life, with monasteries at Glastonbury, Muchelney and Athelney. The monks began reclamation in 12c, though coordinated drainage began only in 1770. The result is rich grassland, peat extraction and willows grown for basket making, but the water levels have to be carefully controlled with sluices and pumps.

TIC Cheddar (01934) 744071
YHA Cheddar (01934) 742494

Congresbury - Bristol

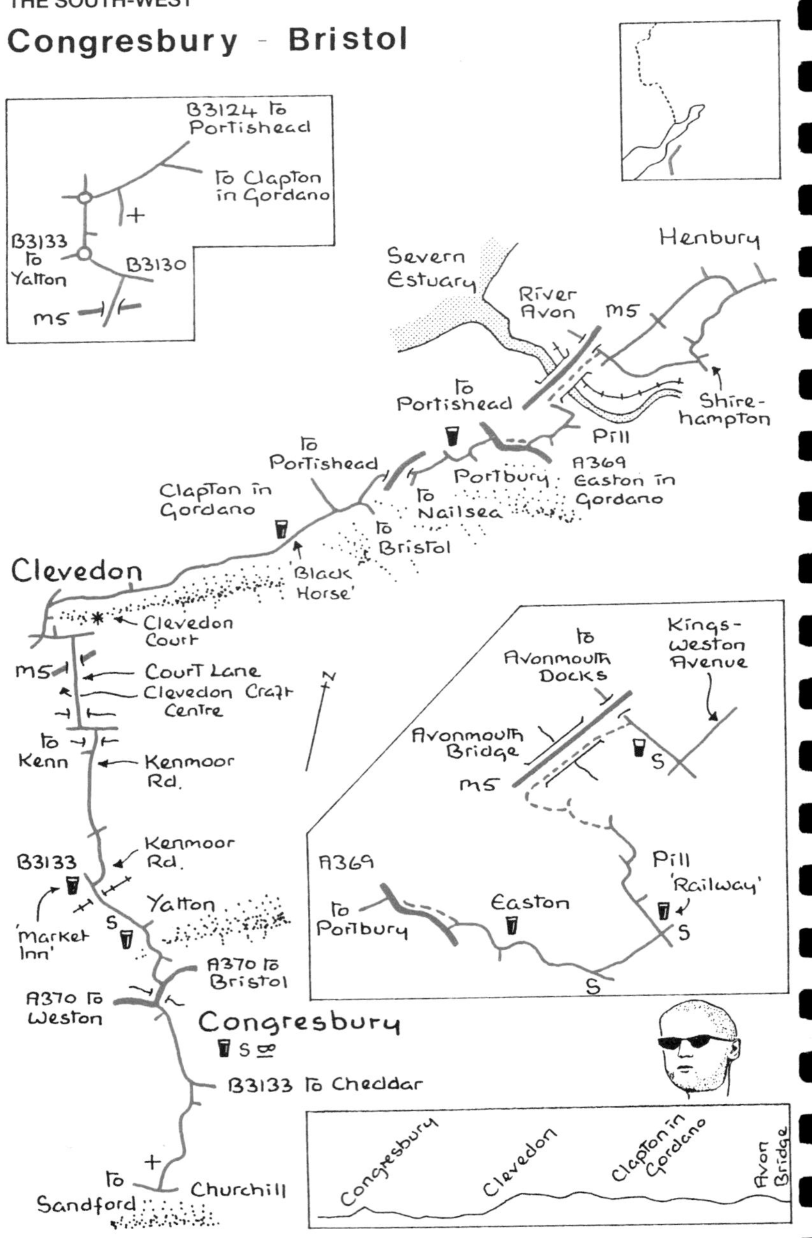

CONGRESBURY – BRISTOL 12 miles

A diorama of moving vegetation as the cyclist weaves through wooded waves. This is an easy run through leafy suburban countryside, assisted by Avon County Council's excellent cycle waymarking.

Clevedon **S** A fashionable Victorian seaside resort with a Victorian pier. Clevedon Court is a 14c manor house in the care of the National Trust.

Avon cycle routes. Avon has a circular 'Cycleway', with various link sections, as well as a series of other city and suburban cycle routes. The County Council deserve praise.

TIC Bristol (0117) 9260767
YHA Bristol centre (01272) 221659
Somerset Bike Centre, Congresbury (01934) 834441
A B's Motorcare, Yatton (01934) 838168
Bikeking, Clevedon (01275) 873551
Clevedon Cycles (01275) 341025
The Buycycle Shop, Portishead (01275) 818427
Velo-C, Pill (01275) 372314

Bristol - Severn Bridge

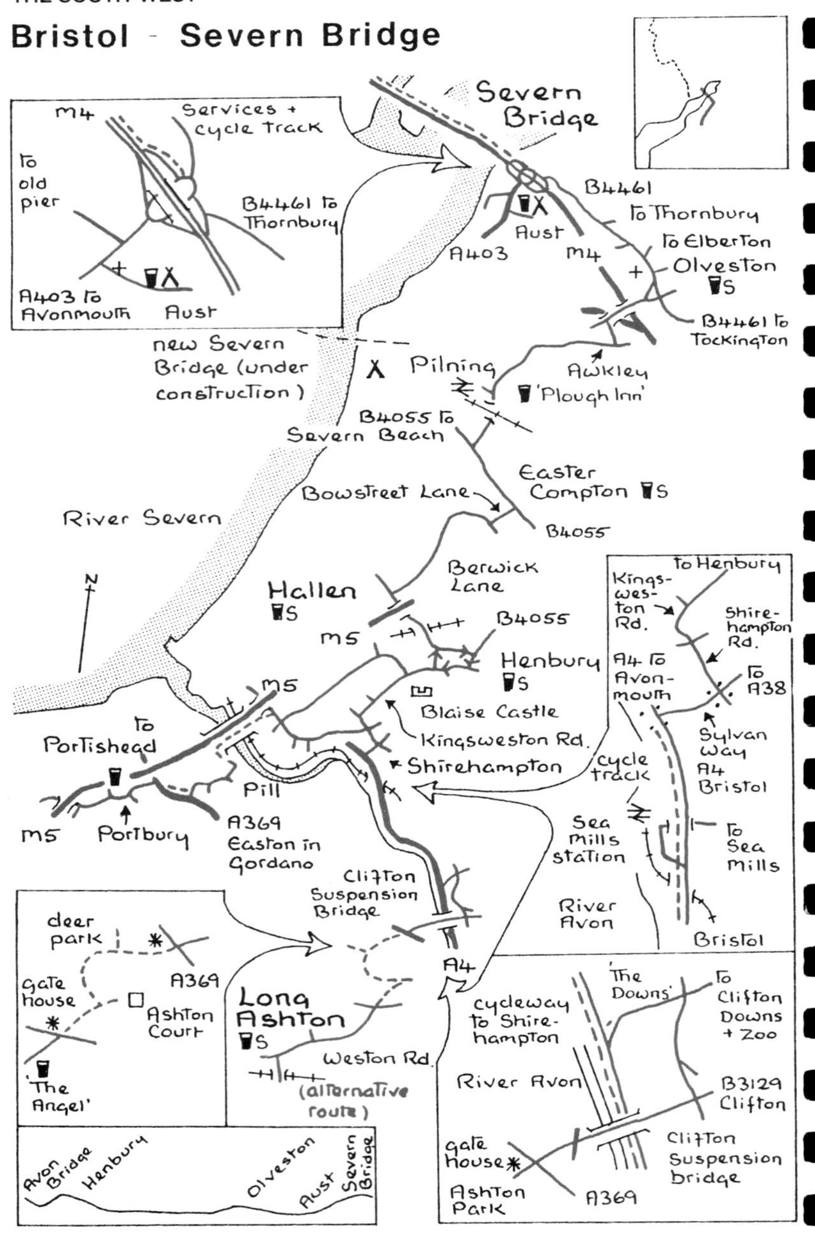

BRISTOL – SEVERN BRIDGE 14 miles

A painless and interesting ride through Bristol, edging into chemical-land at Hallen. By Pilning the city has been shaken off, apart from 'farm gymnasia', 'farm golf driving ranges' and 'horse farming' in profusion.

Bristol S An ancient commercial city and port. The Merchant Venturers were incorporated in 1552, and ships sailed the world from here, giving rise to the phrase "all ship-shape and Bristol fashion". There are lots of places of interest, especially the wharves and docks, including the SS Great Britain, the first large iron ship in the world, and the first to be propelled by a screw rather than paddles. It was launched in 1843 and salvaged in 1970.
Brunel's Clifton Suspension Bridge, 1864, is as impressive an engineering feat as the Severn Bridge.

Henbury S Blaise Castle House Museum is a late 18c House with a West Country museum, and a mid 18c Gothic Castle. Blaise Hamlet is a cluster of thatched cottages built in 1812 by JS Harford for his retired servants.

The Severn Bridge, completed 1966, has a central span of 3240feet (988m). A second road crossing is planned to be completed in 1997. The cycle path is an experience to savour, not only for the sheer volume of vacant space beneath your wheels, but you must also stop and put your feet down to experience the vibration and swaying of the bridge itself.

TIC Bristol (0117) 9260767
YHA Bristol Centre (01272) 221659
Chas Bland, Long Ashton (01275) 393696
Autopoint, Henbury
Harvey's Cycle Exchange, Westbury on Trym (0117) 629520
Pete's Cycles, Thornbury (01454) 281548
Thornbury Cycles (01454) 419225

ALTERNATIVE

Willand - Holman Clavel (the Blackdown Hills)

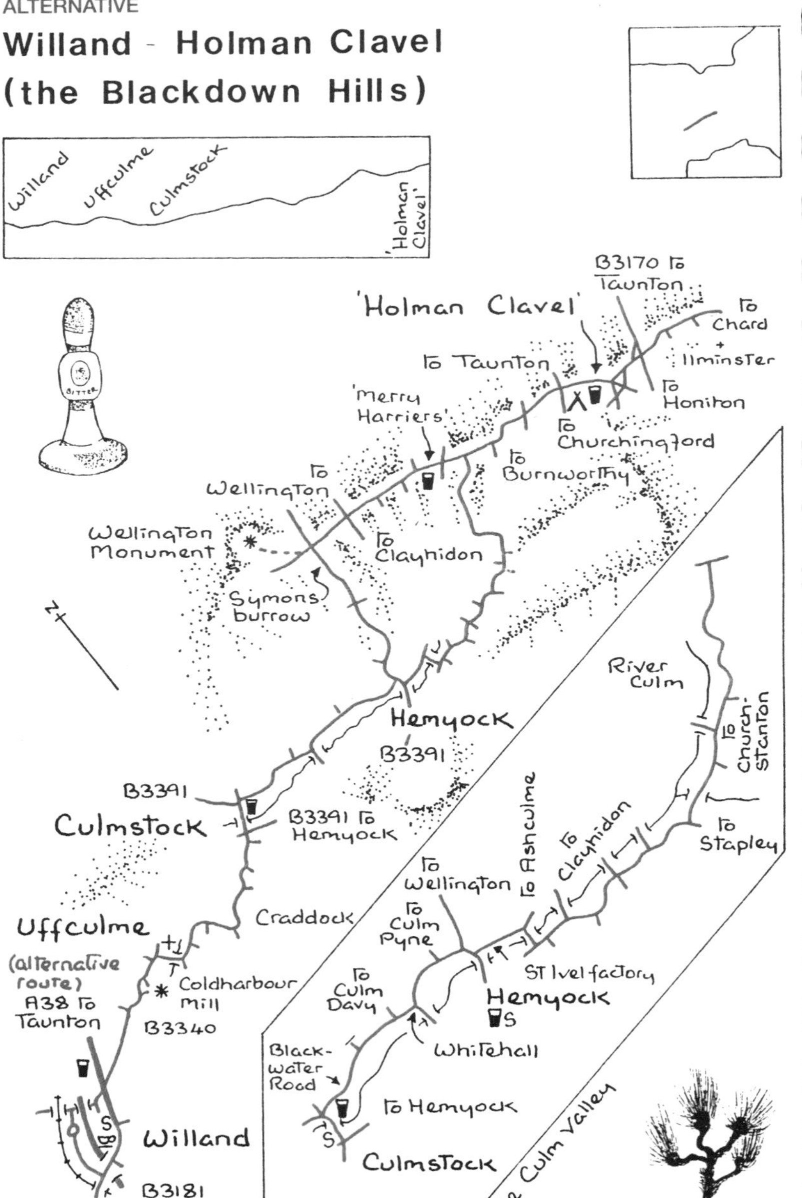

WILLAND – HOLMAN CLAVEL
(The Blackdown Hills) **11 miles**

A magic, arboreal valley with hidden corners round every corner. The minor roads become extra-minor as the climb begins to bite, culminating in a lovely pull-out at the top. A word of warning on the Blackdown Hills. They seem to form a vortex which plays havoc with direction finding.

Uffculme **S** Coldharbour Mill was a working woollen mill until 1981. It is now an award-winning working museum.

The 'Holmen Clavel Inn' has a hearth spirit called Chimbley Charlie. His seat is on the 'clavey', the beam above the fireplace, which is made of 'holman', the local word for holly.

The Blackdown Hills are known for the abundance of well-preserved fossils dating back seventy million years. The hills are layered flint, greensand and clay.

The Wellington Monument. The present one was erected in 1892. A fair called the 'Wake of Waterloo' was held around the base of the monument in 1819 but never repeated because of alleged 'drunkeness and debauchery'. The cannon was one of fifteen ordered in 1818, remnants of the Battle of Waterloo. It was finally delivered in 1985.

ALTERNATIVE

Holman Clavel - Muchelney

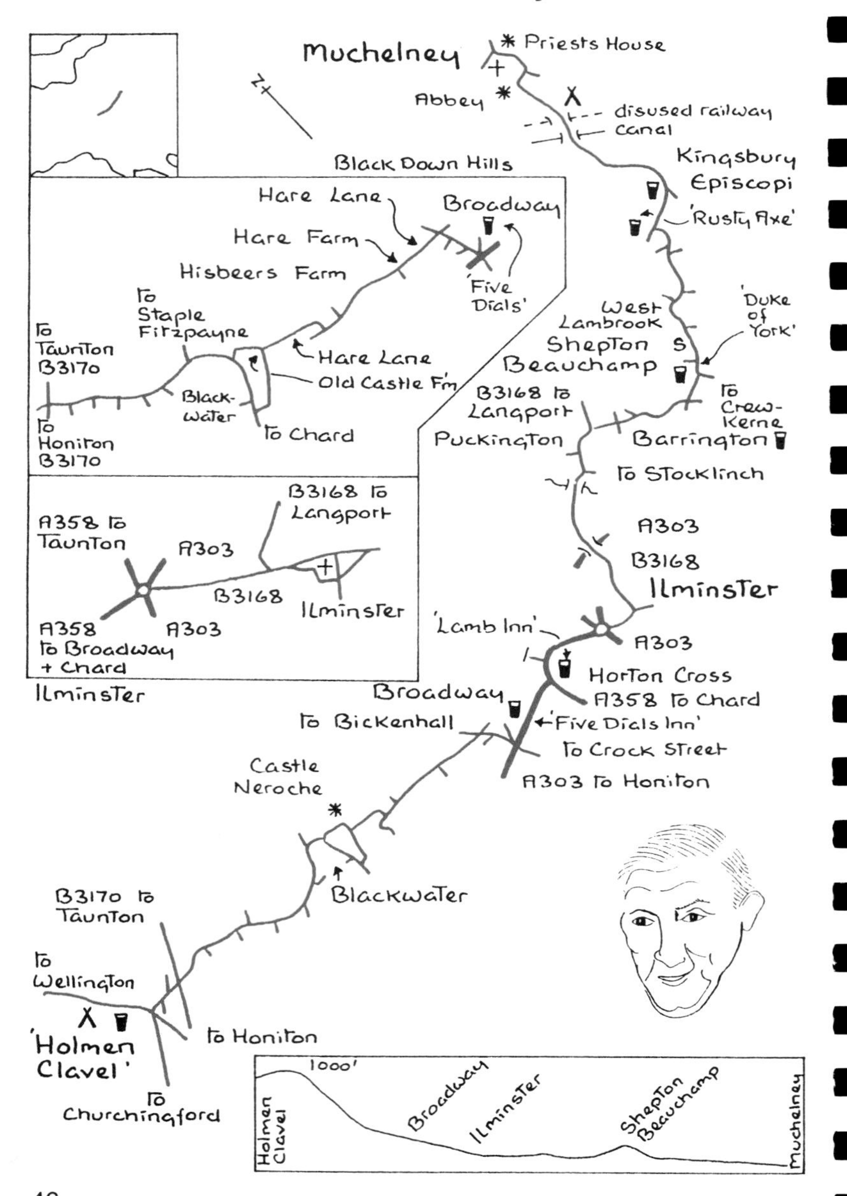

HOLMAN CLAVEL – MUCHELNEY 20 miles

South Somerset is a delicious part of the world for cyclists, flat, with warm stone villages, market gardening, willow growers, and orchards. Even the locals cycle.

Blackdown Hills. Gerard, in 1633, called the eastern end "the dirty forest of Rache". It includes the earthworks of Castle Neroche, an 11c fortification of William the Conqueror's half brother, the Count of Mortain. The ramparts were used as sand and gravel pits in the 19c and the trees planted from 1878. Many of these were felled in the Second World War, and replaced by the Forestry Commission.

Ilminster **S** Once a major Roman centre on the Fosse Way (Exeter to Lincoln). The Minster has one of Somerset's best towers. There is a small museum.

Barrington Court. Restored by the Lyle's of Tate & Lyle, the gardens are by Gertrude Jekyll.

Kingsbury Episcopi. Set in an area of small orchards, this village has an ancient lock-up on the green. The church is magnificent.

Muchelney. The Abbot's House is all that remains of the Benedictine Abbey, which was one of the great ecclesiastical settlements of the Middle Ages. Opposite is the home of John Leach, the potter. The Priest's House is late medieval with a large Gothic hall window.

Huish Episcopi. The church, built around 1505, belongs to the Bishops of Wells and has another wonderful tower.

Langport **S** It's prosperity was founded on the River Parrett, made navigable to Langport in 1836. The Navigation was abandoned forty years later, but is still used by small craft. The shops lean because of the sinking clay soil. The 'hanging chapel' was originally a 15c tradesmen's guildhall, then a chantry, grammar school and museum of stuffed birds. Langport is celebrated for its eels.

TIC Chard (01460) 67463

ALTERNATIVE

Muchelney - Wells

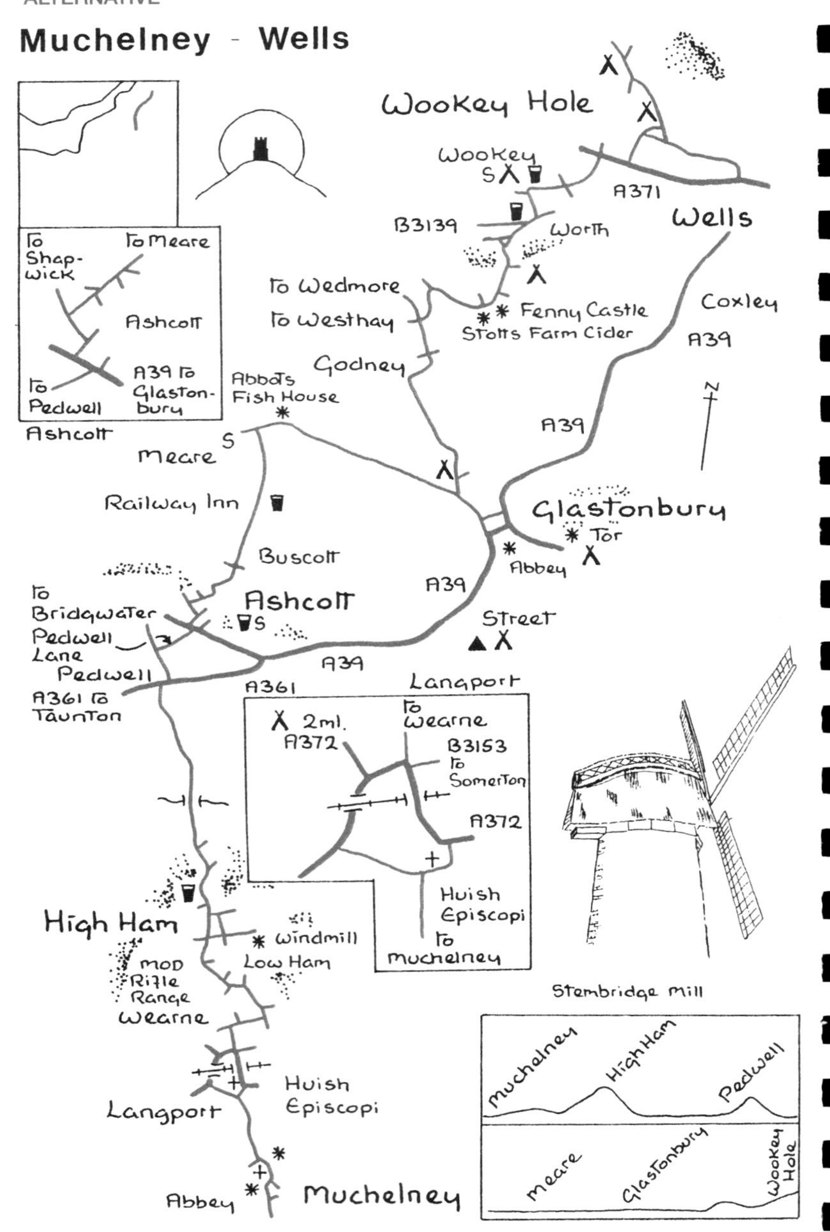

MUCHELNEY – WELLS 20.5 miles

Wheel from 'island' to 'island', High Ham, Polden Hills, Glastonbury, along a route guarded by pollarded willows in a 'sea' of bog and sedge. Watch for heron and surviving brick 'pill' boxes. The Mendips rise ominously ahead.

High Ham Stembridge Windmill is the only surviving thatched mill in the country. It dates from 1822 and operated until 1910. The 15c church of St Andrew has a row of gargoyles including a trumpeter, a man throwing stones and a monkey nursing a baby.

Meare **S** Until the 18c a huge marshy lake lay between Meare and Godney. A village of huts on stilts and brushwood mounds existed on and around the lake. The Abbots Fish House, 14c, was where fishermen, employed to supply the monks at Glastonbury, lived, salted and stored their catch. The Manor House, 1340, was the summer residence of the Glastonbury abbots.

Glastonbury **S** Until recently Glastonbury was an island in a shallow sea. The monastery was the second most wealthy in England after Westminster Abbey. It flourished from its refoundation in 943 to its dissolution by Henry the Eighth in 1593, when it's remains were plundered. Glastonbury is reputed to be the seat of King Arthur's Court, and the burial place of Arthur and Guinevere.
The Tor. In Arthur's day it was the island fortress of Melwas, King of Somerset. A post-Roman fort has been excavated, and the present tower, 15c, belongs to St Michael's Church.
Wearyall Hill. The site of the original winter flowering 'Holy Thorn' where Joseph of Arimathea landed and thrust his staff into the ground in AD60.
The Abbey. The ruins are the last of a series of buildings begun in AD633. The 13c Chalice Well is said to be the burial site of the Chalice Cup, or Holy Grail, sought by Arthur's Knights.
The Abbey Barn, 14c, houses the Somerset Rural Life Museum.
The Tribunal, 14c, a Courtroom, is now a museum.
See also the Glastonbury Lake Village Museum. Expect to meet crowds.

TIC Glastonbury (01458) 832954
YHA Street (01458) 42961
Franks Auto Needs and Cycles, Langport (01458) 250348
On Your Bike, Street (01458) 43048
Street Cycle Co (01458) 47882
TJ Cycles, Street (01458) 841715
Pedalers, Glastonbury (01458) 83117

ALTERNATIVE

Wells - Bristol (Mendip Hills)

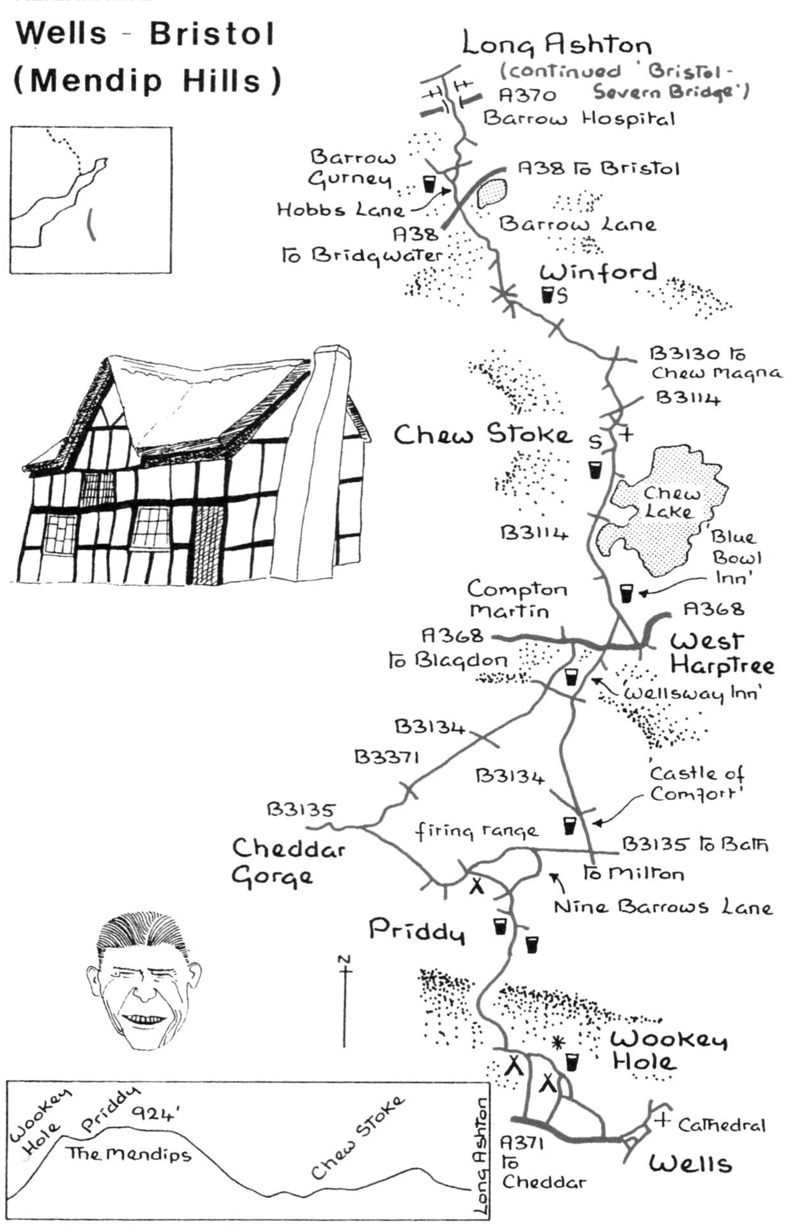

WELLS – BRISTOL (The Mendip Hills) 24 miles

The climb is steep, but not tremendously so, the views are spectacular and the descent to the north less challenging. Whilst ascending ponder the fact that the Mendips were the 'mountains green' in Blake's 'Jerusalem'. The approach to Bristol is relatively painless.

Wells **S** In the shadow of its cathedral, Wells is a beautiful town. The medieval ecclesiastical precinct is the best in the country. The wonderful cathedral was begun around 1180, and contains a remarkable 14c clock. See also the Bishops Palace (fortified and moated) and the Wells Museum.

Wookey Hole **S** The village is completely swamped by the car park for the caves, one of the major cave complexes in Britain. In 1852 six layers of habitation were found, including humans, mammoth, woolly rhinocerus, hippopotami, sabre-tooth tigers, wolves and buffalo. There are fantastic stalagmites and stalactities. The Caves are behind the Papermill, which dates from the early 17c, and still operates. There is also a collection of fairground carvings and relics, and moulds for Madame Tussauds.

Priddy Nearby are Swildon's Hole and Eastwater Cavern, popular with cavers. This plateau once housed a Roman leadworks and, much later, an annual fair held during the days of the Black Death, when locals climbed up here to escape the plague. The lead mines closed down completely at the beginning of the 20c by which time the neighbouring calamine (zinc oxide) deposits, worked for the British brass industry, had also expired.

TIC Wells (01749) 672552
Bristol (0117) 9260767
YHA Bristol Centre (01272) 221659
Bike N'Bits, Wells (01749) 670260
City Cycles, Wells (01749) 675096
Chris Bland, Long Ashton (01275) 393696

THE WELSH MARCHES

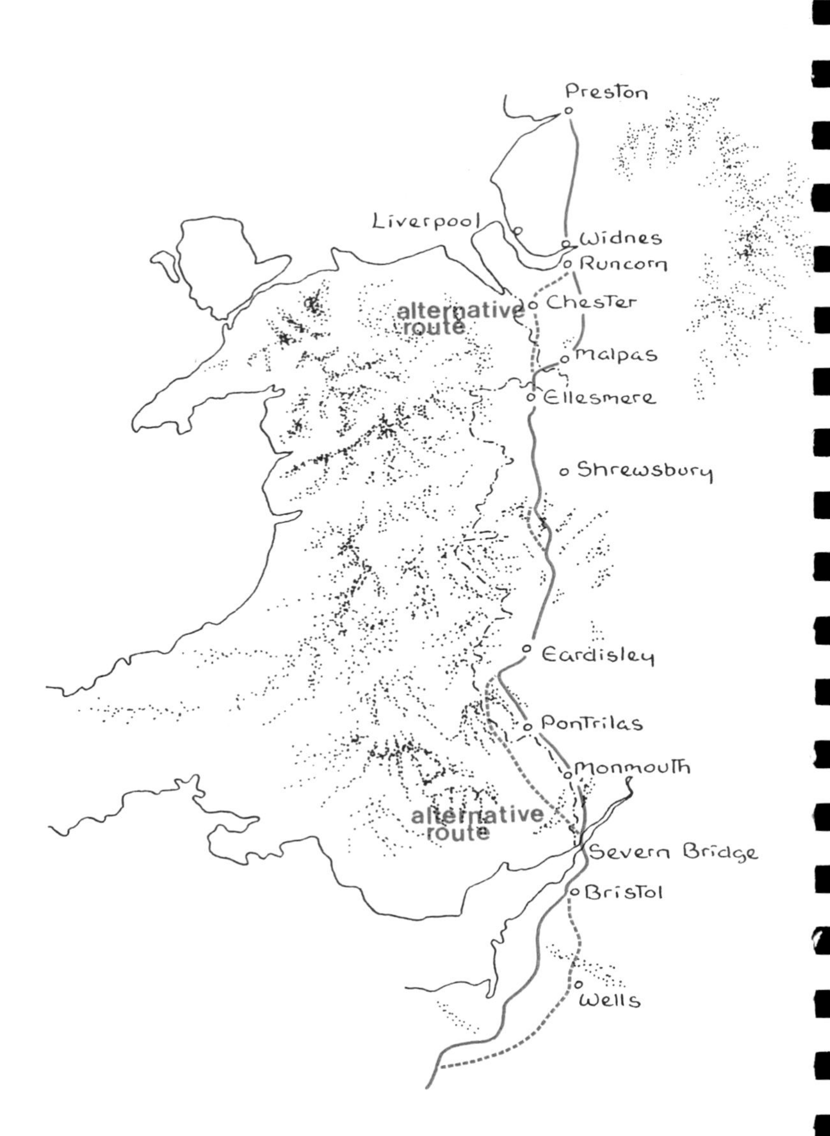

THE WELSH MARCHES

Route Choice For the next 50/60 miles there is a choice of route. Both have attractions.
The direct route follows the river valleys; the Wye to Monmouth, with its unique bridge; the Monnow to Pontrilas, taking in the castles at Skenfrith and Grosmont; and the Dore, past Abbey Dore and Peterchurch; to rejoin the Wye near Hay-on-Wye. This route has, in the main, gentle gradients, and what it lacks in grandeur and panoramas, it makes up for in discreet charm.
The alternative travels across country into Wales, taking in the border strongholds at Raglan and White Castle, before plunging deep into the Black Mountains along the Vale of Ewyas to Gospel Pass (1770ft), affording magnificent views of the Marches. This route is hilly.
Either alternative begins with a further choice. The Wye Valley is deeply cut into a plateau of between 700 feet and 900 feet elevation. On the English side the B4228 leads to the youth hostel at St Briavels, on the Welsh side the B4293 takes a high level route to Monmouth or Raglan. The road running along the Wye Valley is the splendid, but busy, A466, which also passes one of the finest abbey ruins in Britain, at Tintern.
At the northern end of the Marches the route choice is simple, between the more pleasant Malpas-Tarporley route, and the desire to visit Chester (and stay in the youth hostel there).

The Marches. Following the Norman invasion of Britain in 1066, William the Conqueror created the Marcher Earldoms along the Welsh border (March = mark or boundary). These, and numerous lesser Lordships, he gave to the most unruly of his followers, with a promise that they could keep any land which they could wrest from the Welsh, and they could rule by creating their own laws.

French Culture. The french culture was as alien to the 'English' Saxons as to the Welsh, but the Normans came in strength. Castles were built, large-scale farming introduced, new towns founded, market centres created and the ancient Celtic church brought under the rule of Canterbury and Rome.

The Boundary. The first demarcation between Wales and England was drawn by the Romans with their road between Chester and Caerleon (near Newport, Gwent). Welsh resistance to the Romans and the Saxons led to their being known to the Saxons as 'Wealas' and to themselves as 'Cymry' (fellow countrymen). The Welsh language emerged in AD400-600. In AD757-796 the Saxon King Offa marked the boundary with a dyke.

Resistance. Even though King Edward the First, in 1282, completed the conquest of Wales, the Welsh continued their resistance, typified by Owain Glyndwr (1400-1415). Peace finally came in 1536 when the marcher lordships were abolished and private Lords no longer had the power of life and death over the inhabitants.
Under the Tudors the woollen industry flourished and many of the timber-framed houses and the churches in the Marches date from this time (late 15c and 16c). The Industrial Revolution coupled with the Enclosures brought rural depopulation, which has continued until recently.

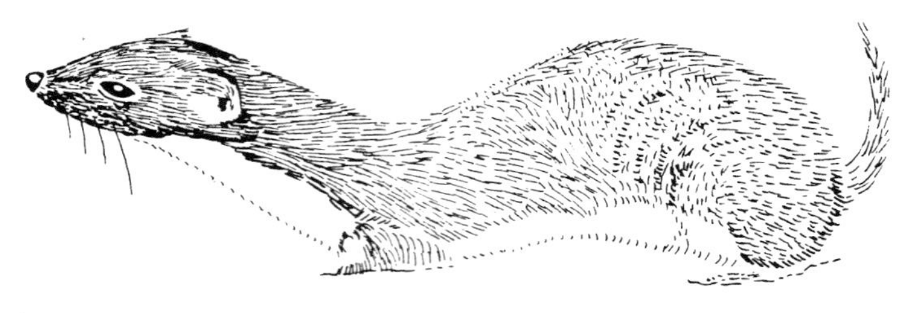

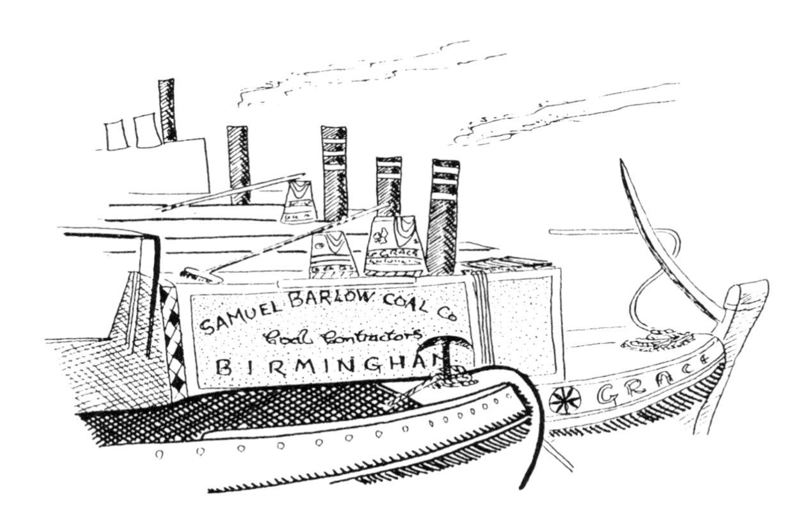
SAMUEL BARLOW COAL Co
Coal Contractors
BIRMINGHAM
GRACE

Severn Bridge - Monmouth

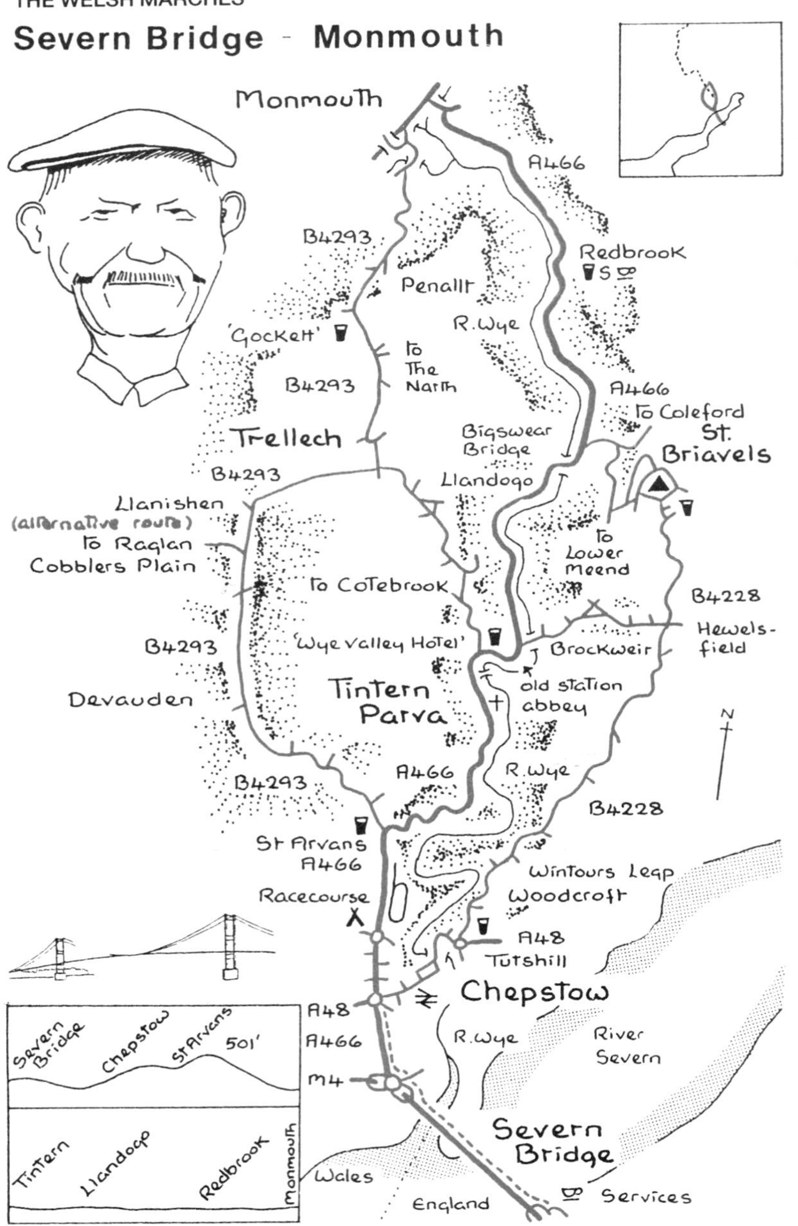

SEVERN BRIDGE – MONMOUTH
(The Wye Valley) 18 miles

The Wye Valley is a delight, but the A466 can be unpleasantly busy. An alternative from the magnificent Tintern Abbey is to climb up to Trellech (Treleck? – the road signs are not of one accord), and drop down again to Monmouth, or to take the B4293 from St Arvans all the way to Monmouth. The youth hostels are at St Briavels Castle, a not inconsiderable climb up the east side of the valley, and at Monmouth.

Chepstow (Casgwent) S Built on the Roman town of Castell Gwent, Chepstow's glory is the castle, the oldest stone castle in Britain. It was built by William Fitz Osbern, of whom it was said he built "the castle for his protection, the priory for his soul, and the town for his insurance". Chepstow Museum, local history: the Bulwarks, an Iron Age fort; Brunel's railway bridge and an iron bridge of 1816; stocks, 19c bow windows etc.

Wintour's Leap. Legend has it that a horseman made the prodigious leap to the river to escape his pursuers in the Civil War.

Tintern S The dramatic ruins of the Abbey date mainly from the 13c. In the 18c iron furnaces and wire works surrounded the Abbey, with river vessels bringing copper ore from Cornwall for the smelters and tinplate works. The railway opened in 1876. Look for the water wheel by the 'Royal George' (the last of over 20 in Tintern), Quay House and the restored railway station.

Monmouth S A pleasant market town based on a street plan unchanged since 1450. The town grew around a 12c castle and Benedictine monastery. The fortified bridge is unique. The town is associated with Charles Rolls (of Rolls Royce), Lord Nelson and King Henry the Fifth.
Monmouth Castle and Regimental Museum; the Nelson Museum, the life, loves and death etc.

TIC Chepstow (01291) 623772
Monmouth (01600) 713899

YHA St Briavels Castle (01594) 530272
Monmouth (01600) 715116
Full details of accomodation, including bed and breakfast, 'backyard' camping, hostels etc, on and around the Offa's Dyke Path from the Offa's Dyke Association, West Street, Knighton, Powys (01547) 528753.

Rough Riders, Chepstow
Monmouth Cycles Centre (01600) 772779
Overmonnow Garage, Monmouth (01600) 712632

Monmouth - Abbey Dore

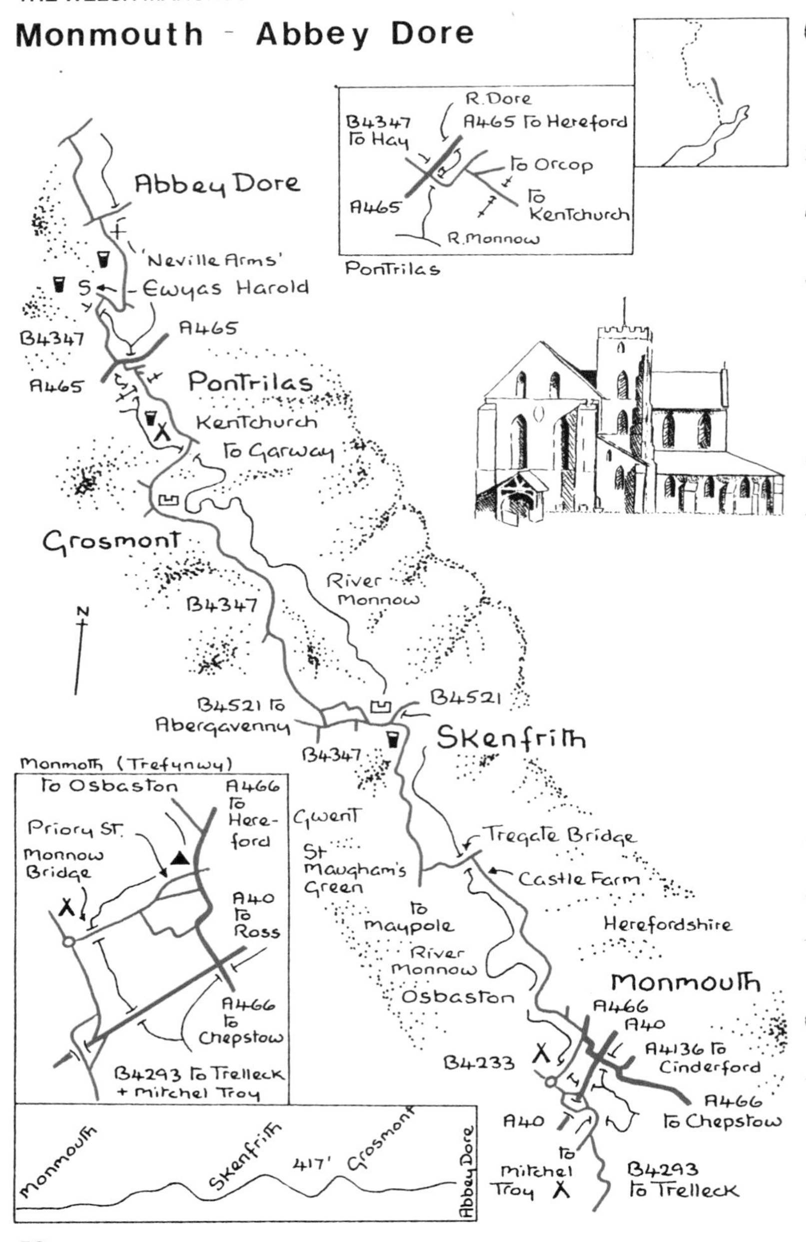

MONMOUTH – ABBEY DORE 16 miles

The valley to Skenfrith is a country-person's delight; mewing buzzards, vineyards, orchards, spinneys and copses in the discreet valley of the Monnow. A small climb at Skenfrith is followed by one at Grosmont, leading to the next valley, that of the River Dore.

Skenfrith The smallest of the 'three castles'. All three were granted to Hugh de Burgh in 1201, and all are worth exploring. The semi-fortified church tower has an impressive dovecote.

Grosmont **S** The small Town Hall indicates that this village was a borough from Norman times to the 19c. The street lighting is by old style lanterns hanging from the cottages. The impressive castle, the third of the 'three', saw Henry the Third flee under cover of darkness when it was attacked by Llewellyn the Great's army in the 13c.

Kentchurch The 14c castle was rebuilt by Nash in the 19c.

Ewyas Harold **S** Before the Norman Invasion of 1066 some of the Wessex nobles sensed trouble and began to 'dig in' on their new English estates. 1051 saw the first of the motte and bailey castles which became such a feature of the post-Conquest landscape. This was one of the first three. We know that the site was occupied after the Conquest by William Fitz Osbern, the Conqueror's right-hand man in the west, and that it was later equipped with a stone keep and gatehouse, but that is all.

Abbey Dore In 1632 the ruins of a 'dissolved' abbey (Cistercian, founded 1147) were sheltering cattle when rescued by a local squire. The atmospheric result has exceptional carvings.

TIC Monmouth (01600) 713899
YHA Monmouth (01600) 715116

Abbey Dore - Eardisley (the Golden Valley)

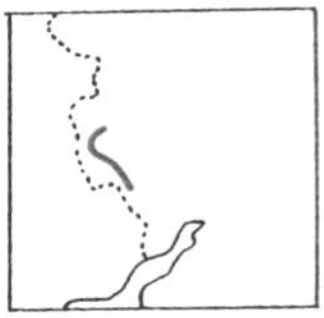

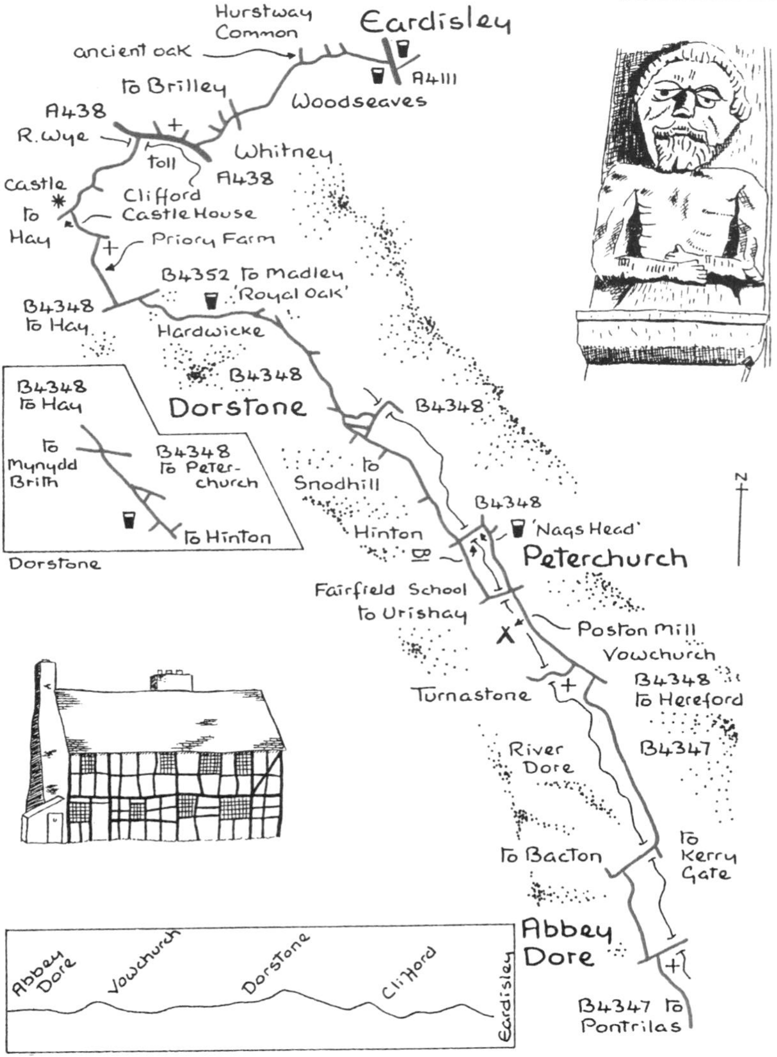

ABBEY DORE – EARDISLEY
(The Golden Valley) **18.5 miles**

Gentle cycling, floating along the mellow Golden Valley with its brick farms and orchards. The cafe is at Hinton. Sheltered by the Black Mountains, the Normans built more churches than castles here, and the 'Golden' is presumably from the french "d'or" (River Dore), but why 'Golden'?

Vowchurch. The hill-fort is prehistoric, the church rebuilt in the 14c and 15c.

Turnastone. Note the large enamelled Raleigh sign, a replacement for an earlier one in the 1920's.

Peterchurch **S** The Norman church is early, stark and bleak, with hardly any decoration but great size and majesty. One day local monks, both poor and hungry, went fishing in the River Dore. They caught an enormous trout with a golden chain around its neck, thus solving both their problems. Look also for Wellbrook Manor, a 14c Hall, and Urishay Castle, once a medieval fortress house, then a Jacobean Manor, now a ruin.

Dorstone **S** The church, 'restored' in 1889 is linked with Richard de Brito, one of the four knights who killed Thomas Becket in 1170. The Pandy Inn also has connections, having had Oliver Cromwell on its guest list. Above the village is Arthur's Stone, a burial chamber from 3000BC.

Clifford. The castle was built by William Fitz Osbern the first Marcher Earl of Hereford in 1067.

Whitney. Up the hill at Brilley is the 17c Cwmmau Farmhouse (National Trust).

Eardisley **S** A village of black-and-white houses. At the time of the Domesday Book it was at the centre of a vast forest, the last surviving tree being the Great Oak on Hurstway Common. In the mid-12c this district saw the emergence of the Herefordshire School of Sculpture, an example of which is the best Romanesque font in Britain, in the church, with high relief carvings of Christ despoiling Hell, battling Knights etc. The castle was once held by the Baskervilles and the area to the south is said to be haunted with ghostly black dogs. On May Bank Holiday the whole place is transformed into the Wild West, with stetson-hatted cowboys enjoying the stampede.

TIC Hay on Wye (01497) 820144

Joyrides Cycles, Peterchurch.

ALTERNATIVE

Severn Bridge - Raglan

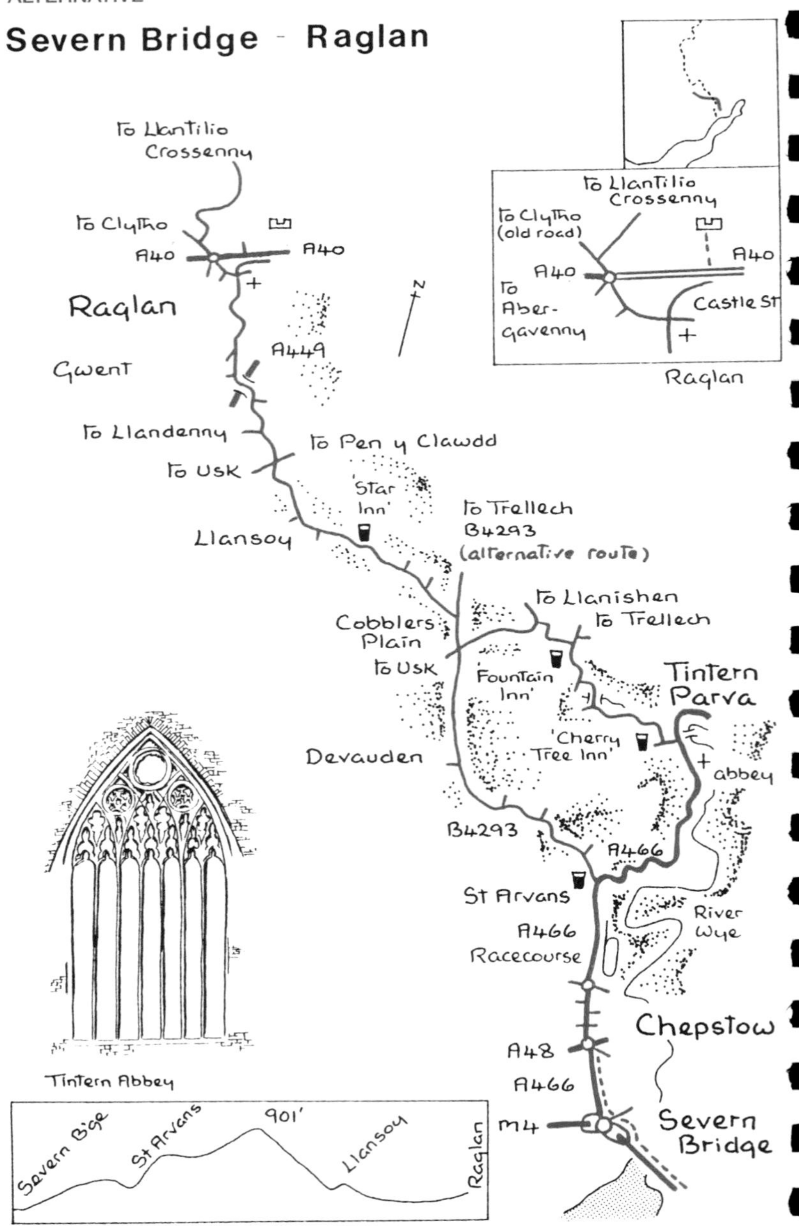

Tintern Abbey

SEVERN BRIDGE – RAGLAN 15 miles

A liquid, yielding land, well wooded with pockets of Morris Minors. The route climbs to St Arvans, and then up to Cobblers Plain, before descending to the impressive fortress at Raglan. Cyclists detouring to visit Tintern Abbey will have a few hundred feet of extra climbing. The occasional vineyard reinforces comparison with parts of France.

Raglan (Rhaglan) S The castle is the last example of medieval fortification to be built in Britain, mainly 15c and 16c. It was taken by Cromwell's New Model Army during the Civil War on 19 April 1646. The precise destruction wrought by the cannon can still be envisaged.

TIC Chepstow (01291) 623772
Abergavenny (01873) 857588
YHA St Briavels Castle (01594) 530272
Rough Riders, Chepstow

Raglan - Llanthony

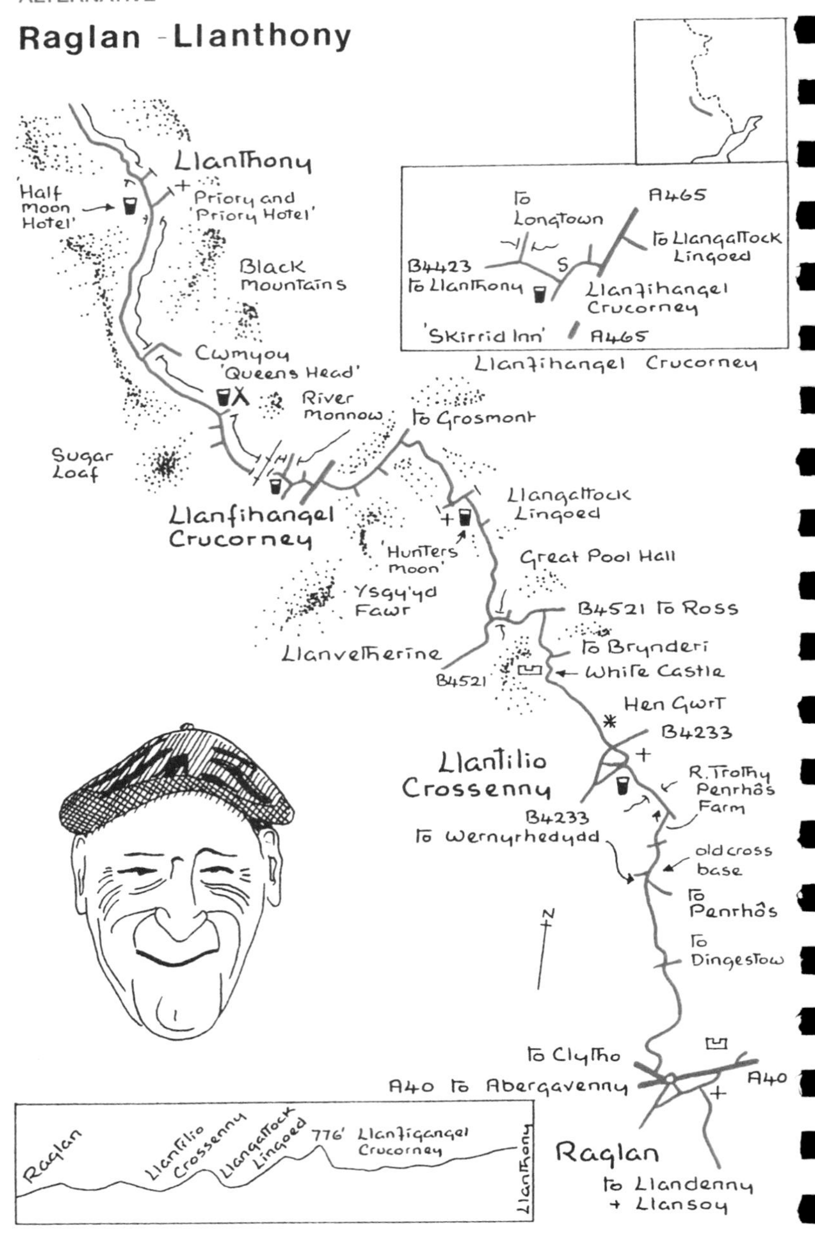

RAGLAN – LLANTHONY 19 miles

Cycling you have to graft at, across the swells and troughs of Gwent, before the waves part for the Vale of Ewyas. This is timeless, meandering, 'not-in-a-hurry' country, as Welsh as this route gets. The view from the summit above Llanfihangel Crucorney is panoramic.

Llantilio Crosseny The church is of 12c/13c origins. Note also Hen Gwrt, a moated, late medieval, hunting lodge (private).

White Castle The finest of the Three Castles guarding the Monnow Valley, granted to Hugh de Burgh in 1201. Around it is an abandoned medieval settlement.

Llanthony Priory An Augustinian priory dating from 1175. The remnants include a pub.

TIC Abergavenny (01873) 857588
Hay on Wye (01497) 820144
Accomodation – Bunkhouse barn, Court Farm, Llanthony (01873) 890359

ALTERNATIVE

Llanthony - Eardisley

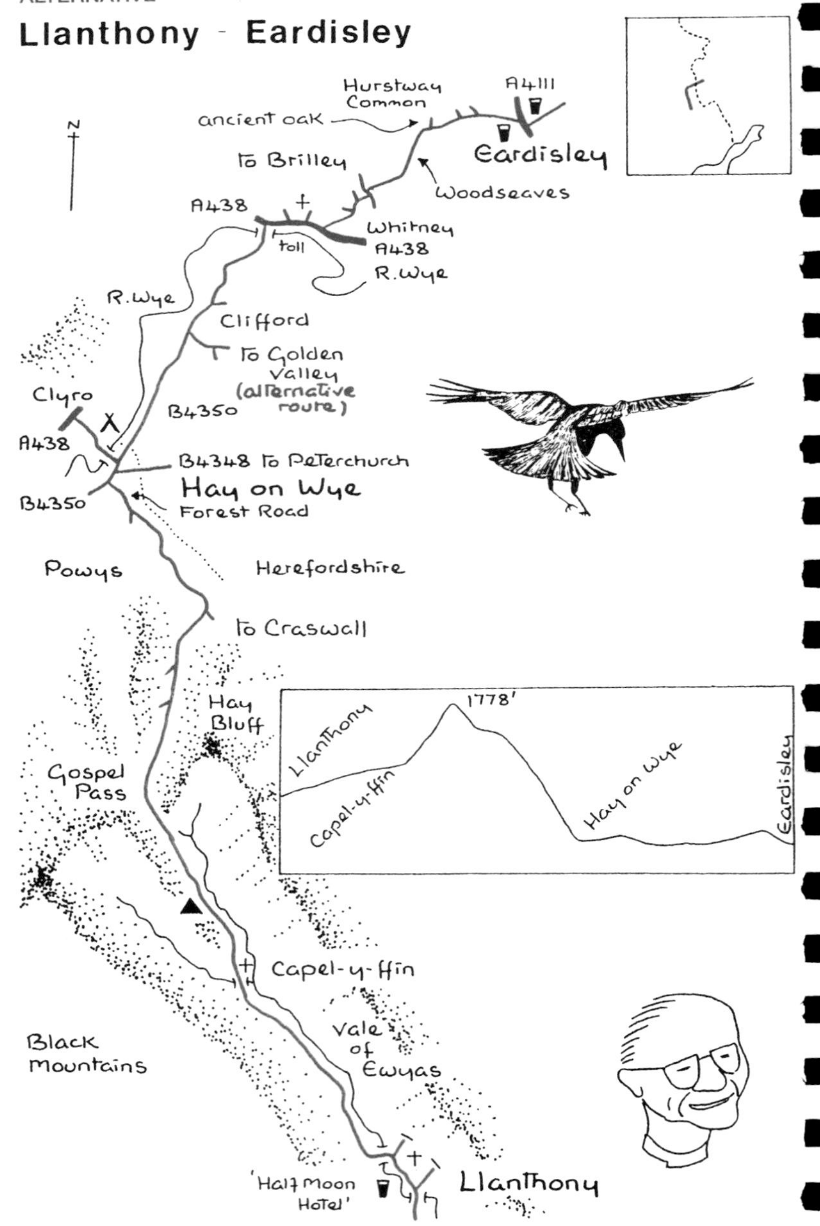

LLANTHONY - EARDISLEY
(The Black Mountains) **20 miles**

The brilliant, long valley running through the peaceful grandeur of the Black Mountains becomes effervescent as the cyclist grapples with the steep, muscular, sections ("worn out by the climbing, knocked out by the view"), approaching Gospel Pass. A big descent leads to civilisation, well, to Hay on Wye. This alternative links with the 'main line' at Clifford.

Capel-y-ffin. A small chapel, founded by the Rev. Joseph Leycester in 1870, is now a Roman Catholic retreat.

Hay on Wye (Y Gelli) S A small, eccentric, border market town with the remains of an 11c motte castle. It is famous nowadays for the plethora of secondhand bookshops.

Clyro. Here Francis Kilvert wrote his mid-Victorian diary of parish life.

TIC	Hay on Wye (01497) 820144
	Presteigne (01544) 260193
YHA	Capel-y-ffin (01873) 890650

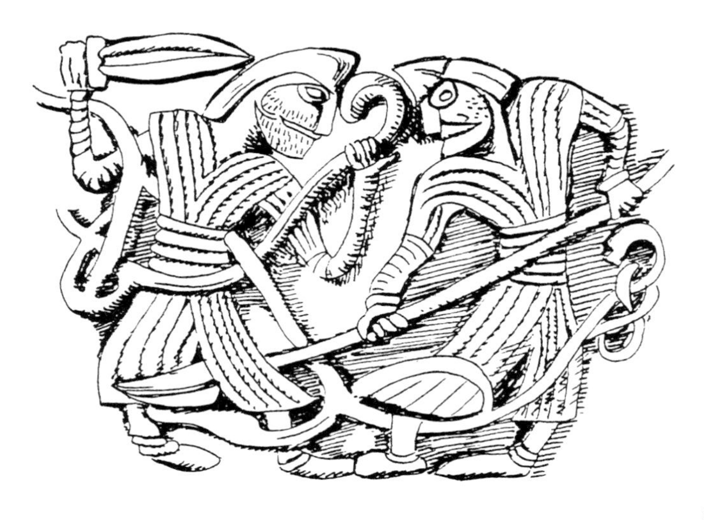

Eardisley - Bucknell

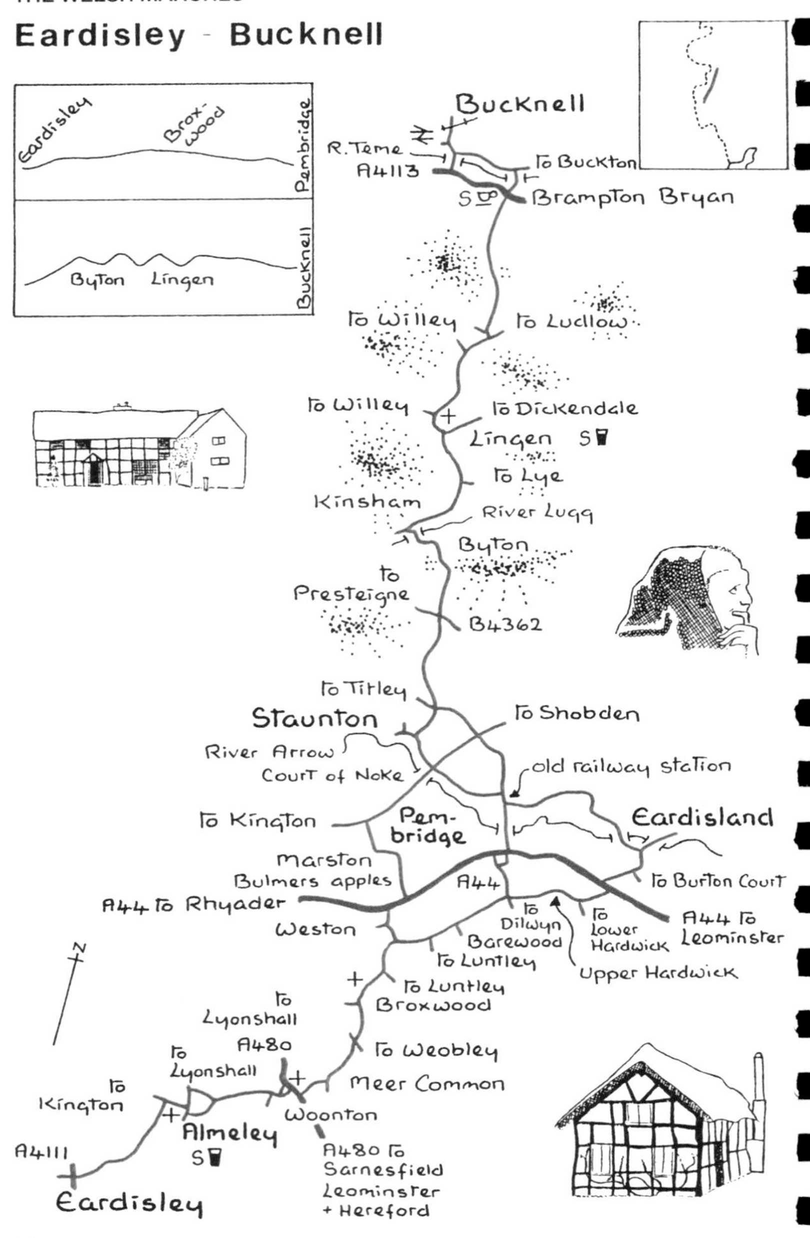

EARDISLEY – BUCKNELL 20.5 miles

Float along, with hedgerows upholstering the landscape, and almost every building a delight. Watch for ancient buildings, ancient people, ancient trees, ancient cider presses and ancient bicycles. The cyclist can choose, if they so wish, to detour to Pembridge and Eardisland. At Staunton there is an abrupt change from the fertile Arrow Valley, littered with apple blossom, to hill country. The pulse rate quickens.

Pembridge **S** An amazing village with houses from every period from the 14c. The church has a three-storey detached belfry; the 16c Market Hall has an open ground floor.

Eardisland **S** Another stunning 'black and white' village with houses spread along the river, including Staick House with its great hall, built around 1300.

Staunton-on-Arrow. This small village includes the 18c Court of Noke and the 16c Old Court.

Brampton Bryan S Another wonderful village. Bryan de Brampton built a fortress here in the 13c. His daughter, Brittiana married Robert Harley (of the Harley Street in London family), who added a castle, the ruins of which remain. The Hall has one of the seven wonders of the hedge world. Across the river is Coxwall Knoll, the site of a prehistoric camp, and said to be the site of the last battle between the Welsh Caractacus and the Romans.

Bucknell **S** Note the ornate G.W.R. signal box and station on the Mid-Wales line, alas, now surplus to British Rail's requirements and sold off. The local W.I. magnanimously maintain what is left of the station.

TIC Presteigne (01544) 260193
Knighton (01547) 528753
Leominster (01568) 611046

Bucknell - Ratlinghope

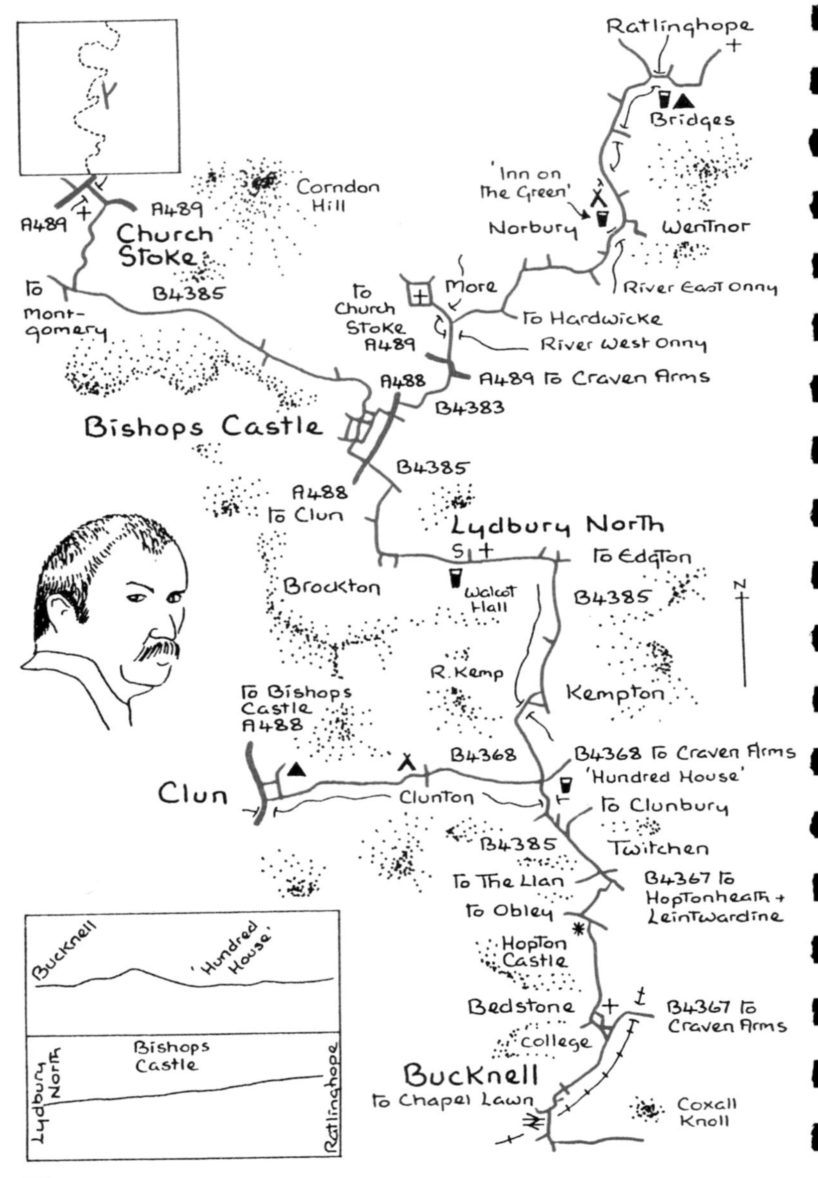

BUCKNELL - RATLINGHOPE 21 miles

Perfect cycling country. The landscape is as varied as a good salad. Relax at the end of the day with a pint of fine beer, soaking up the last embers of the summer sun, and feel at peace.
At Bishops Castle there is an alternative. Ahead are the Stiperstones, involving a climb of 700ft. These hills roll around deliciously and make a welcome break from the farmland. They are the last hills you will encounter before the Lake District. If you still insist on a low-level route, cycle through Church Stoke and Chirbury.

Hopton Castle. During the Civil War Col. Samuel More, with thirty fellow Parliamentarians, held out against a siege by five hundred Royalists for three weeks. On surrender, all were shot.

Clun Valley. This was a major droving route, with Craven Arms developing a large market for the sheep from Wales. The black-faced Clun sheep produce high quality wool and meat.

Lydbury North **S** An exceptionally pleasing Norman church was harmonised by Micklethwaite's restoration earlier this century. Walcot Hall was built for Clive of India in the late 18c.

Bishops Castle **S** Built on the ecclesiastical estate of the Bishops of Hereford, this 13c 'new' town once returned two Members of Parliament. A personal favourite is the 'Three Tuns', a home-brew pub dating from 1642.

More. One of the 'lost villages' of Middle England. This small settlement, dependent on the Castle, was probably founded soon after the Conquest.

TIC	Knighton (01547) 528753
	Ludlow (01584) 875053
	Welshpool (01938) 552041
YHA	Clun Mill (01588) 640582
	Bridges (01588) 61656
	Castle Garden and Leisure, Bishops Castle (01588) 638690

Ratlinghope - Melverley

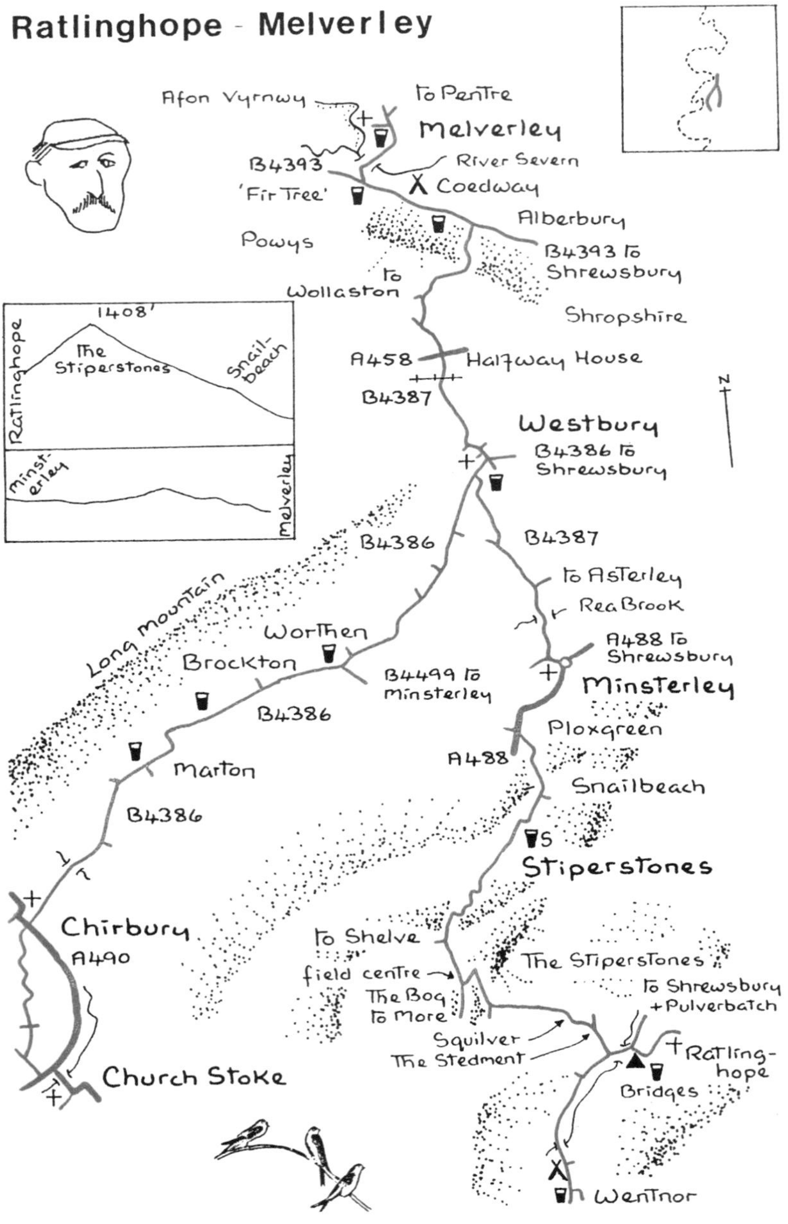

Afon Vyrnwy
To Pentre
Melverley
B4393
River Severn
'Fir Tree'
Coedway
Alberbury
Powys
B4393 To Shrewsbury
To Wollaston
Shropshire
1408'
Ratlinghope
The Stiperstones
Snail-beach
Minst-erley
Melverley
A458
Halfway House
B4387
N
Westbury
B4386 To Shrewsbury
B4386
B4387
Long mountain
To Asterley
Rea Brook
Worthen
A488 To Shrewsbury
Brockton
B4499 To Minsterley
Minsterley
B4386
Ploxgreen
A488
Marton
Snailbeach
B4386
S
Stiperstones
Chirbury
To Shelve
A490
The Stiperstones
field centre
The Bog
To More
To Shrewsbury + Pulverbatch
Squilver
The Stedment
Ratling-hope
Church Stoke
Bridges
Wentnor

RATLINGHOPE – MELVERLEY
(The Stiperstones) **15.5 miles**

All the interest is at the beginning and the end. The pull up the Stiperstones is steep, to the old mining country, where present day inhabitants eek out a living somehow. The second crossing of the River Severn is handy but not inspiring, on an old railway bridge, but Melverley Church is astonishing. Between is rather nondescript.

Stiperstones. This band of quartzite was subject to much frost shattering in the last Ice Age, giving rise to this wild, rugged landscape. The Romans discovered and mined lead, and extensive mining of the lead and zinc began around 1784. These few square miles produced ten per cent of Britain's lead ore. What remains are collapsed pumping houses and overgrown waste heaps. The acid moor is now a National Nature Reserve.

Snailbeach. In the 1850's five hundred people were employed in mining here. The Snailbeach District Railway began at Crowsnest Dingle.

Minsterley **S** Inside the 17c Baroque brick church are the Seven Maidens Garlands (18c) which were carried at the funerals of young women who had died before marriage.

Alberbury. The remains of the castle are linked to the church with a massive 14c saddleback tower. Nearby are the remains of Alberbury Priory, founded in 1225.

Melverley. The church is wonderful, 15c, timber, wattle and daub, with pegs not nails throughout.
The Tontine Inn. A tontine was a favourite form of insurance among the river men of the Severn, the subscriptions going to the last survivor. The Severn was navigable for some miles upstream of here.

TIC Welshpool (01938) 552041
Church Stretton (01694) 723133
YHA Bridges (01588) 61656
Stan Jones Cycles, Shrewsbury (01743) 343775

Melverley - Ellesmere

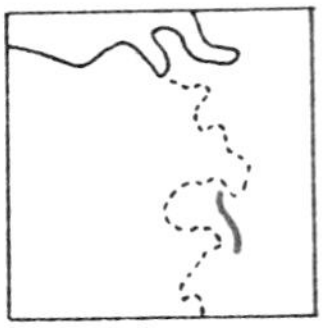

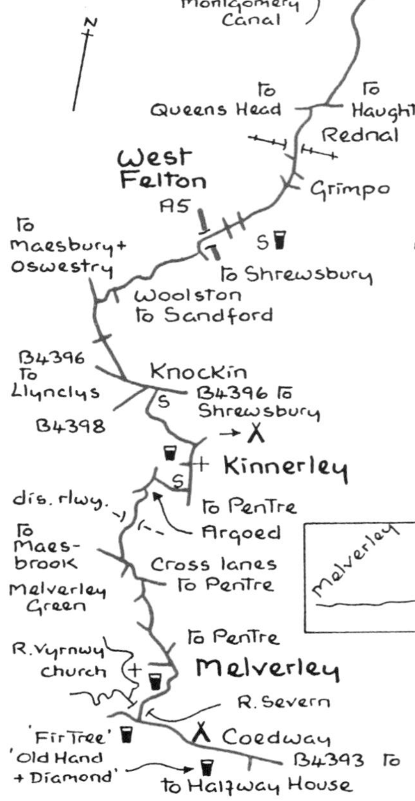

A528 to Wrexham
Swan Hill
Cemy
mere
Watergate St.
Canal basin
A495
A495 to Oswestry
'White Hart'
Llangollen Canal
to Tetchill
Ellesmere

To Penley
A528
Greenacres
The Mere
Ellesmere
A495
A495
To Hordley
Llangollen Canal
Ellesmere College
Tetchill
Welsh Frankton
Hordley
Montgomery Canal
N
To Queens Head
To Haughton
Rednal
West Felton
Grimpo
A5
To Maesbury + Oswestry
S
To Shrewsbury
Woolston
To Sandford
B4396 To Llynclys
Knockin
B4396 To Shrewsbury
S
B4398
Kinnerley
S
dis. rlwy.
To Pentre
To Maesbrook
Argoed
Cross lanes
To Pentre
Melverley Green
To Pentre
R. Vyrnwy
church
Melverley
R. Severn
'Fir Tree'
Coedway
'Old Hand + Diamond'
B4393 To Shrewsbury
to Halfway House

Melverley
West Felton
Hordley
Ellesmere

MELVERLEY - ELLESMERE
(North Shropshire) 14.5 miles

Looking north the plain stretches out like a green, fuzzy blanket. It contains nothing remarkable, and hardly any rivers, just the odd wartime relic, an occasional hamlet or village, perhaps a fellow cyclist, but the rider bowls along, gently undulating, through countryside at peace with itself. It would not always have been like this, for the Welsh, looking down from the austerity of the blue hills in the West, were tempted by the English wealth.

Welsh Frankton. Between 1791 and 1803, at the time of 'canal mania', navigable canals were built from Ellesmere Port to Chester and on to Ellesmere, Llangollen and Newtown, Powys. Welsh Frankton is the junction between the popular cruising canal to Llangollen and the Montgomery Canal, abandoned in 1936, but now beginning to be restored to navigation. Sixty years ago, and for a hundred and forty years before that, this junction would have been alive with commercial boats, carrying stone, coal, grain etc to canalside wharves and mills.

Ellesmere **S** The surrounding countryside contains drumlins, meres and peat mosses left by a retreating ice sheet during the Ice Age. The meres attract many species of wild duck, geese, grebes, gulls cormorants and rarer birds.

North Shropshire Villages Nearly all of the present day settlements were mentioned in the Domesday Book, although much of the area in the Middle Ages was kept as wilderness by powerful landlords for deer parks and game reserves. Although the Welsh occupied the area from time to time, land cultivation can be traced back to the Dark Ages.

The Enclosures. The Montgomery Canal was built primarily to improve the agriculture in the Severn Valley. Thousands of acres were improved in the late 18c. The large estates flourished, but the losers were the peasants, deprived of their grazing rights by the enclosures. Famine resulted in 1817, and rural depopulation, with many moving to the expanding towns or abroad.

TIC Shrewsbury (01743) 350761
Ellesmere (01691) 622981

M. Butler, Ellesmere (01691) 622101

Ellesmere - Beeston

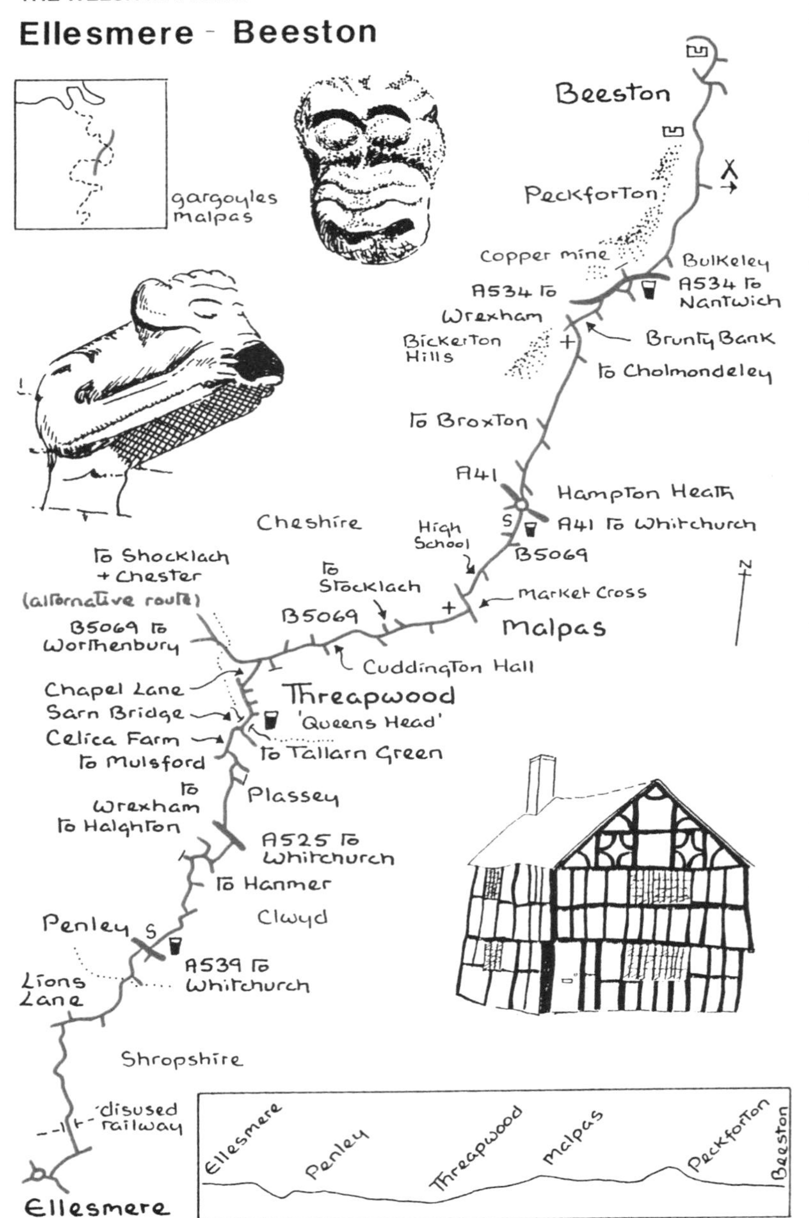

ELLESMERE – BEESTON 20.5 miles

Unrelentingly pastoral; lush and green; birds singing; horses neighing; fresians munching; glorious tree-lined hedgerows, pleasant villages. To the north the wood-cloaked sandstone hills provide a welcome break, and in Peckforton watch for the ultimate in garden ornaments, a huge elephant bearing castle.
At Threapwood 'master choice' once again rears his ugly head. On the one hand there is the pleasant rural route through Malpas, via the sandstone hills (deftly navigated) to the Forest of Delamere and thence to darkest Lancashire, OR, on the other, the not-quite-so pleasant ride up the River Dee to Chester, and the decidedly-not-pleasant-at-all ride to join the main route at Runcorn. The jewel of this route is Chester, which contains not only a youth hostel, but ranks high among historic British cities.

Malpas S An ancient parish originally called Depenbach, but taking its present name from a bad pass on the old Roman road. The church of St Oswald is atmospheric, with oddities deserving exploration. Bishop Reginald Heber was born here. He wrote the hymns "Holy, holy, holy" and "From Greenlands icy mountains" before becoming Bishop of Calcutta.

Peckforton Castle. Medieval in design, built 1844-50 for Lord Tollemache. 'Robin Hood, Prince of Thieves' was filmed here.

Beeston Castle. Built 1220 by Randle Blunderville, Earl of Chester. In December 1643 three hundred Roundheads were holding the castle when a surprise attack by eight Royalists sent them fleeing. They in turn were beseiged, and, on surrender, Parliament ordered the castle to be devastated. It is now a haven for wild flowers.
Beeston Hall is a moated farmhouse, the ancient home of the Beestons of Beeston.
Between the hills is the ancient manor of Horsley. Here is a spring used in the 18c as a bath for the cure of rheumatism.

Cheshire. This is the richest and most beautiful part of Cheshire, known for its cheese, red, white and 'old blue'. It was often overrun in the past by the Welsh. An odd knob of land remains Welsh, now part of Clwyd, formerly 'part of Flint'.

TIC Ellesmere (01691) 622981
Whitchurch (01948) 665761

Beeston - Runcorn

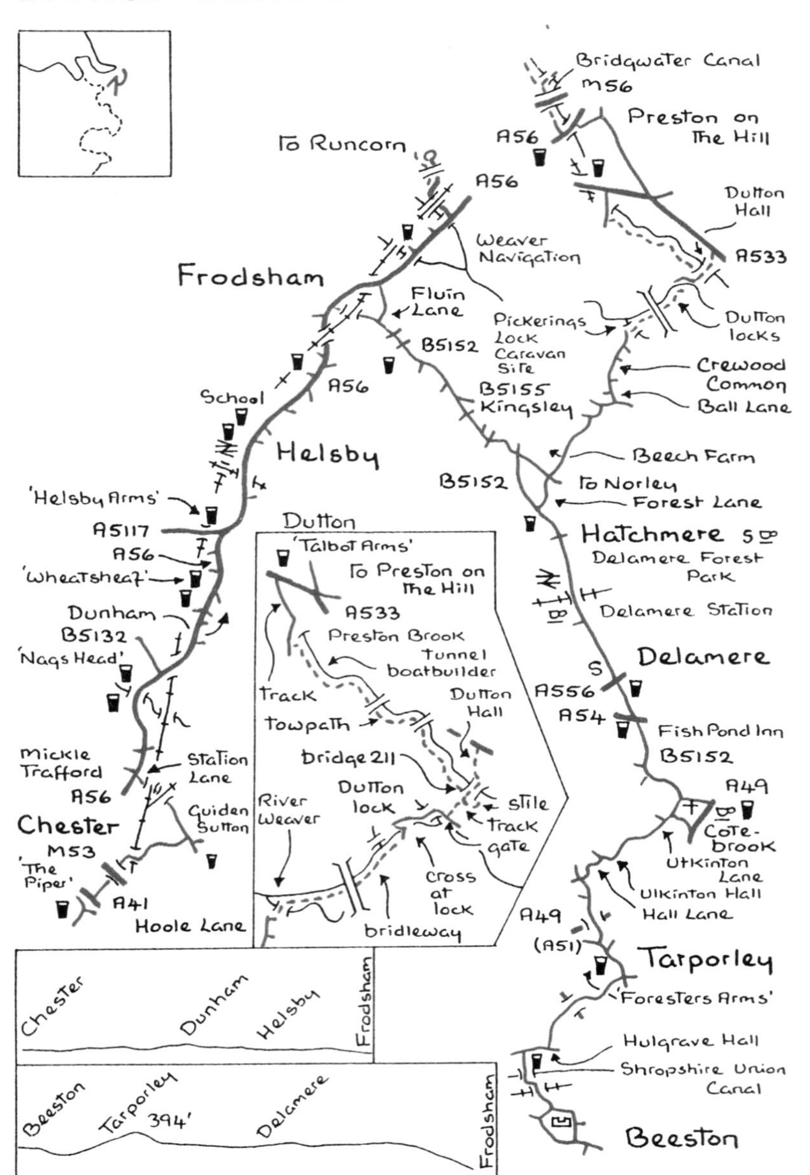

BEESTON – RUNCORN 16.5 miles

Lush, green and horsey, a countryside well suited for broughams, gigs and traps; unfortunately the combustion engine is well in control. Be warned, Cheshire is not the best signposted of counties. You are fast approaching the busiest section of the whole route, and hence there is choice within choice. The fast (if you don't get lost) direct line drops you into Frodsham and, via the A56, onto the rather confusing cycle network of Runcorn. The alternative is the peaceful, interesting route utilising the towpaths of the Weaver Navigation, Trent and Mersey Canal and Bridgwater Canal, on which you will be accompanied by heron, coot and narrow-boats. It is decidedly slower, and, in wet weather, muddier.

Tarporley **S** An important staging post for the London-Chester mail coaches, with a turnpike as early as 1743. The 'Rising Sun' is medieval. The 'Swan Hotel', 1769, is the meeting place of the Tarporley Hunt, the oldest hunt club in England. The great homes in this area bear witness to a prosperous past, though many have become country clubs, or, at Oulton Park, a motor-racing circuit.

Utkinton. The Hall, now a farmhouse, was formerly the seat of the Drones, who were Chief Foresters for the King at Delamere Forest, in the days when the sovereign visited the Vale Royal for hunting. The Forest Museum is near Delamere Station.

Frodsham. Once a major port at the mouth of the Weaver before it was canalised. It is an ancient borough, though the Norman castle was burned down in 1654. The 'Bears Paw', of 1632, survived as a coaching inn. The 15c church has a memorial to Peter Banner, a local carpenter, who died of the dropsy in 1749, but who "in 33 months was tapp'd 58 times, and had 1032 quarts of water taken from him".
It is also famous for its vicars, including WC Cotton, who sang 'God Save the Queen' for the Prince of Wales at Waterloo as a duet, with his parrot Papagay.

Weaver Navigation. This still carries commercial traffic for the salt and chemical industries. It became fully navigable in 1732.

TIC Chester (01244) 317962/351609/318916/322220
Warrington (01925) 442180/444400
Runcorn Cycle Centre (01928) 560727

Threapwood - Chester

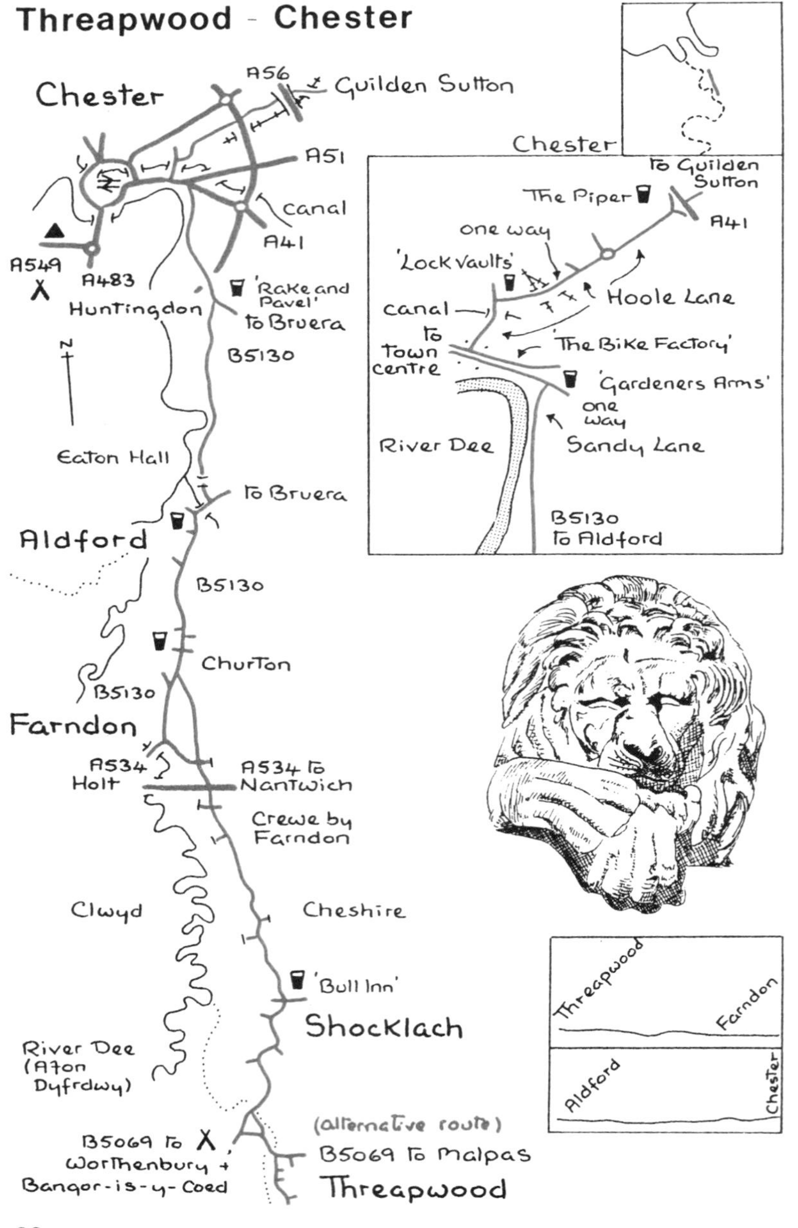

THREAPWOOD – CHESTER
(The Dee Valley) 14 miles

This modest section has much to be modest about. Cheshire is a car-borne county, making these roads to Chester, Helsby and Frodsham not particularly dangerous, but not pleasant. The landscape is unambitious, and you look down on Wrexham and the petrochemicals industry of Ellesmere Port. Farndon is a commuter village specialising in Scotties and Pekenese, Helsby a busy working town and Frodsham is busy but surprisingly pleasant.

Farndon. A village famous for its strawberries and plums. In the church, stained glass commemorates the Civil War. This area 'saw much action' as fortunes swayed. In every border conflict Farndon Bridge has been important, and during the Civil War Roundhead batteries in the churchyard pounded the Royalist-held Holt Castle.

Aldford. An estate village for the Duke of Westminster. There are lots of obscure moates and mottes hereabouts providing refuge from the rising flood water and the Welsh.

Chester. Founded by the Roman, Julius Agricola. The four Roman gates in the city walls survive. The Anglo-Saxons arrived to stay in 680AD and in the 9c Lady Ethelfleda, Lady of Mercia, rebuilt the walls against the attacking Danes. It then became a royal city, with a mint and palace, and was an important stronghold against the Welsh, and in the Civil War. Fire, civil war damage and Victorian 'improvements' have changed the town but much remains.
City Walls; Grosvenor Museum (Roman remains); Dewa Roman Experience; Roman amphitheatre and hypercaust; the Rows; Chester Cathedral and St John's Church; Chester Heritage Centre; St Mary's Centre; Castle Street Georgian House; King Charles Tower; 'On The Air' the Broadcasting Museum.

TIC Chester (01244) 317962/351609/318916/322220
YHA Chester (01244) 680056
🚲 The Bike Factory, Chester (01244) 317893/320173
Chester Cycle & Pram Centre (01244) 381177
Cycle Centre, Hoole, Chester (01244) 340421
Davies Bros (Cycles), Chester (01244) 319204/318899
K. Davis, Chester (01244) 373408
Dave Miller, Chester (01244) 326508

Runcorn, Widnes and Warrington

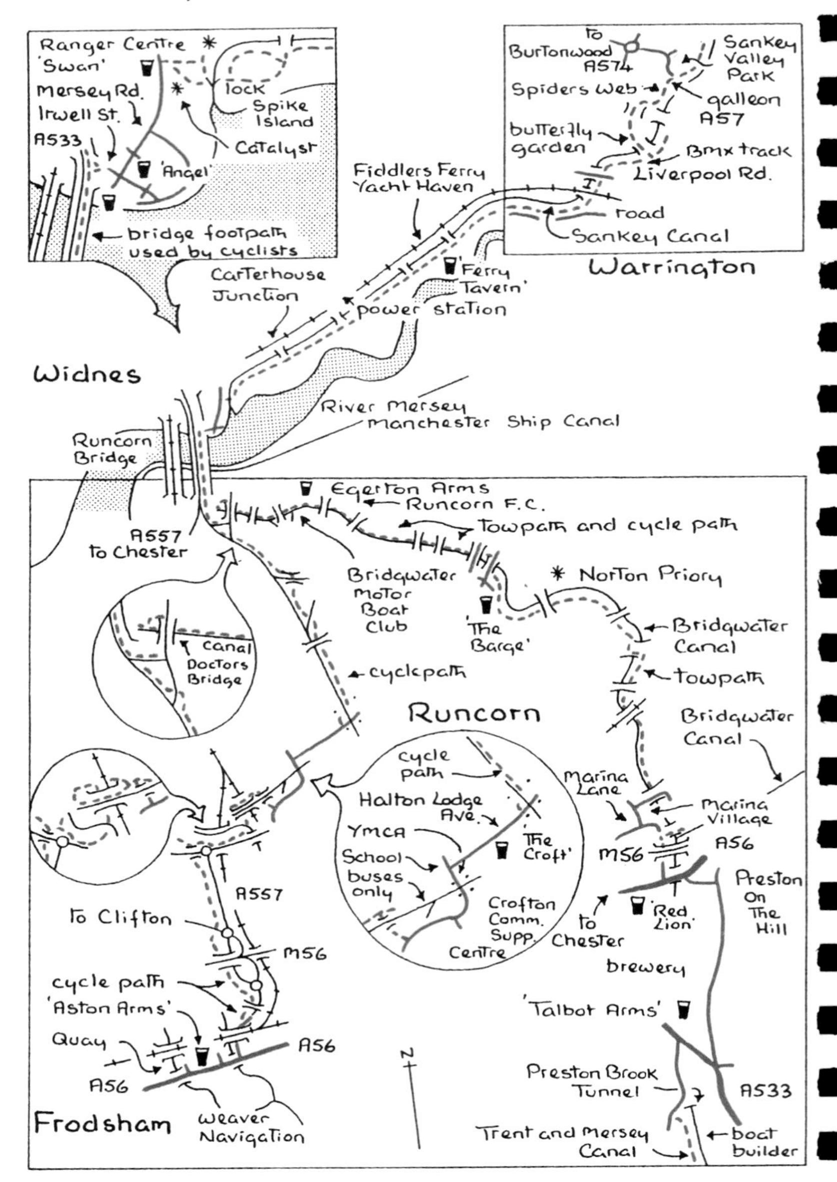

RUNCORN, WIDNES AND WARRINGTON 9 miles

Runcorn buzzes with traffic noise, though both routes avoid most of the vehicles. The canal towpath is straight-forward, and of good quality; the cycle paths unsigned and confusing, but, if you get it right, quick and not unpleasant.

The Runcorn Bridge is the second major river crossing, but, in contrast to the Severn Bridge, it is older, seedier, more cramped and a bit smelly. The footpath is used by local cyclists, though the sight of them steaming towards you can be a bit daunting.

The Sankey Canal towpath is reasonable and well used by cyclists and fishermen. This is a remarkable section with, on the one hand, a plethora of heron and the majesterial Mersey, and on the other, industrial might and the air redolent with elemental odours.

Runcorn. A 'New Town' with a massive road system. Piers, warehouses and wharfs remind us of its status as a 19c port, with the Bridgwater Canal, Weaver Navigation and Manchester Ship Canal connecting with the Mersey. The river was not bridged until 1864-9 by the railway bridge. A road Transporter Bridge was replaced by the 1082 feet suspension bridge in 1956-61.

The Manchester Ship Canal. Less than 2,000 years ago all the land on the south bank of the Mersey was swamp and mud-bank. The Manchester Ship Canal, completed in 1894, permanently protected the land from inundation.

Widnes. In the late 19c Spike Island was dominated by Hutchinson's and Gossage's huge chemical factories. It is now a recreation area, with a visitor centre. 'Catalyst' is a 'hands on' chemical museum.

Fiddler's Ferry. Powergen's coal fired power station. At full capacity 19,000 tonnes are burnt each day.

Sankey Navigation. England's first true canal of the Industrial Revolution, opened in 1757, with all the bridges able to swing to accomodate the Mersey Sailing Flats. The canal became the St Helens Canal in 1845 when the Railway Co. took over, and its main traffic was sugar. Final closure was in 1963. The towpath forms part of Sustran's 'Trans Pennine Trail' cycle route.

TIC Warrington (01925) 442180/444400

🚲 CharlesBingham, Widnes (0151) 424 2391
Chestnut Lodge Cycles, Widnes (0151) 424 1886
John Geddes (cycles), Widnes (0151) 420 7797
Eric Linekar, Widnes (0151) 424 4925
D & M Cycles, Great Sankey, Warrington (01925) 653606

THE NORTH COUNTRY

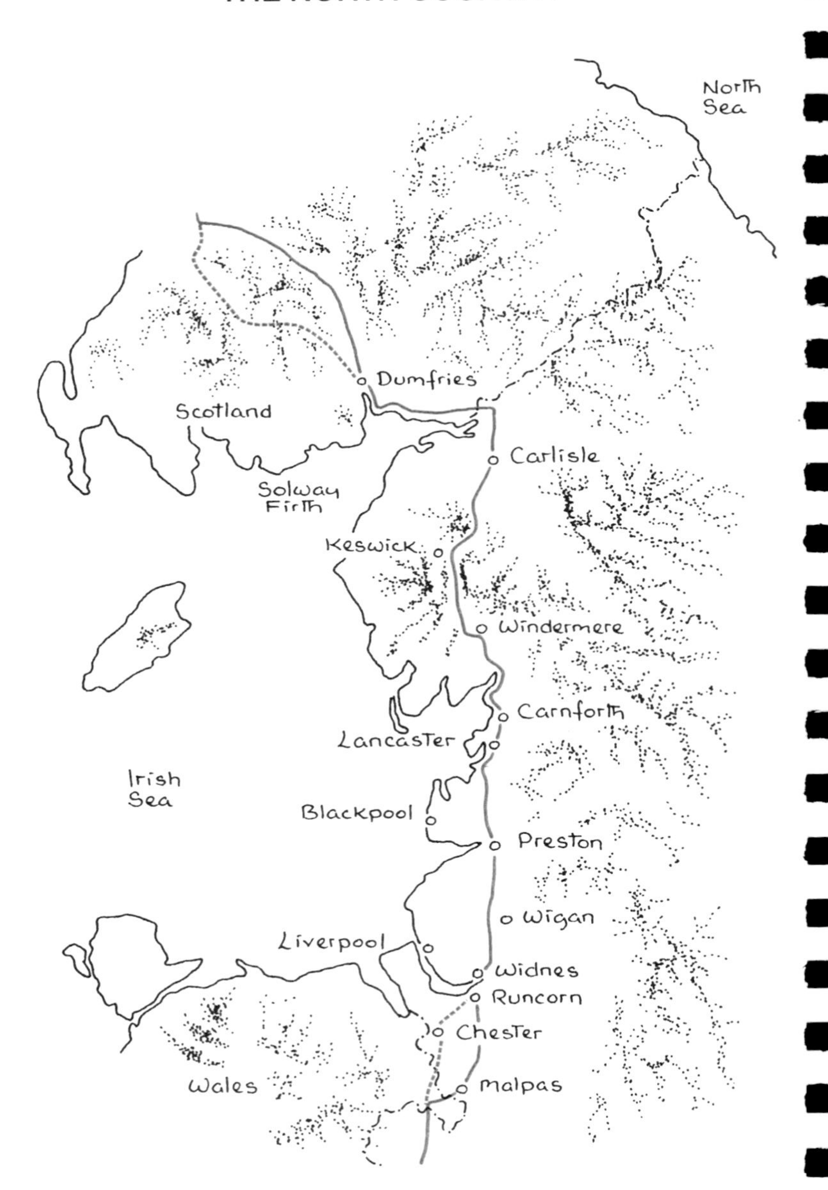

THE NORTH COUNTRY

This is the most heavily populated section of the entire route. It begins by picking its way through the industrial Liverpool-Manchester conurbation, and ends by negociating the beautifully dramatic mountains of the Lake District.

Footprints Lancashire and Cumbria have pretty well copped the lot over the years, and whilst some places seem to have been mugged and left for dead, others are groaning under the weight of visitors.

For a long while this was not hospitable country, with large areas of bog, swamp, moss, mere and exposed moorland. Early communication was via the Irish Sea but there has long been a north-south land route used by, among others, the Romans, raiding Scots, the Jacobite advance and the Royalists and Roundheads. Romans, Picts, Vikings, Ango-Saxons and Normans have all settled here, as shown in the place names (eg Croston is from the Scandinavian 'cros' and the old English 'tun', a village with a cross, and Lancaster is from 'caster', a Roman fort, on the 'Lune', a Celtic river name), and the dialect ('claggy' meaning sticky, and 'lug', an ear, are both Scandinavian).

It wasn't until the 16c that drainage, land reclamation and peace on the northern frontier led to more prosperous settlements. Since then the cotton industry, the development of the coalfields, the growth of the chemical industry, and tourism have all left big footprints.

Bald Mountains. Opinions differ on why the northern uplands are so bald. It is possible that Mesolithic Man prevented the advancing wildwood from recolonising after the last Ice Age, but more likely that, by 4000BC, these fells were covered with a mixed pine, birch and hazel forest. Some scientists believe that the cool, damp cyclonic weather which persists today led to a degeneration of the forest and directly to the open upland moorland, others, that man removed the trees, and his grazing animals allowed the upland blanket bog to gain a grip.

The Locals. The local dialects have many words for 'cowd' weather, whether it be 'teemin dahn' or not; 'parky' (chilly), 'mucky' (dull), 'nesh' (wet), 'slape' (slippery), 'starvation' (cold), and 'rag' (hoarfrost); and not so many for 'melsh' (warm) weather. This is the North, though, and all the myths are, at least partially, true. They eat hot pot, black pudding, tripe, faggots and wet nellies. The people wear flat caps, shawls, have allotments, keep pigeons and ferrets, watch rugby league, wear anoraks to walk the dog, and are 'dead friendly'.

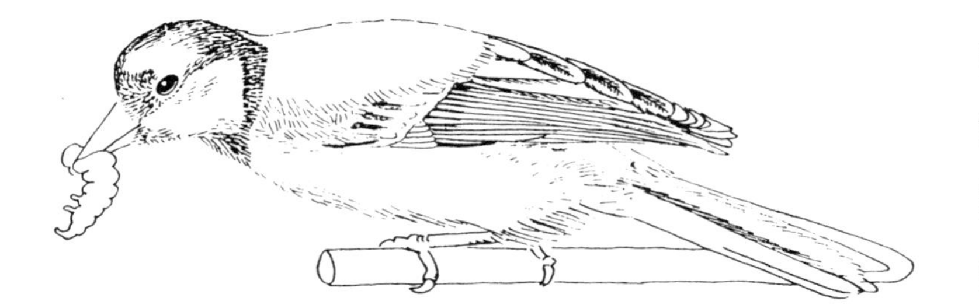

BURNLEY
BREWERY LTD

Warrington - Appley Bridge

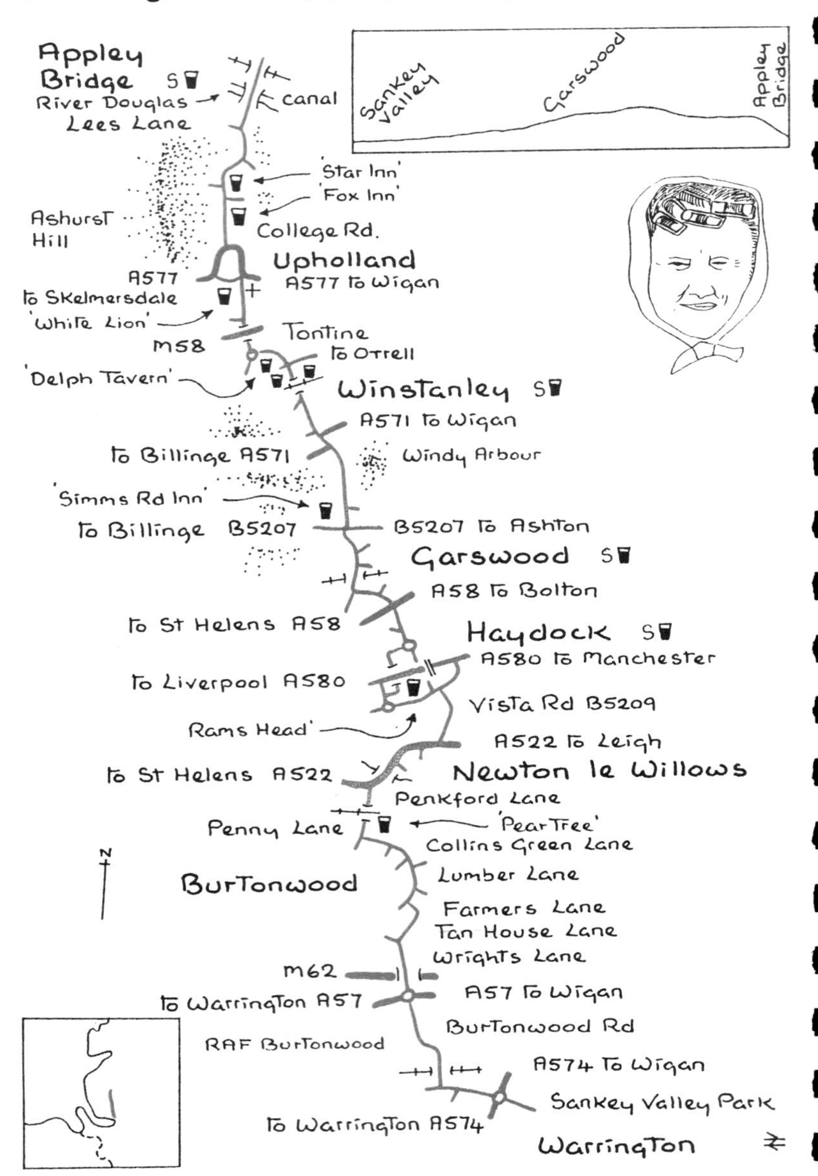

WARRINGTON – APPLEY BRIDGE 15.5 miles

Deepest Lancashire, battle-scarred by factories and industrial waste, though most of the heavy industry is now gone. The cyclist is tempted to push on, especially if the cloud lurks around Billinge Beacon, and the 'Lancashire drizzle' seeps through the Goretex, but most of the locals are extremely friendly. Lancashire cyclists tend to hunt in packs.

RAF Burtonwood. An ex-airfield earmarked as an industrial estate for USA factories. One wonders 'why'?

Newton le Willows **S** Watch out for the ghosts of Royalists caught and hanged by Cromwell in 1648, who still march to their doom.

Windy Arbour. The site of an old colliery, dramatically transformed into a picnic area.

Upholland **S** The 14c church incorporates the remains of an earlier Benedictine priory.

Billinge Beacon and Ashurst Hill. The summits are marked by stone beacons, part of a chain built right across England during the Napoleonic War, which would blaze to raise the alarm of an imminent invasion.

Industry. South Lancashire, in the 19c, was described as "featureless, filthy, cratered like a battlefield", and "a vast ocean of ugliness, hopelessly, helplessly depressing, miles of derelection". The St Helens-Widnes-Warrington triangle is one of the three major chemical producing areas in Britain. The early chemicals were made from salt, limestone and coal. Much of the desolation wrought on the landscape was due to the Leblanc Process (using sulphuric acid), in particular the problem of getting rid of the noxious black waste material known as 'galligu'. Here can be found the early canals, the Bridgwater and the Sankey Navigation, and the first complete railway, the Liverpool and Manchester.

TIC Warrington (01925) 442180/444400
Wigan (01942) 825677

Jack Carter, Newton le Willows (01925) 224300
Rogersons Cycle Centre, Orrell (01942) 214437

Appley Bridge - Preston

APPLEY BRIDGE – PRESTON 9 miles

A bit of a pull out of Appley Bridge, to keep those leg muscles toned up, and the greyness of the last few miles is replaced by dramatic, beckoning, vistas of the (flat) land to the North. This is a rural area well into transition, from farmland to the super-imposition of a 'semi-urban' population with immaculately groomed properties and carborne inhabitants, and, closer to Preston, urban farming, horticulture and horses.

Appley Bridge **S** The village developed on the back of the Leeds and Liverpool Canal. In 1740 the first 'cut' took coal from Wigan to the Ribble, bringing in return lime, bricks from Tarleton and slates from Wales and North Lancashire for the new houses of the spreading towns. The canals to Leeds and to Liverpool were begun in 1770 and took 40 years to complete. At 127 miles it is the longest single canal in Britain. Railway competition reduced traffic, and the hard winter of 1962/63 finished off most of the working boats.

Mawdesley. Famous for its basket making, using buff, green and white willows from the local mosses.

Eccleston The Smalleys opened a weaving mill here in the 19c. The 'Blue Anchor' may seem a little misplaced until you read:

Croston **S** An ancient settlement (the cross was originally set up in 651AD by Aiden's missionaries) in a sea of bog, mere, watery waste and tidal estuary. Often the church could only be reached by boat. Drainage started in the 18c and the 19c brought the railway, brickworks and cotton mills.

TIC Wigan (01942) 825677
Preston (01772) 253731

Preston

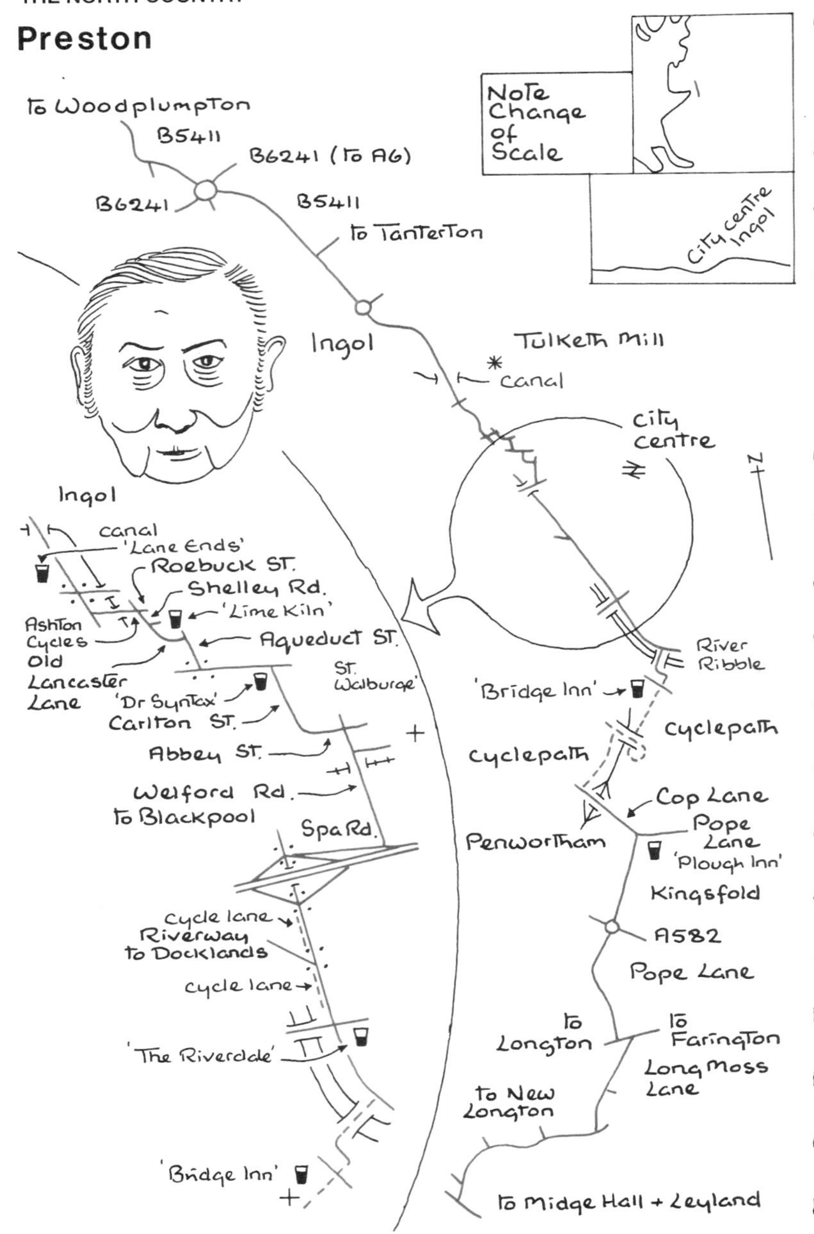

to Woodplumpton
B5411
B6241 (to A6)
B6241
B5411
to Tanterton
Note Change of Scale
City centre
Ingol
Ingol
Tulketh Mill
canal
City centre
N
Ingol
canal
'Lane Ends'
Roebuck ST.
Shelley Rd.
'Lime Kiln'
Ashton Cycles
Old Lancaster Lane
Aqueduct ST.
'Dr Syntax'
Carlton ST.
ST. Walburge'
Abbey ST.
Welford Rd.
to Blackpool
Spa Rd.
cycle lane
Riverway to Docklands
cycle lane
'The Riverdale'
'Bridge Inn'
River Ribble
'Bridge Inn'
Cyclepath
Cyclepath
Cop Lane
Penwortham
Pope Lane
'Plough Inn'
Kingsfold
A582
Pope Lane
to Longton
to Farington
Long Moss Lane
to New Longton
to Midge Hall + Leyland

PRESTON

9 miles

To the cyclist from the south, there is a relatively painless entrance to a town not known for its cycle-friendliness. Among the swirling new roads and tarmac'd acres, the cycling provision is decidedly skimpy, but what can you expect from a town whose bypass was Britain's first motorway. The route to the north is a bit of a fight.

Preston. First shot to fame in 1648 when Cromwell, having inflicted a decisive defeat on the Royalists at the 'Battle of Preston', promptly retired to the 'Unicorn' at Darwen Bridge for a pint.
Then, in 1768, local boy Richard Arkwright invented the spinning-frame, but he had to move to Nottinghamshire to avoid attack. The introduction of machinery lessened the demand for hand labour, and coupled with bad harvests and Corn Laws, Preston became a centre of rioting. The Industrial Revolution gathered pace, and a hundred years ago, steel girders were used to build huge weaving sheds, including Centenary Mills and Tulketh Cotton Mill, with its large engine house, chimney and ornamental water tower.
Joseph Livesay (1794-1884) founded the Temperence movement here. The word 'tee-total' came from a friend of his with a stammer, who had trouble with "total abstinance".
Places of interest include the Arkwright Heritage Centre, the Harris Museum and Art Gallery, the Lancashire County and Regimental Museum and Centenary Mill, built by John Horrocks in 1895. St Walburge's Church in Weston Street is an astonishingly garish, Roman Catholic, Victorian church by JA Hansom, with the third tallest spire in England. Preston also boasts Europe's largest bus station.

TIC Preston (01772) 253731

🚲 Broadgate Cycle Stores, Penwortham, Preston (01772) 746448
Ashton Cycles, Preston (01772) 735664
Ribble Cycle Co., Ashton, Preston (01772) 721721/736136
Fulwood Cycles, Preston (01772) 713042
Pedal Power Cycles, Preston (01772) 719129

Preston - Garstang (the Fylde)

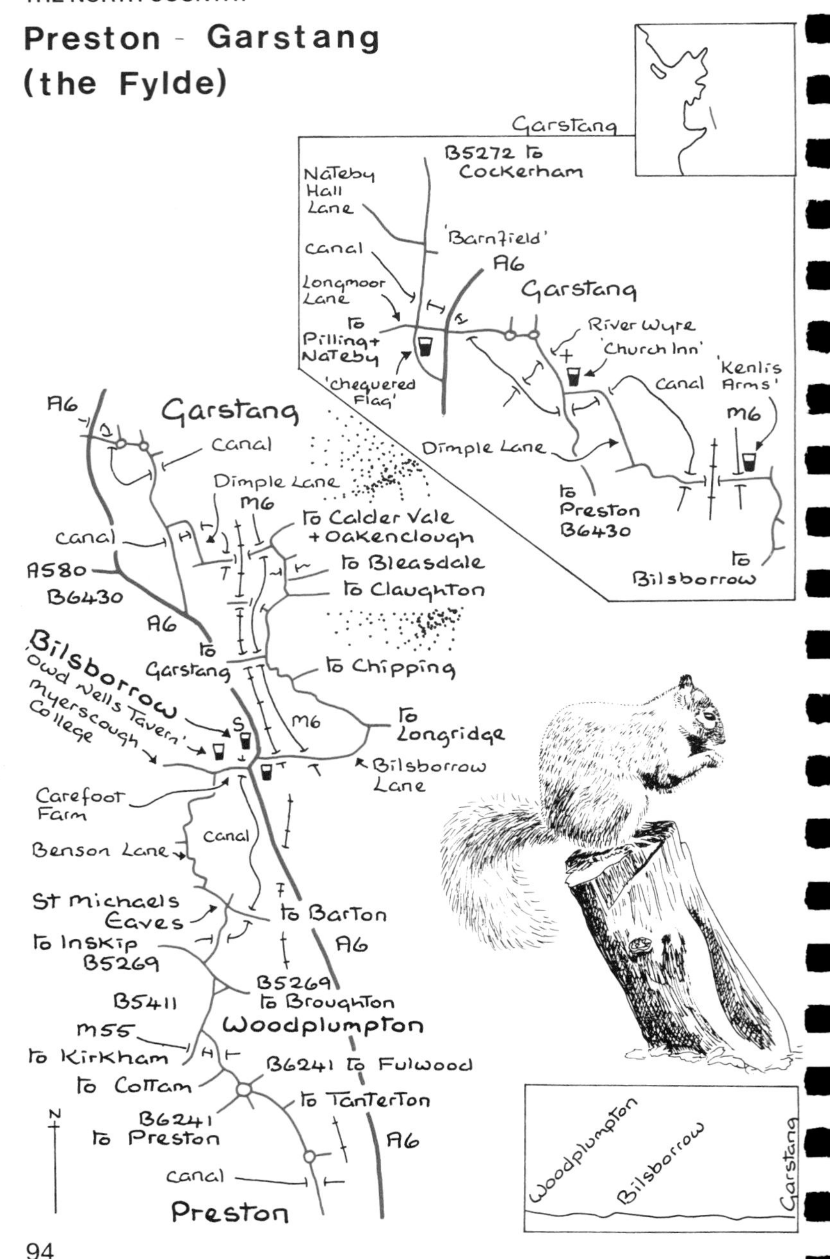

PRESTON – GARSTANG (The Fylde) 10.5 miles

Cycling in the 'corridor', with the M6, A6, West Coast main railway line and the Lancaster Canal all within spitting distance of each other. None make a good cycle route, so we wiggle around a little on the old lanes.

Woodplumpton **S** The birthplace of Henry Foster, a 19c Navigator who drowned in the Gulf of Mexico.

Garstang **S** An unbearably busy little town. For centuries it has been the Fylde and Wyresdale market centre, with Fylde corn and cattle, fish from the Wyre and yarns, linens and cottons from the surrounding cottage industries.

The Fylde. In the 11c much of this land was uninhabited bog, swamp, moss and mere, and much of the rest was King William's hunting preserve. Farming began in the 14c, and 16c drainage resulted in the good farmland you see today. The Fylde of Amounderness was an area of large landowners, the 'gentry' including the monarch as the 'Duke of Lancaster'.
The villages in the 'M6 corridor' have long been on a through route to Scotland, and in the way of raiding Scots, the Jacobite advance and the comings and goings of Royalist and Roundhead.

Cotton. Two hundred years ago, the availability of cotton from the New Colonies, and a growing market for cheap cloth meant a rapidly growing industry. With Liverpool as the premier port, on the back of the slave trade, and the exploitation of the Lancashire coalfield, new mills brought a boom to the Lancashire towns. 'King Cotton' produced monumental mills, with particularly spectacular chimneys, but the concentrated mechanisation meant a dreary landscape of cheap terraced housing and mills belching out black smoke. There were social distortions too, with women finding it easier to find work than men, and strong traditions of non-violent protest and religious observance. When the 'Cotton Famine' hit Lancashire in 1862-5, as a result of the American Civil War, there was a great boom in public works, financed by public subscription in other parts of the country. The industry recovered but thereafter began to decline.

TIC Garstang (01995) 602125
Discovery Bikes, Garstang

Garstang - Lancaster

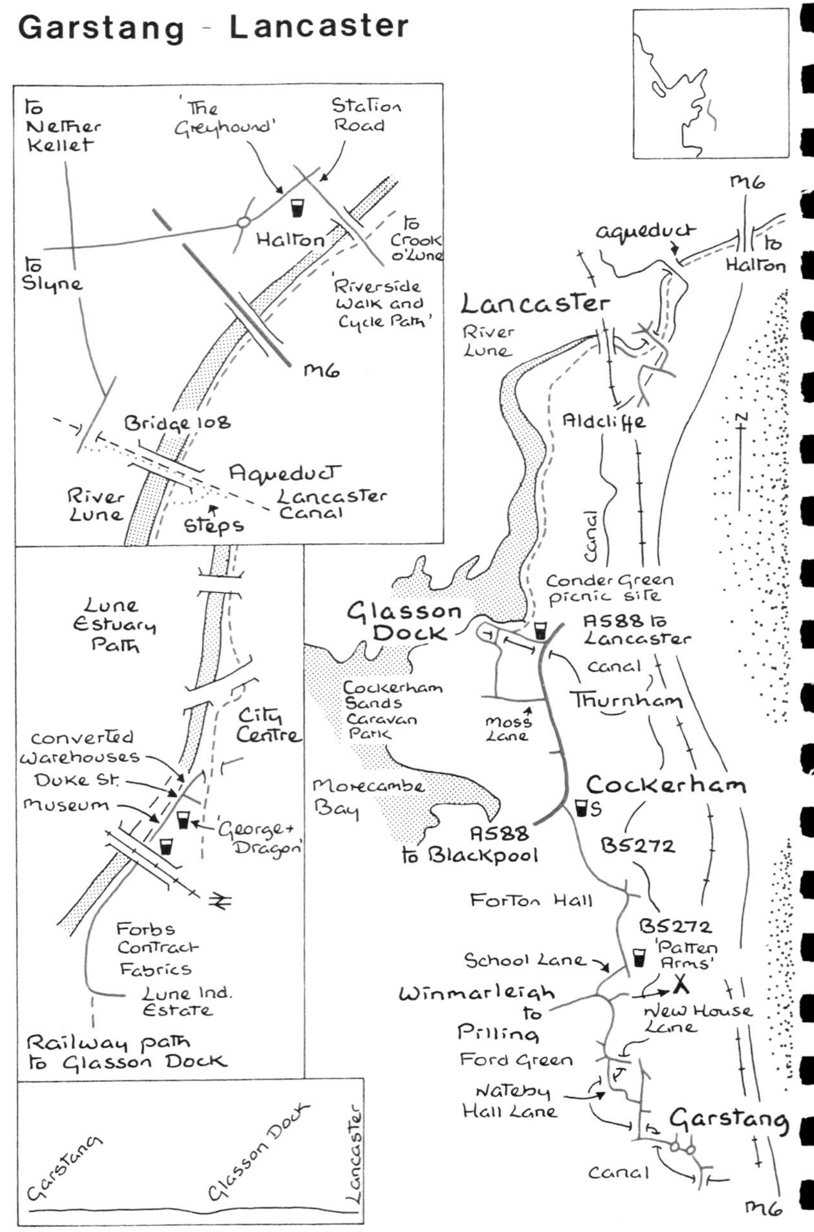

GARSTANG – LANCASTER 11 miles

Not outstanding riding, but Glasson Dock cheers the spirits, and the old railway line on and through Lancaster is redolent and straightforward, but prone to mud in places.

Glasson Dock **S** The oldest existing tidal dock in England, it boomed in the 18c when the Lancaster canal was linked to the dock basins. It remains a fascinating village.

Lancaster **S** In 1170 Roger de Poitou built a keep, which still stands, on the site of a roman camp. The castle was improved and in 1322 Robert Bruce burnt the town but could not take the castle. It was a Parliamentary stronghold in the Civil War, and George Fox, the Quaker, was twice imprisoned here. It is still an assize court and jailhouse.
See also the Maritime Museum; the Ashton Memorial and Butterfly House; the City Museum and the Judge's Lodgings (Gillow and Town House Museum and Museum of Childhood).

Morecambe Bay. Fishing has long been important here, especially for cockles and flounders. Lancaster, as a port, eventually gave way to Glasson Dock, and Heysham. At present there are gas platforms out there.

TIC Garstang (01995) 602125
Lancaster (01524) 32878

Cycle 2000, Lancaster (01524) 381414
Lancaster Cycles (01524) 844389
Smalley's, Lancaster (01524) 63478

Lancaster - Levens Bridge

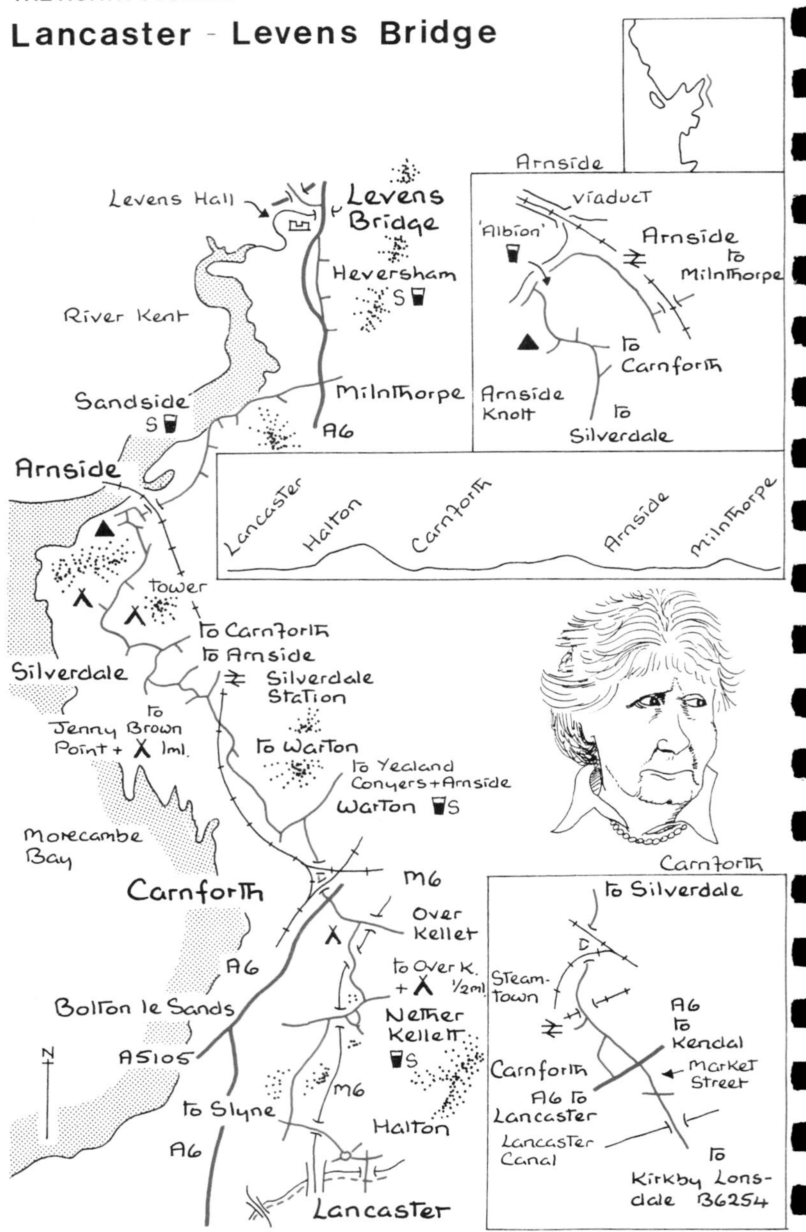

LANCASTER – LEVENS BRIDGE 20 miles

An outcropping of limestone; ride past escarpement, pavements, old kilns and quarries, exuberant with wildlife, and, for the old train-spotter, Steamtown is a 'must'.

Carnforth S Steamtown.

Silverdale S Prior to 1850 the home of fishermen, wildfowlers, mossmen, stonegetters and furnacemen from the local iron forges, and a cattle drovers crossing point of Morecambe Bay. Now it is Costa Geriatrica, and a birdwatchers paradise. Mrs Gaskell lived here. Leighton Hall has a birds of prey collection.

Arnside S Once a busy port, now an unspoilt little resort. The viaduct, built 1856/7, crosses the Kent quicksands. The Kent Channel crossing was once the main route north, before the Levens Bridge turnpike was opened in 1820. It can be treacherous, but is still walked today with local guides, varying from 5 to 7 miles depending on tides and currents.
Arnside Knott, a rich limestone woodland, one of many in this area.
Arnside Tower, one of a chain of 14c forts built against Scottish raiders.

Milnthorpe S Before the M6 was built, this was a notorious traffic bottleneck on the A6. It is an ancient settlement, colonised by the Celts, Romans, Angles and Normans, which once boasted nine coaching inns and a port on the River Bela.

Levens Hall. An Elizabethan house built on a 13c pele tower, it has one of the oldest landscaped parks in Britain, including a topiary garden. The Hall is said to be haunted by a lady in pink and a spectral black dog.

Morecambe Bay supports the largest population of wintering waders in Britain. In the 1970's it was proposed to build a barrage here, topped with a motorway.

Lancashire Cycle Way. The route coincides in places with this circular 'cycleway'.

TIC Lancaster (01524) 32878
Kendal (01539) 725758
YHA Arnside (01524) 761781
Dyno-Start Cycle Centre, Carnforth (01524) 732089

Levens Bridge - Hawkshead (the Lake District)

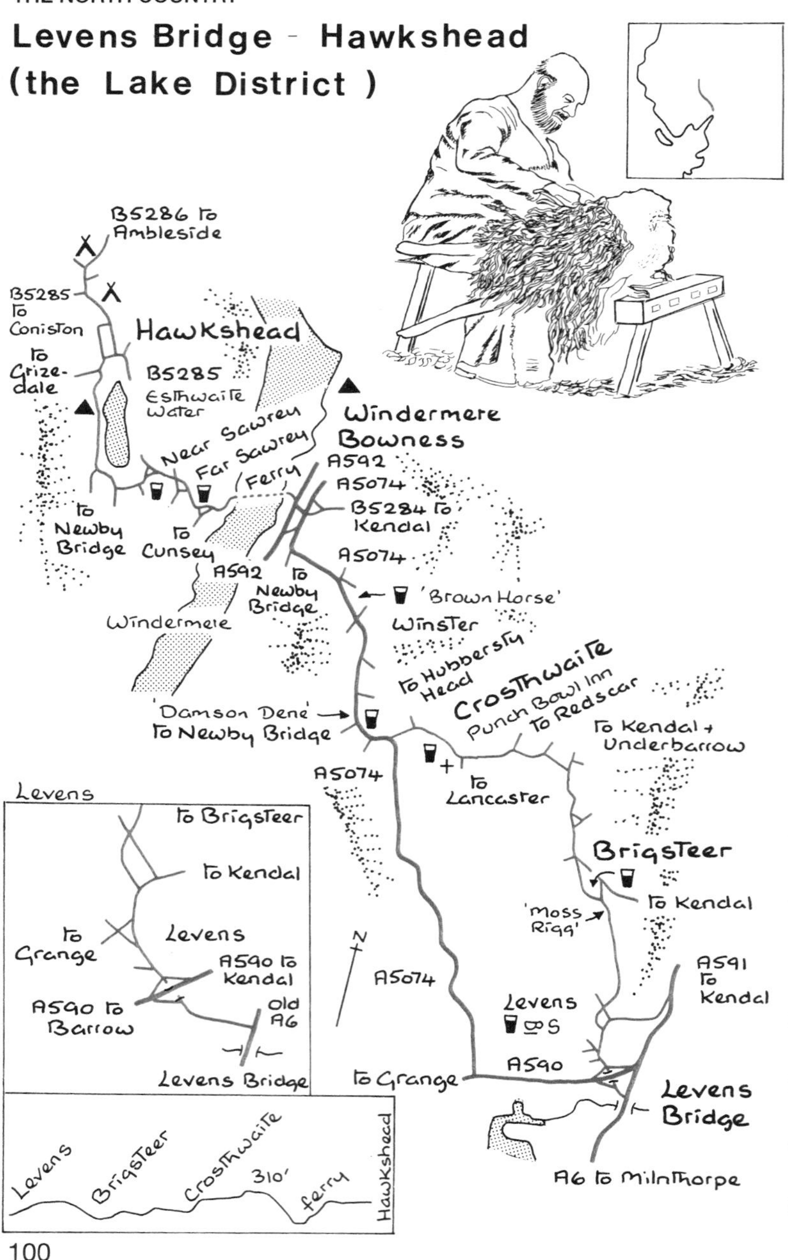

LEVENS BRIDGE – HAWKSHEAD
(The Lake District) **15 miles**

A cracking run among the boisterous, wooded foothills of the Lake District. There is plenty of gear work but nothing serious.

Brigsteer. Note the old Quaker Meeting House.

Lyth Valley. A centre of plum growing.

Windermere and Bowness **S** are best avoided unless you like crowds. Windermere has a steamboat museum. The lake is the longest of the Lake District lakes, with an end to end 'steamer' service. In 1930 Sir Henry Seagrave set a new water speed record here, of 98.76mph.

The Ferry. Cumbria C.C.'s M.V. 'Mallard' operates year round. There has been one recorded sinking, in 1635, when a wedding party floundered, drowning forty eight people and eleven horses. To the north of the ferry is Claife Heights, the haunt of red and roe deer. The deer population is controlled by culling, to limit tree damage, the natural predators having been exterminated long ago.

Near Sawrey This is "Potterland", the home of Beatrix Potter. The 'Tower Bank Arms' is featured in 'Jemima Puddleduck'.

Hawkshead **S** A busy village with the Courthouse Museum of Local Life, Anne Tyson's cottage and the School. The poet William Wordsworth was at school here 1778-1787. He then lived at Dove Cottage and Rydal Mount and is buried in St Oswald Church, Grasmere.

The Cumbria Cycle Way crosses this route at Levens.

TIC Bowness (015394) 42895
Hawkshead (015394) 36349
YHA Windermere (015394) 43543
Hawkshead (015394) 36293
Ashton, Bowness (015394) 44479

Hawkshead - Thirlmere (the Lake District)

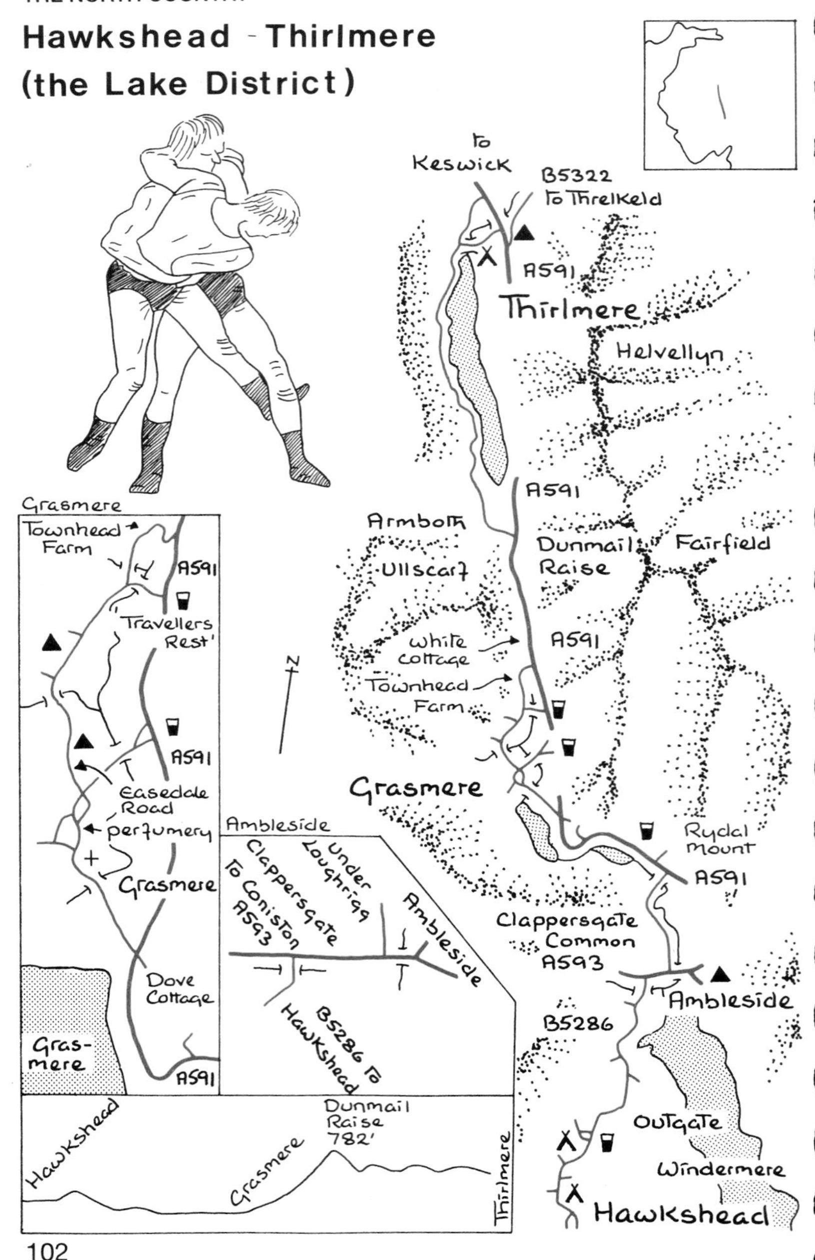

HAWKSHEAD – THIRLMERE
(The Lake District) 17 miles

The heart of the Lake District; brooding fells, soaring rock faces, imperial beauty. Put your head down only for the traffic-plagued pull up Dunmail Raise.

Ambleside **S** A tourist honeypot, with the Lake District History Centre and Bridge House.

Grasmere **S** Since 1852 the mid-August Grasmere Sports have been held, including Cumberland and Westmorland wrestling, hound trailing and fell running. The wrestling is said to date back to the days of face to face combat among Border inhabitants.

Dunmail Raise. The A591 is the main north-south route in the Lake District, and from the 1930's drastic widening has been proposed and completed in patches only. In the 1970's the A66 was engineered to take most of the heavy traffic, following a Public Inquiry and irresistable political pressure.
In AD 945 the last Celtic King of Cumbria, Duvenald (Dunmail) is said to have been defeated at a battle commemorated by a cairn at the summit of Dunmail Raise. The Viking immigration followed soon afterwards.

Thirlmere. In 1879 Manchester Corporation received permission to extract fifty million gallons of water a day from Thirlmere, which thus became the first reservoir in the Lake District. The dam raised the water level by fifty feet, flooding houses and farms, especially at Armboth. The school and pub were subsequently demolished. The water in Thirlmere is exceptionally pure, and untreated, so public access is limited. The afforestation which accompanied the reservoir was also the first large scale conifer planting; another contentious issue.

Helvellyn at 3118ft, is England's second highest mountain.

The Sheep is 'Queen'. Farming walks a thin line between subsidised husbandry, and a janitorial role for a landscape we have chosen to fossilise.

TIC Ambleside (015394) 32582
Grasmere (015394) 35245
YHA Ambleside (015394) 32304
Grasmere – Butterlip How (015394) 35316
Thorney How (015394) 35591
Thirlmere (017687) 73224
Biketreks, Ambleside (015394) 31245
Ghyllside Cycles, Ambleside (015394) 33592

Thirlmere - Hesket Newmarket

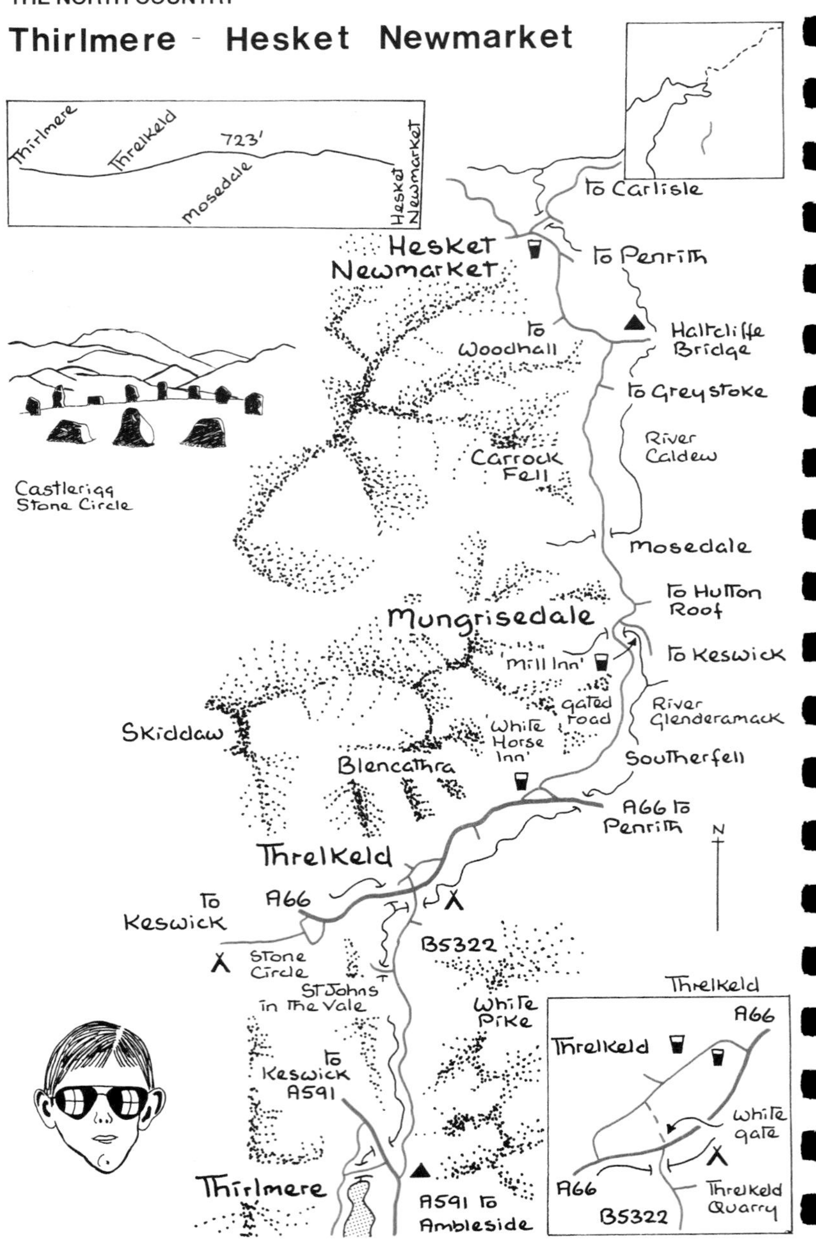

THIRLMERE – HESKET NEWMARKET

(The Lake District) **14 miles**

Fine wheeling, skirting the majesterial mountains, apart from a couple of nasty miles on the busy A66.

Threlkeld The centre of the local fox hunt, with the huntsmen in grey, and on foot.
The Castlerigg stone circle dates from around 1500BC.

Keswick **S** Another town heaving with tourists, with a Museum and Art Gallery, Pencil Museum and Moot Hall.

Carrock Fell There have been mines here since the Middle Ages, now mostly overgrown, but a tungsten mine opened as recently as 1972.

Hesket Newmarket **S** The 'Old Crown' is an excellent home-brew pub.

Natural Beauty vs Tourism. The Lake District rocks were uplifted into a dome, which a new river system began to erode in a radial pattern, but much of the scenery we see today was carved out during the last Ice Age. The tourist explosion began with the railway to Windermere. On Whit-Monday 1883 ten thousand day trippers came to town. The conflict between a National Park as an area of natural beauty, as a place of tourist recreation, and as a place of work is unresolved, but inevitably the landscape suffers from man's interference.

TIC Keswick (017687) 72645
YHA Carrock Fell (016974) 78325

Hesket Newmarket - Carlisle

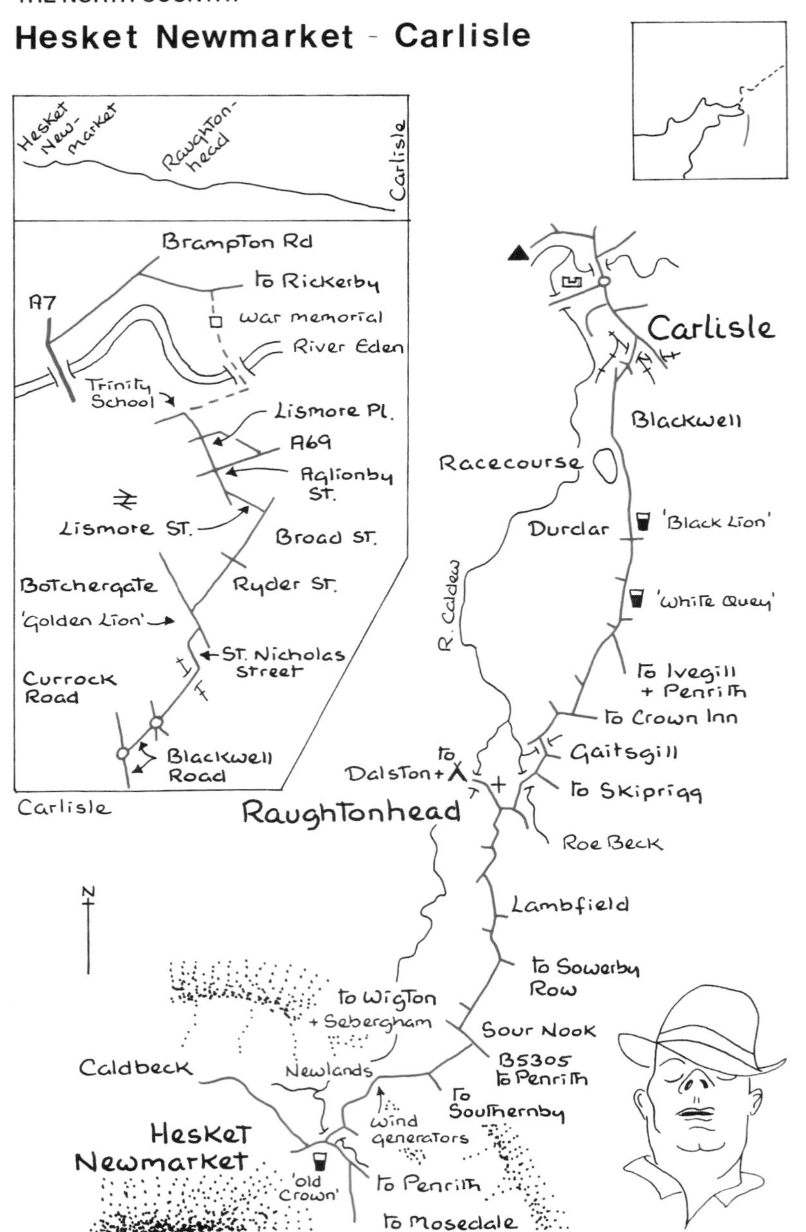

HESKET NEWMARKET - CARLISLE 12 miles

Rural Cumberland; an intricate ride along quiet backroads, past old sandstone farms, to the industrial city of Carlisle.

Caldbeck **S** The Howk is a limestone gorge with a ruined bobbin mill. The church of St Kentigern has a norman doorway, a medieval tower, and the graves of John Peel, the huntsman, and the Maid of Buttermere.

Carlisle **S** Carlisle was the important Roman town of Luguvallium, commanding the western end of Hadrians Wall. When the Romans withdrew (410AD) peace reigned with the emergence of the greatest Celtic British leader, Urien of Rheged, based in Caer Luel (Carlisle). Many believe him to be the role-model for the King Arthur stories. One of the least known and least documented turning points in history was in 573AD, at the battle of Ardderydd (Arthuret?), when the Christians defeated the Pagans. The poet and prophet Myrddin (Merlin?) lost his wits when his Lord was slain.
The Castle dates from William Rufus, (12c) and the Cathedral, begun in 1093, was rebuilt following Civil War damage.
Note the Tullie House Museum; the Guildhall Museum; the Border Regiment Museum; and the Industrial Trail.

TIC Carlisle (01228) 512444
YHA Carlisle (01228) 23934
Border Cycles (01228) 36872
Scotby Cycles (01228) 46931
Palace Cycle Store (01228) 23142
Whiteheads (01228) 26890

SOUTHERN SCOTLAND

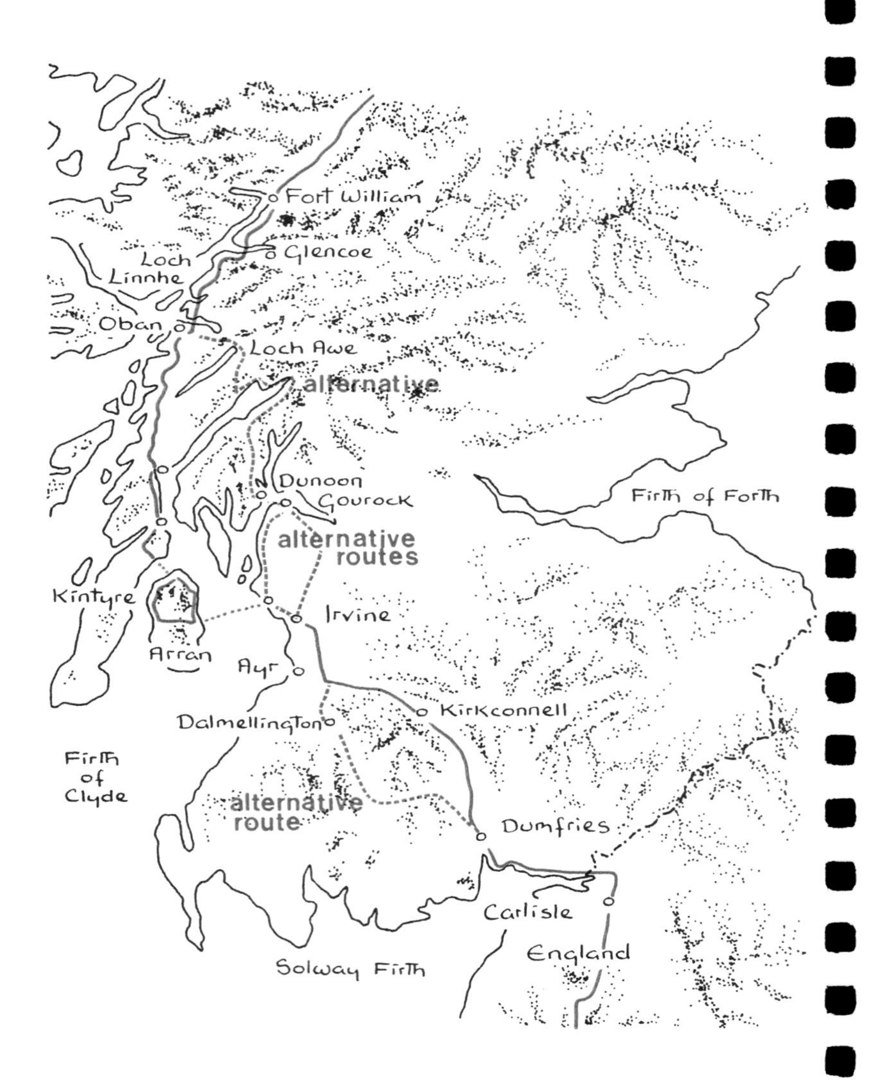

SOUTHERN SCOTLAND

The traditional End-to-End route follows the A7 to Edinburgh and the A9 from Perth to Inverness. Many cyclists today keep to this route, or variations thereof. These involve long, high, uphill climbs on roads more suitable for articulated lorries. This Guide goes West, seeking the magnificent coastal and mountain scenery of Argyll, with similar overall mileage and climbing to the more traditional route.
In Dumfries and Galloway there is choice. The least hilly route is through Kirkconnell and New Cumnock. The alternative, via Dalmellington, takes in the youth hostels at Kendoon and Ayr.
At Irvine there is a major choice, depending on the time of year, for the ferry from Arran to Kintyre is seasonal. The shorter, and better route is via Arran, Kintyre and Oban. The alternative is via Largs or Johnstone to Gourock and on to Inveraray and Loch Awe.

Scotland is a 'foreign' land, with an independent legal and educational system and many cultural differences. Here is a brief guide.

Clans were family groupings, with loyalty owed to the chief, who, in return acted as leader, protector and dispenser of justice. They were largely destroyed by the reaction of the English to the 1745 rising, and then by the Highland clearances.

Tartan is a 19c invention. In the Highlands a coarse, woollen cloth ('Tartaine' in french) was worn, and dyed with vegetable dye.

Scottish Hotels have bars and lounges, and range from austere to plush. They are generally welcoming.

The Midge spends most of its life as a larva providing food for fish, but many become airborne to plague the visitor. Only the females bite.

The Picts. The Romans found the native 'picts' (the painted ones) impossible to subdue, so they built Hadrian's Wall (and very briefly the Antonine Wall between Clyde and Forth) as a northern frontier.

The Scots In the Dark Ages the Scots, who were in fact Irish Celts, formed the Kingdom of Dalriada, north of the Clyde.

The Norse. By the end of the 8c Norsemen had conquered Orkney, Shetland, the far north of the mainland and all the Western Isles including Arran and Kintyre, and held them until King Haakon the Fourth was defeated in the Battle of Largs in 1266.

Bannockburn. In the meanwhile the Picts and Scots united to form the country of Alba, later to become Scotia. It was the English King Edward the First (the 'Hammer of the Scots') who set out on his 'pacification campaigns' (sic.) and the strongholds fell one by one. William Wallace (1270-1305) rallied the resistance but was captured and executed. Robert the Bruce was more successful, and, uniting the various fiefs and lords behind him, defeated the English at Bannockburn in 1344.

The Jacobites. Following the Act of Union in 1707 there were attempts to restore the Stuarts to the throne. James the Eighth, or the Old Pretender, arrived too late in 1715, generally lacked charisma and quickly departed. General George Wade was sent to pacify the Highlands with a programme of road and bridge building to facilitate military access.

The Young Pretender. In 1745 Bonnie Prince Charlie landed at Arisaig, and, with a Highland army, marched south, reaching Derby before retreating and finally facing defeat in the bloodbath at Culloden.

Carlisle - Gretna

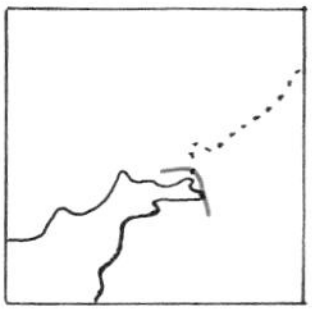

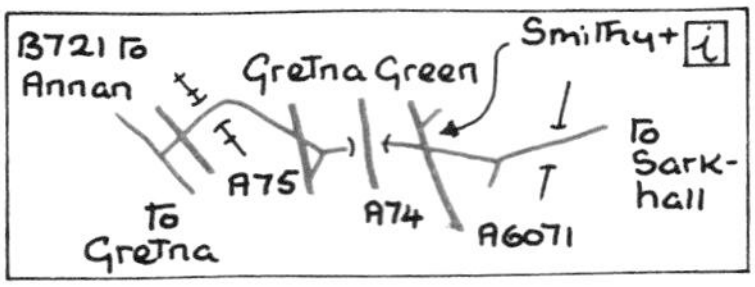

B721 to Annan
Gretna Green
Smithy + i
to Sarkhall
A75
A74
A6071
to Gretna

Gretna Green

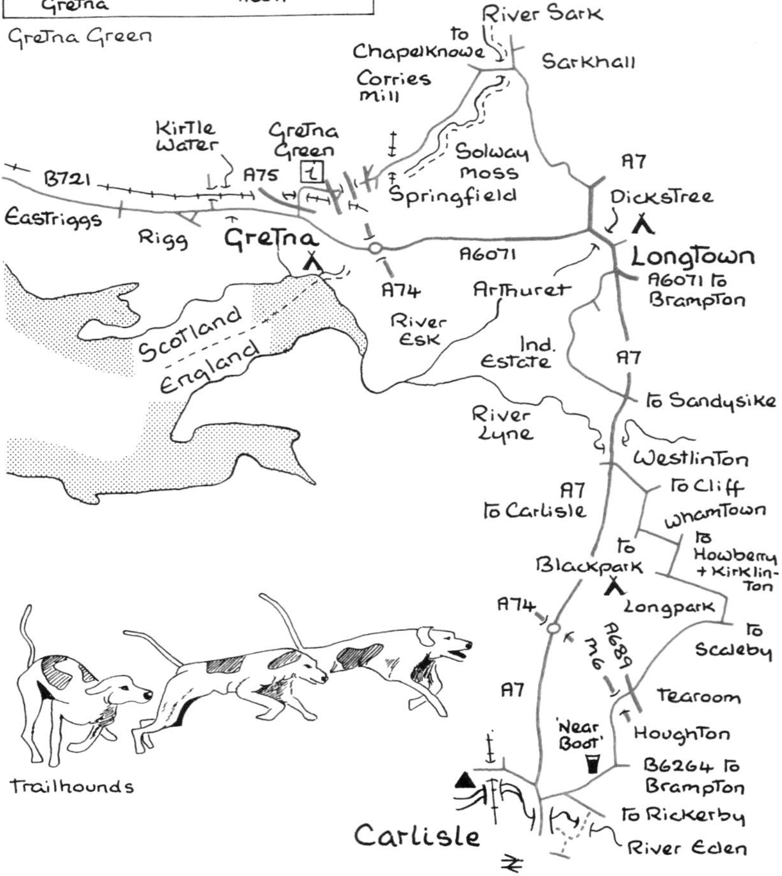

River Sark
to Chapelknowe
Sarkhall
Corries Mill
Kirtle Water
Gretna Green
Solway Moss
A7
B721
A75
i
Springfield
Dickstree
Eastriggs
Rigg
Gretna
Longtown
A6071
A74
Arthuret
A6071 to Brampton
River Esk
Scotland
England
Ind. Estate
A7
to Sandysike
River Lyne
Westlinton
to Cliff
A7
to Carlisle
Whamtown
to Blackpark
to Howberry + Kirklinton
Longpark
A74
A689
M6
to Scaleby
A7
Tearoom
'Near Boot'
Houghton
B6264 to Brampton
to Rickerby
Carlisle
River Eden

Trailhounds

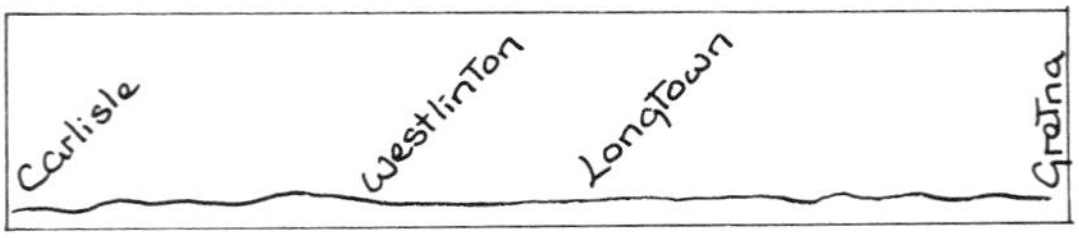

N

Carlisle
Westlinton
Longtown
Gretna

CARLISLE – GRETNA
(The Scottish Border) 20 miles

As with most border crossings, this is undramatic, but there is a strange feeling about this no-mans land. Given a favourable wind this is country to fly through.

The 'A74'. A map will show you the direct route from Carlisle to Scotland is along the A74. That no cycle route accompanies this road is diabolical. On no account cycle the A74; it holds motorway traffic at motorway speeds and is lethal. It was scheduled to be upgraded to a motorway, and a route suitable for cyclists created, but this proposal has been put 'on hold'.

Longtown **S** A small border town, it used to be the territory of the 'Grahams', who had a notorious reputation for cross border raiding.

Solway Moss. Scotlands greatest military disgrace. An army of 18,000 Scots were beaten by Sir Thomas Wharton's 3,000 Englishmen when they were trapped crossing the marshy tideland of Solway Moss.

The Debateable Lands The area between the rivers Sark and Esk had a special border status during the time of border 'reiving'. Border reiving, or cattle rustling, was rife from the Solway to Berwick from the 14c to the 17c. These wild, unproductive lands were inhabited by hordes of 'mosstroopers' who made it their business to harry and despoil their English or Scottish neighbours. The border barons did as they pleased, and yet were constantly at each others throats. They were the Scotts, Armstrongs, Elliots, Kerrs, Maxwells and Douglasses, Johnstones, Grahams and many more. Special border laws were established with rights of sanctuary and retribution. Intermarriage across the border carried the penalty of death.

Gretna **S** During the First World War, Gretna became the base for the Empire's largest arsenal. In 1915 it was also the scene of Britains worst ever rail disaster with 220 killed. A troop train was involved and the accident made worse because the internal lighting was by gas.

Gretna Green **S** The 'First Village' in Scotland, and a mecca for runaway lovers, even to 1969, for in Scotland parental consent was not required after the age of 16. There are two Blacksmiths Shops.

TIC Carlisle (01228) 512444
Longtown (01228) 791876
Gretna Green (01461) 337834

Gretna - Ruthwell

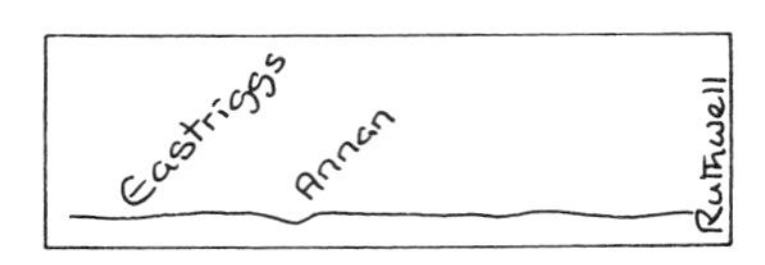

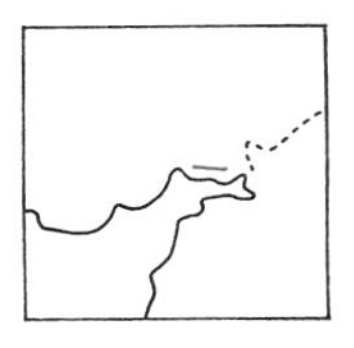

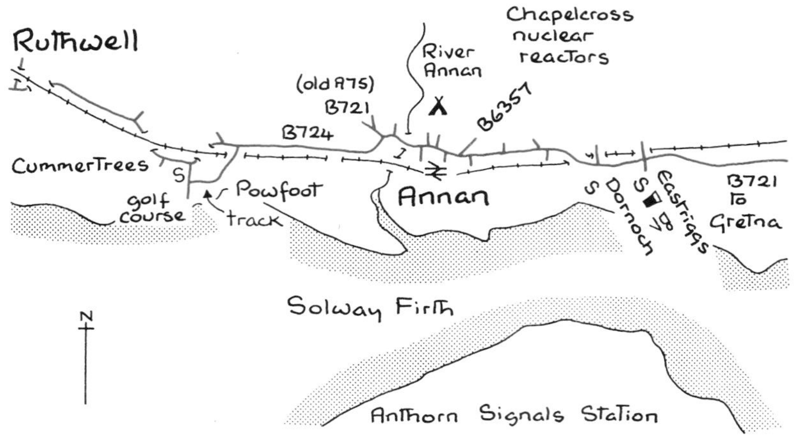

GRETNA – RUTHWELL 9 miles

An open, airy, windswept landscape. There are views across the Solway to the Anthorn radio masts, Silloth and the mountains of the Lake District; and, from the rather dreary old main road between Gretna and Annan, the nuclear reactors of Chapelcross.

Annan **S** An ancient market town, famous last century for Nicholson's shipyard, where 'Queensbury' tea clippers, up to 1,000 tons, were built. Remains can also be seen of the 5,790ft long Solway railway viaduct. Built in 1865, it closed in 1921 following damage by the sea.

Powfoot Once earmarked as the 'Blackpool of the North'.

Ruthwell. Inside the church is Ruthwell Cross, a carved, late 7c Anglian stone cross. Note also the Savings Bank Museum and the Brow Well, where Robert Burns took the curative waters just before his death.

Scotland. In 1413 Aeneas Syvius described Scotland as a "cold country, fertile of few sorts of grain, and generally void of trees, but there is a sulphurous stone dug up which is used for firing. The towns are unwalled, the houses commonly built without lime, and in the villages roofed with turf, while a cow's hide supplies the place of a door. The commonalty are poor and uneducated, have abundance of flesh and fish, but eat bread as a dainty. The men are small in stature, but bold; the women fair and comely, and prone to the pleasures of love. Nothing gives the Scots more pleasure than to hear the English dispraised".

Ruthwell - Dumfries

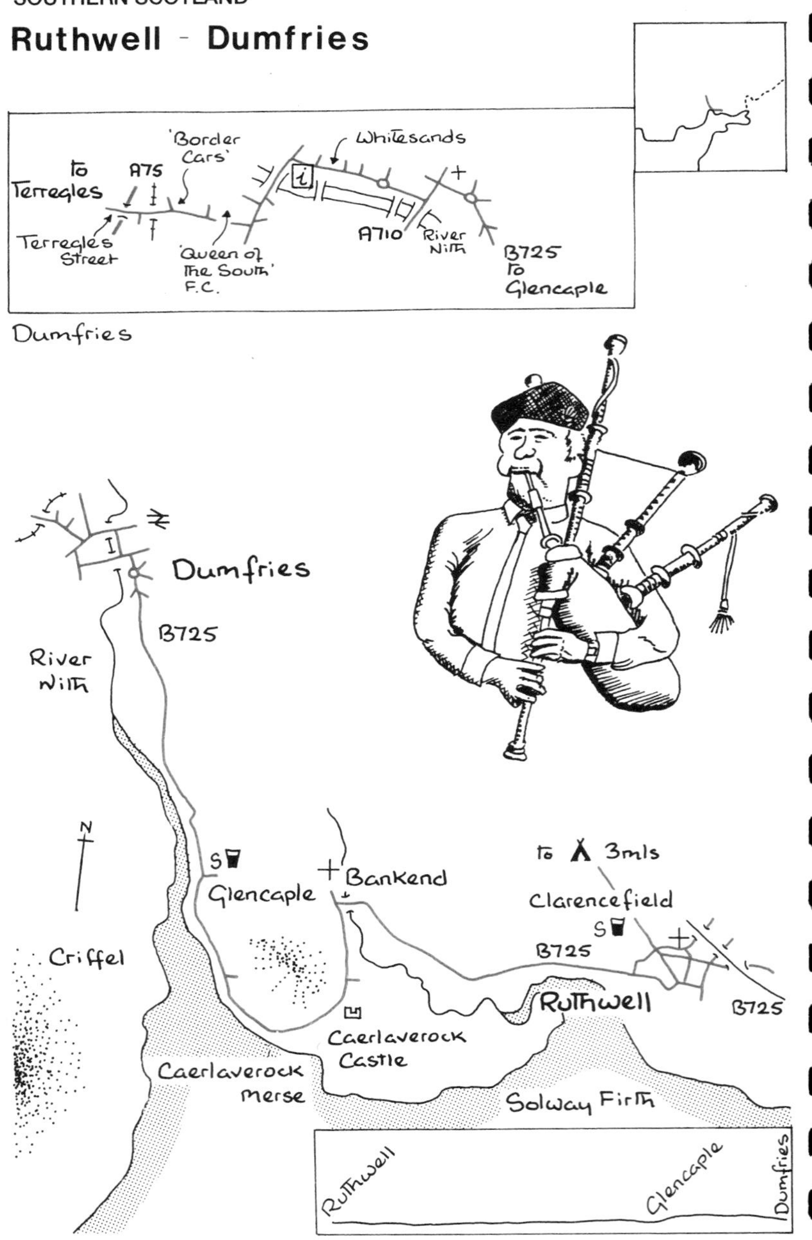

RUTHWELL - DUMFRIES 14 miles

A fine ride around one of the more interesting corners of Britain, with shapely Criffel graceing the estuary of the Nith.

Bankend. The grave of Robert Paterson is in the churchyard. He spent much of his later life erecting stones to Covenanters (he was Sir Walter Scott's 'Old Mortality').

Caerlaverock Castle. A late 13c triangular, moated castle belonging to the Maxwells, Earls of Nithsdale. It faced several sieges, most notably in 1300 when King Edward the First of England landed with a three thousand strong attacking army. The sixty men inside Caerlaverock eventually were overrun.

Caerlaverock Merse. One of the largest, unreclaimed salt marshes in Britain, the wintering ground for Barnacle, Greylag and Pink-Footed geese.

Dumfries **S** Became a Royal burgh with a charter in 1186, but suffered at the hands of the invading English. It has strong associations with the Scottish poet, Robert Burns (writer of Auld Lang Syne etc); the Robert Burns Centre; Burns House; Burns Mausoleum; Burns Statue and the Globe Inn. See also the Old Bridge House and 15c Old Bridge, the Aviation Museum, Dumfries Museum and Camera Obscura, the Crichton Royal Museum and Lincluden Collegiate church.

The Presbyterian Church. From 1638, with a break of thirty years later in the 17c (see Covenanters, page 121), the Presbyterian church was immensely powerful in Scotland. It was the only education and social welfare agency, and a court of morality extending its intolerance not just to its rivals, Catholics, Episcopalians and Quakers, but to all non-conforming people, outcasts, gypsies and troublemakers. Attendance at the Sunday service was compulsory and the Elders and clergy spent an enormous amount of time examining erotic episodes and sexual irrgularities. Discipline was savage. People were branded, flogged and put in stocks, 'witches' were tortured with racks, pulleys, thumbscrews, pincers, sleep deprivation and three inch pins. The events of 13th April 1659 when nine women were strangled and burnt on Whitesands, Dumfries because they were 'witches', were not uncommon.

TIC Dumfries (01387) 253862

Grierson and Graham (01387) 259483
Halfords (01387) 267118
Kirkpatrick Cycles (01387) 254011
Nithsdale Cycle Centre (01387) 254870

Dumfries - Drumlanrig (Nithsdale)

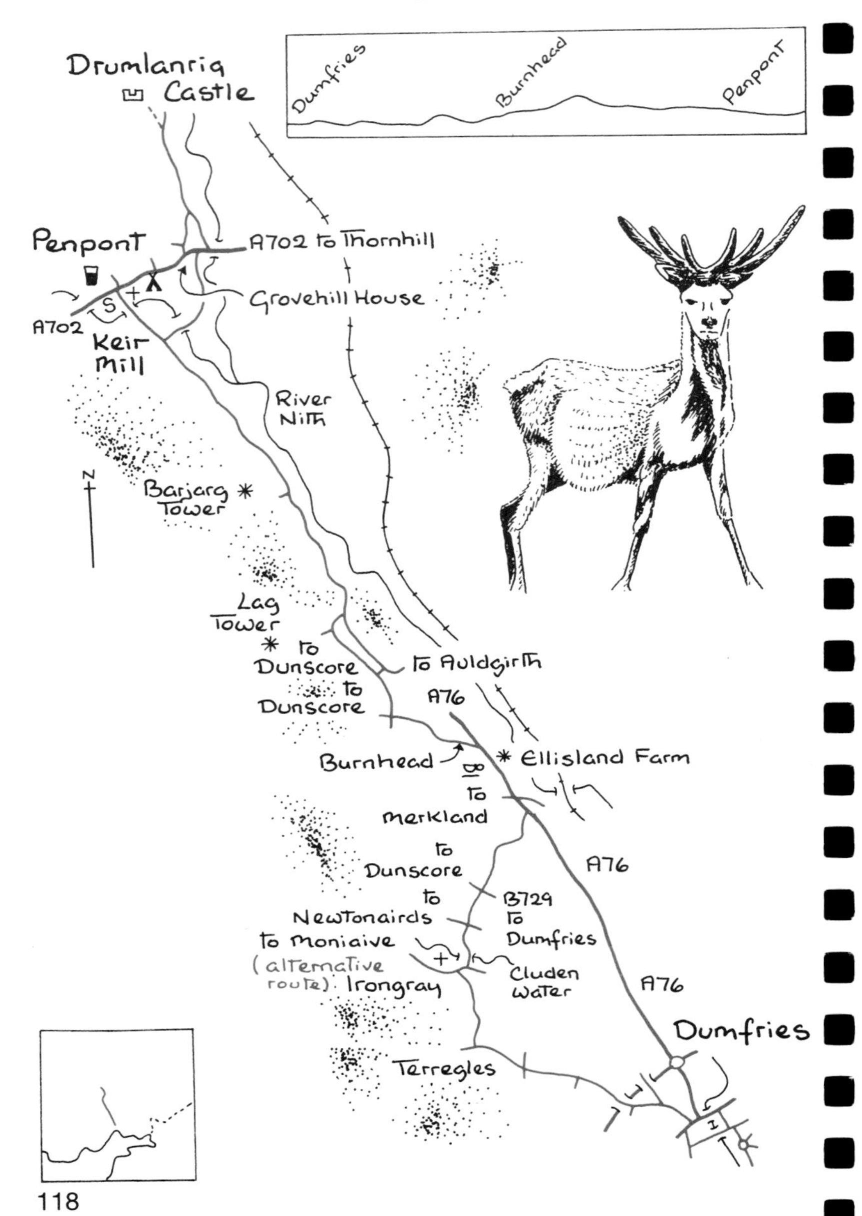

DUMFRIES – DRUMLANRIG (Nithsdale) 17 miles

The route weaves into the valley of the Nith, surrounded by hazy purple hills. This is fine wheeling country, low on traffic, wildlife close at hand, wilderness on the horizon and the occasional skirl of bagpipes drifting from an upstairs window.

Route Choice. From Dumfries the route choice is between (a) following the Nith Valley northwards, then skirting the 'Southern Uplands' into Ayrshire; or (b) (see Pages 124–129) passing through the mountains, including one or both of the Youth Hostels at Kendoon and Ayr.

Irongrey. In 1666 the muster point for Covenanters (see page 121) during the Pentland Rising, which ended in disaster for them. Nearby is a memorial to two Covenanters, Edward Gordon and Alexander McCubben, hanged from a nearby tree.

Lag Tower. A ruined keep, home of Grierson of Lag, scourge of Presbyterians in the 17c. A favourite trick was to put the Covenanters into spiked barrels and roll them down a hill.

Keir Mill, Courthill Smithy Plaques ("He buildeth better than he knew") commemorate the birthplace of the pedal cycle, invented here by Kirkpatrick Macmillan around 1840. A leaflet 'Follow the K.M. Trail' is available from local TICs.

Drumlanrig Castle. Built 1679-90 it is haunted by Lady Anne Douglas, who walks with her head in her hands, and is the home also of the Duke of Buccleuch, reputedly the second largest private landowner in Europe. The Castle houses Alex Brown's Cycle Museum.

TIC Dumfires (01387) 253862

Drumlanrig - Kirkconnel

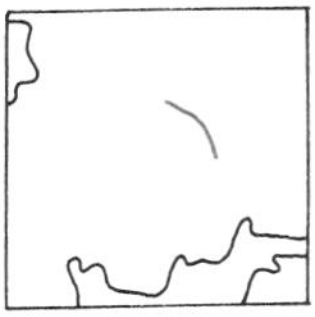

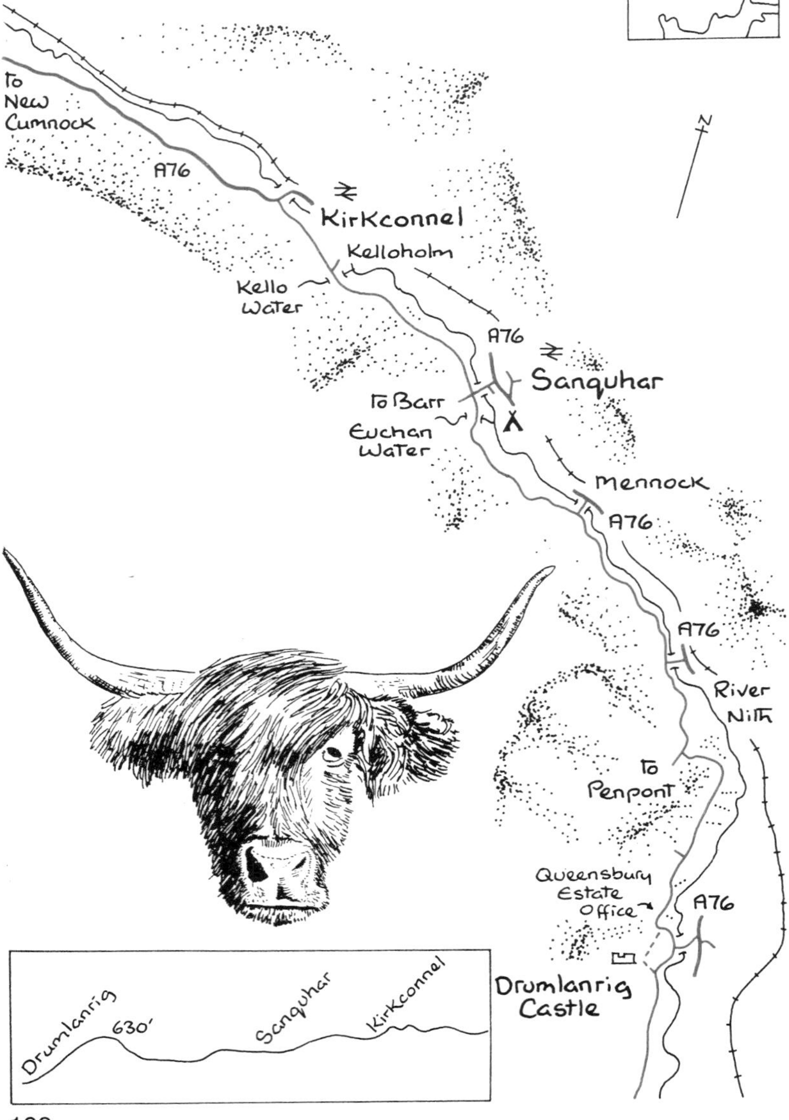

To New Cumnock
A76
Kirkconnel
Kelloholm
Kello Water
A76
Sanquhar
To Barr
Euchan Water
Mennock
A76
A76
River Nith
To Penpont
Queensbury Estate Office
A76
Drumlanrig Castle

Drumlanrig
630'
Sanquhar
Kirkconnel

DRUMLANRIG – KIRKCONNEL
(Upper Nithsdale) **13.5 miles**

The minor road to Kirkconnel is 'one of the best', a flowing ride on quiet roads, offset by a rather unpleasant section thereafter, on the A76 from Kirkconnel to New Cumnock. Amid this fine landscape the broken communities of Kirkconnel and New Cumnock come as something of a shock. In recent times this area was Scotland's worst unemployment blackspot, but the people remain wonderfully friendly to passing cyclists.

Sanquhar **S** The claims to fame are: Britain's oldest post office (1763); the Tollbooth with its visitor centre; the Castle, now in ruins, but once the formidable seat of the Duke of Queensbury; and as the birthplace of medieval adventurer James Crichton ('the Admirable Crichton').

Kirkconnel **S** Coal mining dates back beyond the 18c. The heyday was in the early 1920's and the last pit shut in the 1970's. More recently the home of Brock's fireworks.

Covenanting. In the largely Protestant Scotland of the 17c (see page 117), King James the Sixth attempted to re-establish Episcopacy. In 1638 the 'National Covenant' was drawn up by the Presbyterian Scots to defend 'the crown and true religion'. They took arms a year later, but it was not until the 1680's, when they were persecuted, that the real trouble started. These were the 'killing times', and Defoe estimated that eighteen thousand died and many were sold as slaves to America, imprisoned, fined, flogged, branded and tortured. The Protestant William of Orange became King in 1688, and the Church of Scotland established two years later. This area saw a great deal of the trouble, and many memorials remain.

TIC Sanquhar (01659) 50185

Kirkconnel - Stair

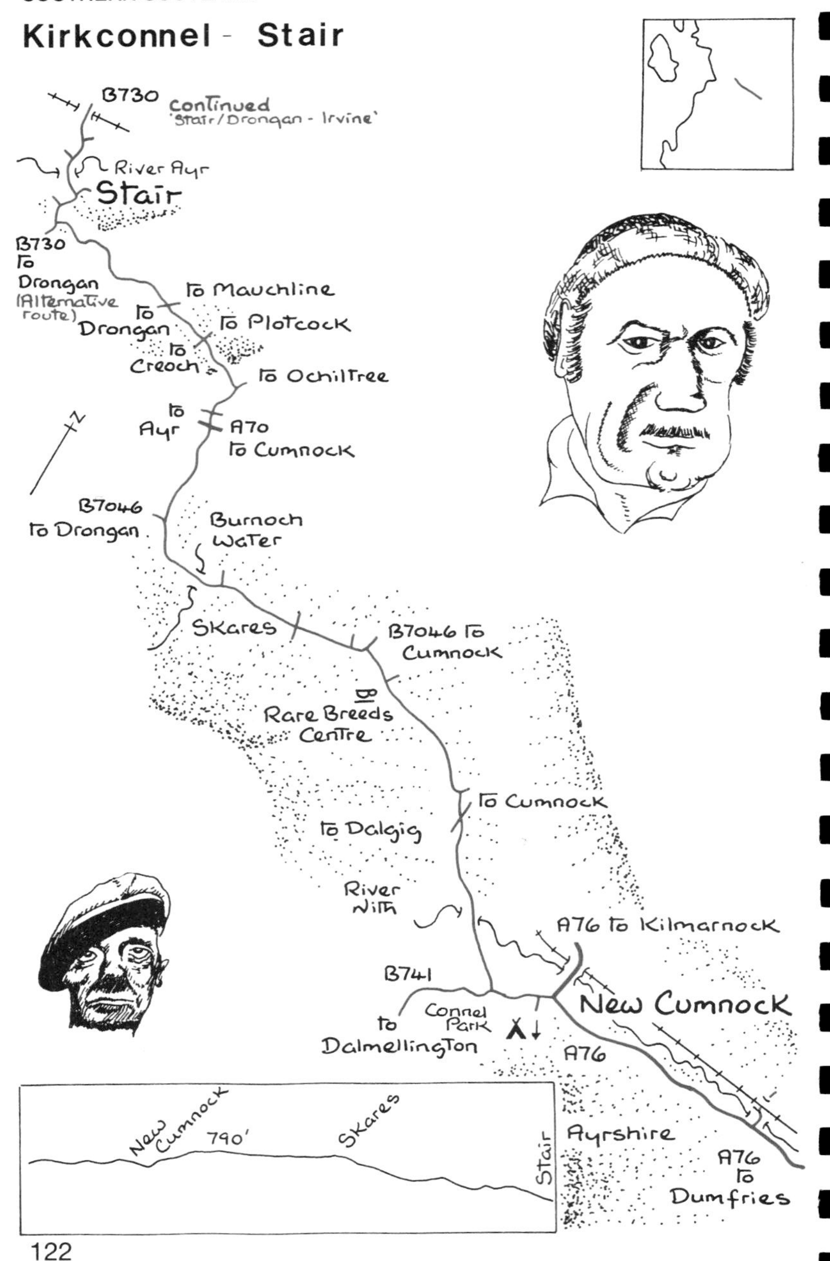

KIRKCONNEL – STAIR 21.5 miles

A transitional ride skirting the towns of Cumnock, Auchinleck and Mauchline. The route blossoms out from the Nith Valley to rich farmland, with the island of Arran hovering on the horizon like a mirage. The industrial scars on the landscape have almost healed, but the old men's faces show the lines of hard lives. Note an impressive lack of signposting.

New Cumnock **S** There is a memorial to 'The Cumnock Mineworkers who lost their lives in the course of duty', in the form of a safety lamp on a plinth made from ebony and granite.

Cumnock. Home of Keir Hardy, founder of the Independent Labour Party in 1893. The town once prospered with the manufacture of snuff boxes.

Auchinleck. From here James Boswell and Dr Johnson set off on their celebrated tour of the Highlands in 1773.

Mauchline. Andrew Kay and Co, Victorian Works, is one of only two curling stone factories in the world.

TIC Mauchline (01290) 551916
Howie Cycles, Auchinleck (01290) 425910

ALTERNATIVE

Dumfries - Moniaive

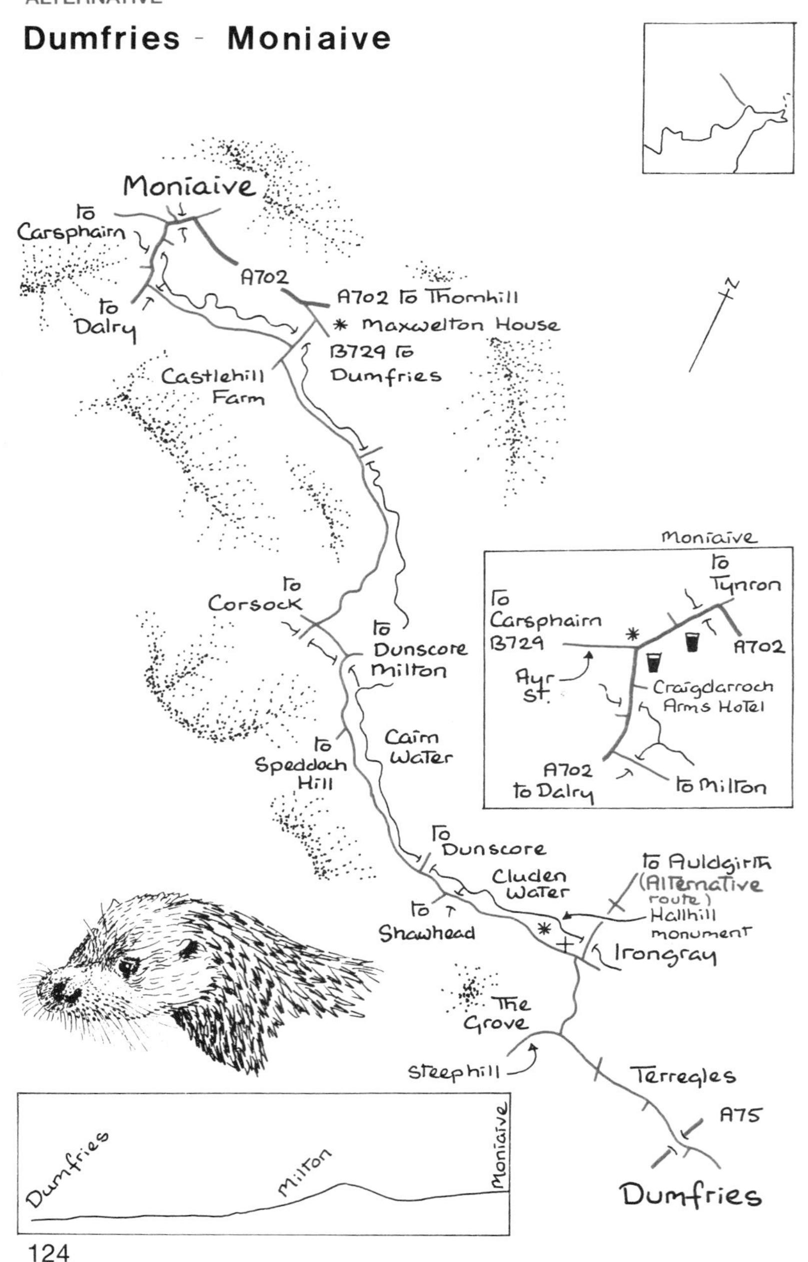

DUMFRIES – MONIAIVE 17 miles

A gentle, intimate, quiet climb alongside the old railway, through mixed estate country, to Moniaive.

Moniaive **S** A village with a mercat cross (1638), one of Scotlands oldest pubs, and a monument to James Renwick, around which many conventicles were held. He was a stout defender of Presbyterianism at the time of the Covenanters, and was captured and killed in 1688.

Scotland, the country. The Roman Emperor, Hadrian, built his wall in AD123, and, although the Picts raided across it, the Romans held this boundary. To the north Scotland was not 'united' as a Kingdom until AD843, by Kenneth MacAlpin. King David the First of Scotland exerted a civilising influence, encouraging trade, a central and local government system, coinage and a feudal system in the lowlands.
Much of the cross-Border animosity can be laid at the feet of King Edward the First of England (the 'Hammer of the Scots'). In 1296 he invaded Scotland, sacking Berwick, killing seventeen thousand people in two days. Retaliation and further invasions followed, including the theft of the Stone of Scone (upon which Scottish Kings and Queens had been crowned). William Wallace led the Scottish retaliation, but he was executed by Edward in 1305. Robert the Bruce followed, eventually achieving in 1314 the famous victory at Bannockburn, followed by a ravaging of the north of England 'with fire and sword'. The borders were not to see peace again for four hundred years.
The Act of union, in 1603, was not accepted by the Scots because it failed to guarantee a protestant monarchy.
Great Britain finally became a reality in 1707, and the last Scottish revolt ended with the massacre at Culloden in 1746.

TIC Dumfries (01387) 253862

ALTERNATIVE

Moniaive – Carsphairn (the Galloway Hills)

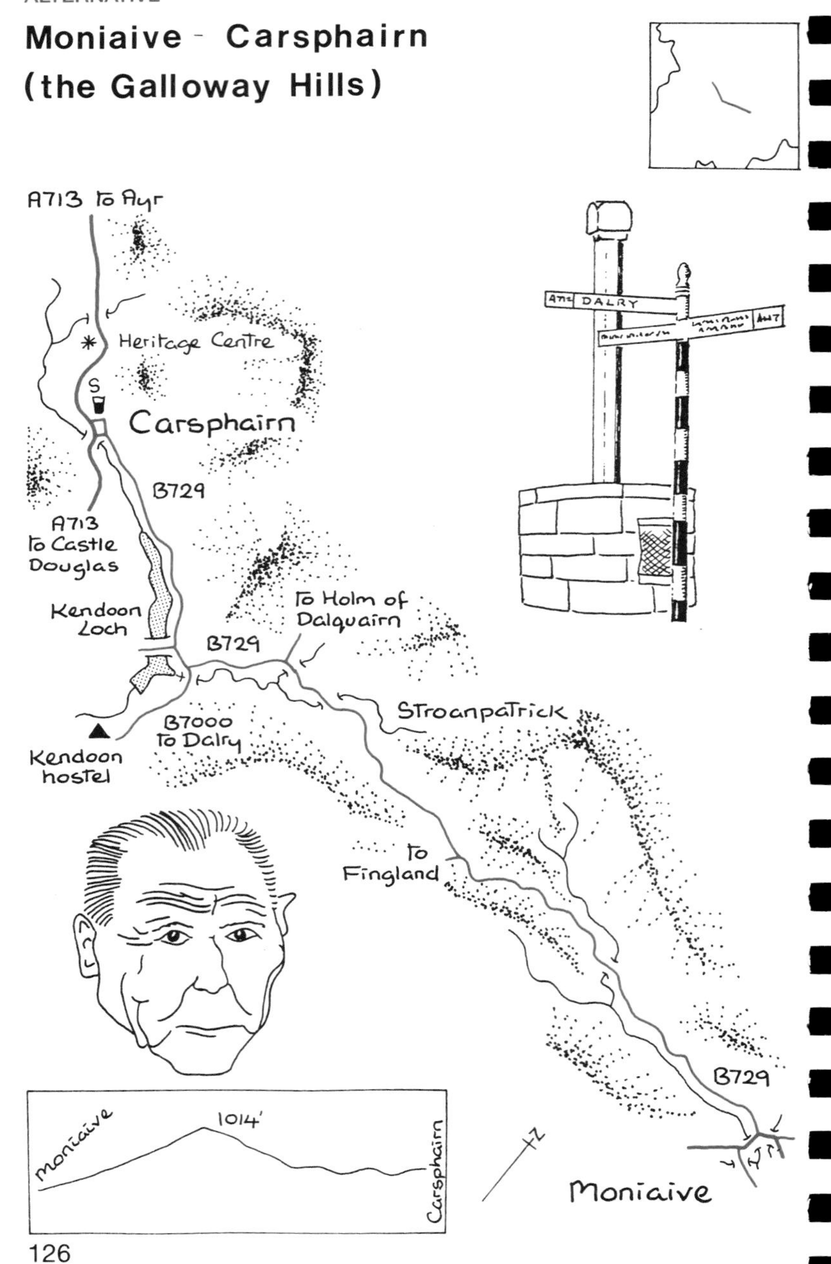

MONIAIVE – CARSPHAIRN
(The Galloway Hills) **14 miles**

A steady pull up alongside the Craigdarroch Water and Stroanshalloch Burn, into the hills, then it is typical Galloway; scrubby farms of sheep and belted Galloway cattle, spacious scrubby fellside and the encroaching Sitka spruce.

Carsphairn **S** The churchyard contains 'skull and crossbones' Covenanters gravestones and the MacAdam family vault (the inventor of 'tarmac'). There is a Heritage Museum.

Kendoon Loch is part of the Glenkens hydro scheme, which predates the more famous Highland ones. Conceived in 1923, the five electricity power-generating stations were built in 1931-35, and still operate successfully.

The Galloway Hills were well settled in prehistoric times. The site of a Mesolithic camp up to eight thousand years old has been discovered recently, and there are plenty of chambered cairns, stone circles, forts and remnants.
In recent times the land has been significantly degraded by over-intensive sheep grazing, and now large-scale conifer planting is in progress.

SYHA Kendoon (no telephone)

Carsphairn - Drongan

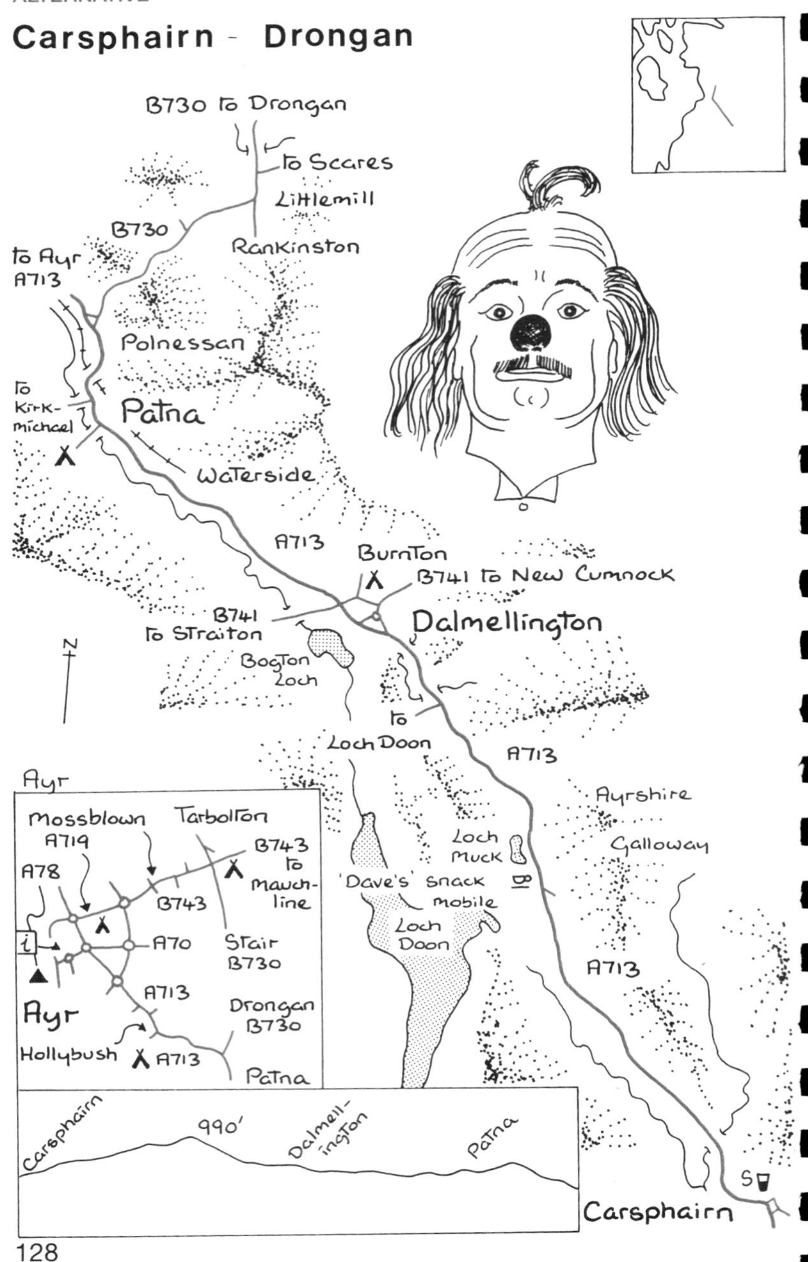

CARSPHAIRN - DRONGAN
(The Galloway Hills) **21 miles**

Steady climbing again, through the hills, this time on the fast, open A713, though it is not a busy road, and gradients are easy. To the east is the Cairnsmore range, to the west the mountains of Corserine and Merrick. The descent into the Doon Valley, with its industrial remnants, is a bit of a shock.

Loch Doon Castle. This 14c castle, originally on an island, was rebuilt when the water was raised for the hydro electric scheme. In the 1980's these hills were saved, by protestors, from becoming an international site for deep-stored radioactive waste.

Dalmellington S A small town enjoying brief prosperity with, firstly weaving, then iron and coal. The Old Minnevey Colliery, at Burnton, houses the Scottish Industrial Railway Centre. Note also the Cathcartson Interpretation Centre, and Covenanters graves in the churchyard.

Waterside The Dunaskin Heritage Centre is on the site of a 19c ironworks.

Ayr. A large industrial town and holiday resort. It is only mentioned here because of its Youth Hostel. The town is not particularly cycle-friendly. Places of interest include: The Land O'Burns Centre, Alloway, and Burns Cottage and Museum; Brig O'Doon; Tam O'Shanter Museum; Auld Kirk and Auld Brig.

Ailsa Craig. Sitting in the Clyde estuary is this 1,114feet high granite volcanic plug, once host to banished monks, now a bird sanctuary. The rock, Ailsite, takes a good enough polish to make excellent curling stones, and by 1970 four thousand pairs were being quarried each year, many to be shipped to Canada.

TIC Dalmellington (01292) 550145
Ayr (01292) 288688
SYHA Ayr (01292) 262322
AMG Cycles, Ayr (01292) 287580
Carrick Cycles, Ayr (01292) 269822
Ranger Trading Ltd, Ayr (01292) 269314

Stair/Drongan - Irvine

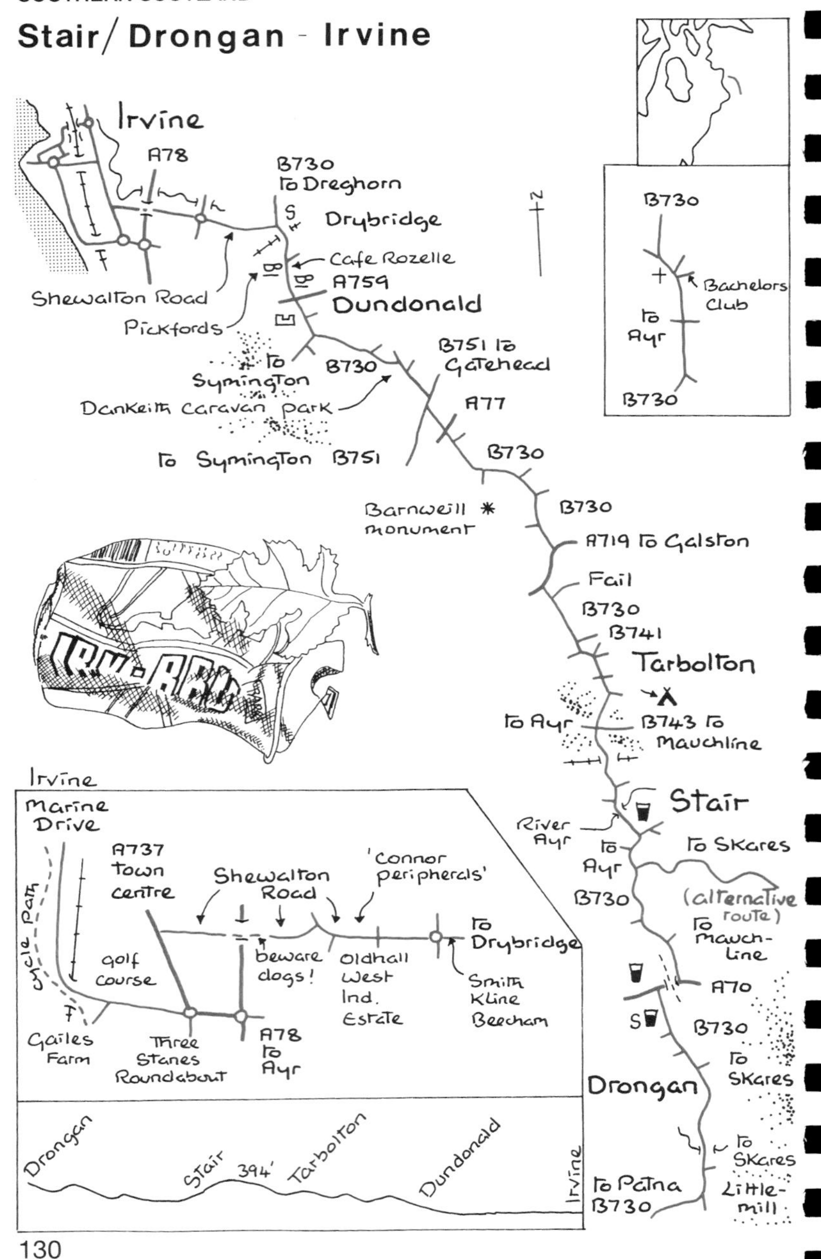

STAIR/DRONGAN - IRVINE 17 miles

'Gain three, lose two' sort of descent into a confusing austere landscape of rich grassland and industrial remnants. Marvel at the milestones passing you on from one old mill to the next, despair at the discarded IrnBru cans. The route follows the B730, shunning much of the development on the coast. Ayrshire's speciality is panorama's, and this route ranks high.

Stair From the 18c bridge you can see the 'Water of Ayr and Tam O'Shanter Hone Works Ltd', where hones were made, used to whet sickles throughout the world.

Tarbolton **S** The Bachelors Club, a thatched 17c building, is famous for the debating club formed here by Robert Burns and friends in 1780. Burns lived here aged eighteen to twentyfour. The church (1821) has a three-stage clock tower, with Covenanter graves and memorials.

Barnweill. In 1855 a tower was built in memory of William Wallace, as it was from here he watched the English garrison burn in 1297 ("the barns o' Ayr burn weill"). Wallace led the first wave of resistance to the English King Edward the First. He scored a notable victory at Stirling Bridge, but in 1305 was betrayed and hung, drawn and quartered in London.

Dundonald **S** The private ruin was built in 1350 by King Robert the Second as a tower-house.

Dreghorn. The Hall commemorates local boy John Boyd Dunlop, the inventor of the pneumatic tyre in 1888.

Ayrshire has a long established agricultural pattern with early potatoes on the coast, dairying inland, based on the Ayrshire cow, and, on the hills, sheep and hardy Galloway cattle.

Textiles were the area's traditional industry, with the manufacture of stockings and bonnets carried out as a village industry.

Coal mining and iron ore brought heavy industry. In 1606 the Scottish Parliament passed an Act which condemned colliers to virtual slavery, miners working underground for up to 16 hours a day, 6 days a week, alongside women and children. It was not repealled until 1799.

TIC Ayr (01292) 288688
Irvine (01294) 313886

Irvine Cycles (01294) 272712

Irvine - Ardrossan Cycle Path

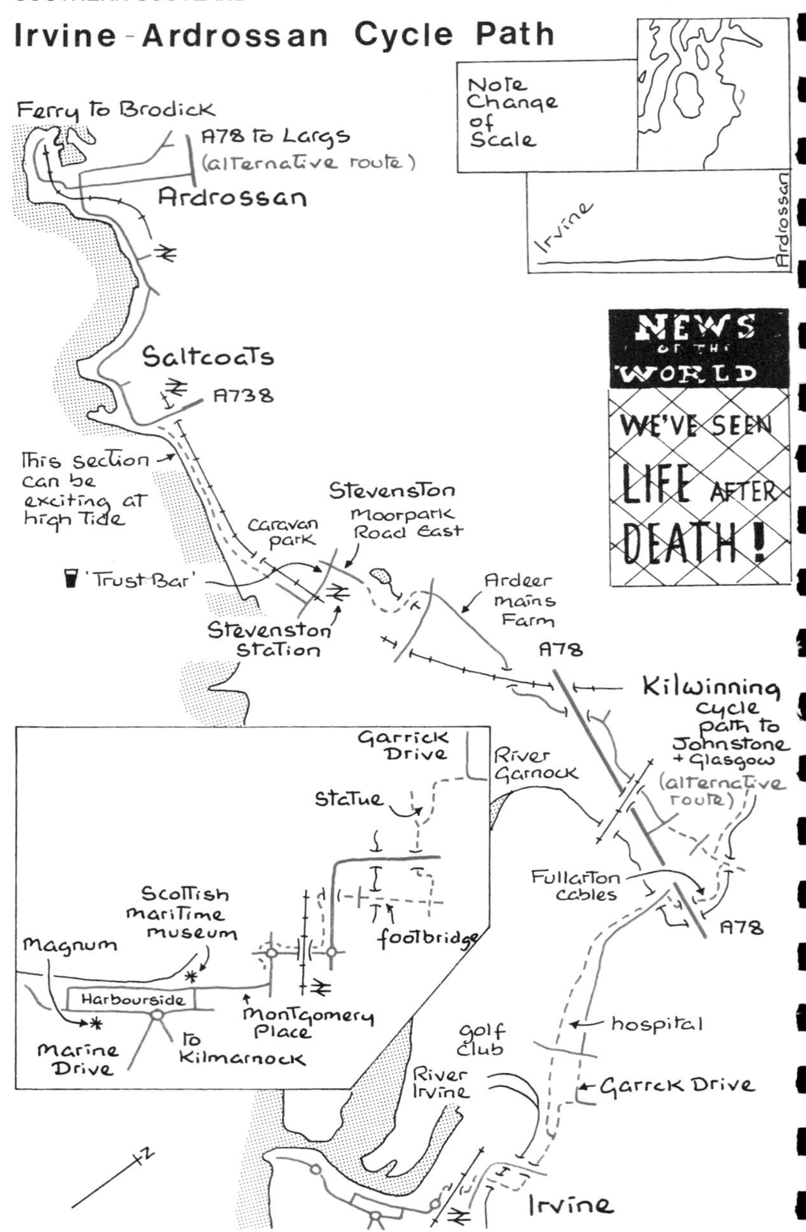

IRVINE – ARDROSSAN CYCLE PATH 8 miles

Much of Ayrshire is a sort of 'subrural' environment, prompting such questions as : why is man's thumbprint on the environment fascinating but ultimately depressing? Is all this necessary? Is Ayrshire the crowning glory of our civilsation, and if not, why not?
Irvine New Town was not built with the cyclist in mind, but Sustrans have done sterling work, and the Irvine Railway Path and Cycle Route is the result, with a branch to Ardrossan. As a result the cycle path is a bit of a hodge-podge and care is needed not to stray off route. All support for Sustrans is welcome: Sustrans, 53 Cochrane St, Glasgow, G1 1HL.

Route Choice. The wild country approaches. To get there you have a choice:

Route 1. Over the sea to Arran. An early gateway to the Highlands. Please note that, although the Ardrossan-Brodick ferry is year round, the ferry from Lochranza at the top of the island operates only from April to October. In addition, in bad weather the Ardrossan ferry is sometimes switched to one of the ports higher up the mainland.

Route 2. North on the mainland to catch the Cyde Ferry at Gourock (year round), reuniting with Route 1 north of Oban. This route involves further choice: Route 2a The coast road is shorter, quicker and flatter, but the A78 becomes most unpleasant as traffic increases above Largs (pages 142–145). Route 2b The northern section of the A78 can be avoided by taking the Glen Road to Inverkip; but this involves an ascent of nearly nine hundred feet (page 144). Route 2c From Irvine the Sustrans cycle path goes via Kilwinning, Johnstone and Greenock to Gourock. The good quality (for the most part) path has gentle gradients and is well used by cyclists (pages 146–149).

Irvine S An old seaport, now a New Town. The Scottish Maritime Museum is constantly developing with a wide variety of craft.

Stevenston and Saltcoats S developed at the end of the 17c with a coal mine and harbour for its export.

Ardrossan S Laid out in 1806 to serve the harbour, with villas along South Bay to create a resort. All these are grey, cementy sort of places.

TIC Irvine (01294) 313886
Ardrossan (01294) 601063

Island of Arran

ISLAND OF ARRAN 22 miles

Both routes to Lochranza involve climbing a pass. If you choose 'The String' then you can enjoy the fabulous coastal run along Brannan Sound, a white shore with seals, deer and birds galore.

The Ferries. Caledonian MacBrayne (Ardrossan (01294) 463470) offer a combined ticket for both ferries (£5.70 in 1995). Ardrossan-Brodick has six sailings a day, and Lochranza-Claonaig ten sailings daily, including Sundays, but the latter operates only from early-April to mid-October.

Brodick **S** The Castle, the ancestral home of the Duke of Hamilton, has been well battered from the 15c, but completely restored in 1844. Note the Isle of Arran Heritage Centre.

Lochranza **S** In the Guinness Book of Records as having the most days in a year without sunshine. In 1847 this was the island's main fishing port, for herring, but by 1905 they were gone, overfished out of existence. The Castle dates from the 13c.

Arran. Pre 1766 Arran was part of the 'Highlands'. Most people lived in 'clachans', little farm villages consisting of 'black houses', stone and thatch, home to man and beast alike, with a communal, patriarchal way of life based on the Clans. In 1766 John Burrel was asked by the Duke of Hamilton to devise better ways of exploiting the island. By 1829 whole tracts of the north were given over to sheep; English began to replace Gaelic; and the island was ruled by a Factor, evicting when he chose, on behalf of a remote landlord. Most of the business enterprises failed, and for many, emigration proved the only answer until tourism arrived.

In the early 19c the Dukes of Hamilton blocked every attempt to make Arran a holiday resort, and only after 1895 were ducal restriction lifted, and villas, shops and boarding houses allowed to spring up. In 1890 the Caledonian Railway Co. set out to wrest the Ardrossan-Brodick trade from their hated rivals, the Glasgow and South-Western Railway. 'Glasgow to Arran in ninety minutes' they advertised. This led to a speed war with magnificent paddle steamers racing each other, with occasional collisions, across the Firth.

TIC Brodick (01770) 302140/302401
Lochranza (01770) 830320
SYHA Lochranza (01770) 830631
Accomodation – Corrie Croft, North High Corrie, Corrie (Sleeps 20) (01770) 302203
Brodick Cycles (01770)302460

Lochranza - Kilmartin

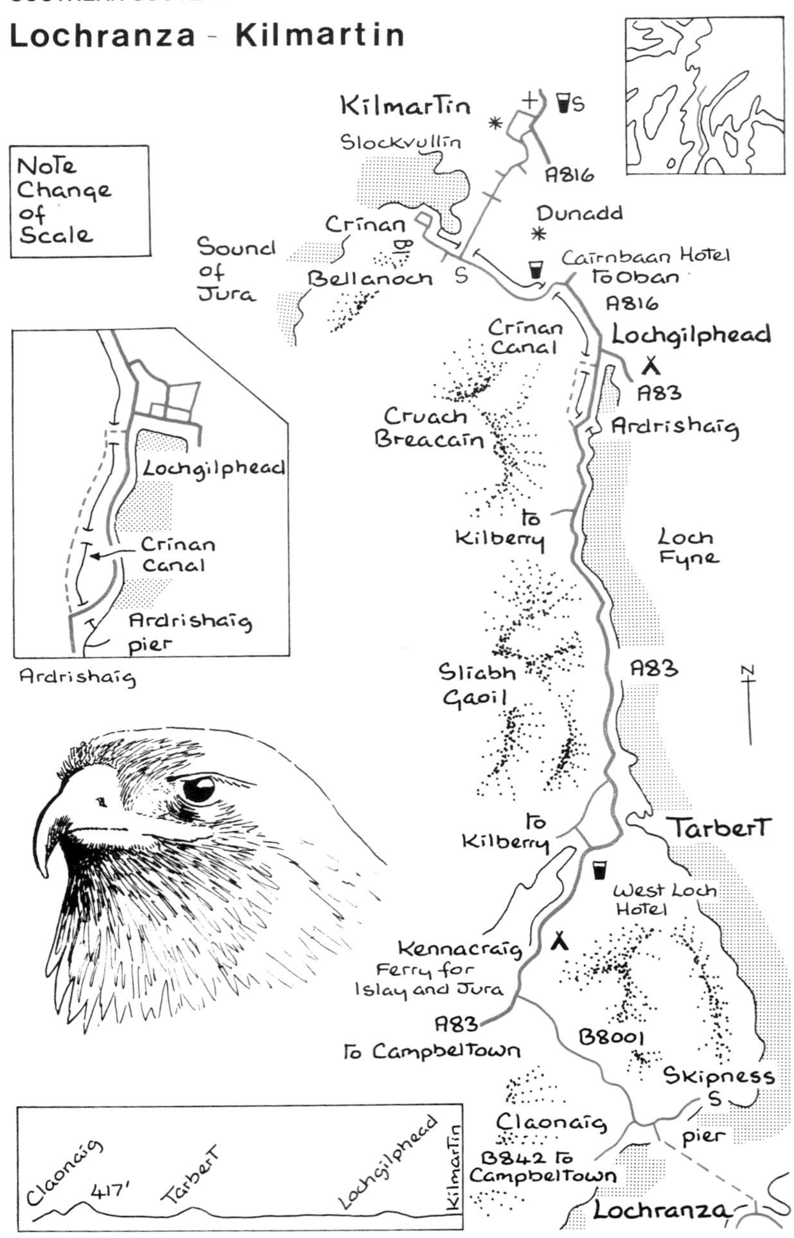

LOCHRANZA – KILMARTIN 31 miles

A fine sea crossing and a lonely climb into Kintyre, so it comes as something of a shock when the A83 is reached. The whole run is full of interest, but perhaps the country has met a few too many people with their own ideas of what to do with it.

Tarbert **S** Once a prosperous fishing port, but the herring are gone. Despite the yachts it is a lovely little town, with a bloody past. Whoever held the castle here commanded the isthmus, so this was regularly fought over between rival Scot's factions, and between the Scots and the Vikings.
When Magnus Barefoot, King of Norway, launched an invasion in 1098 the Scottish King Edgar bought him off by agreeing that Magnus could keep any island around which he could travel. Kintyre was on his list, so he sat at the tiller of his longboat as it was dragged across the isthmus at Tarbert. There is a Heritage Centre here.

Ardrishaig **S** One end of the Crinan Canal, designed by John Rennie, and opened in 1801, it's nine miles saves a one hundred and thirty mile sea voyage.

Lochgilphead **S** No longer a market town and herring port, but a tourist centre. The hospital here treated psychiatric and psychological disorders, and the phrase "He's in Lochgilphead" came to mean a person receiving treatment for alcohol abuse.

Bellanoch. At the old inn, in 1848, nearly two hundred people marched to attack the police and release five of their colleagues. This was one of the few examples of organised resistance to the evictions during the 'Clearances' in Argyll.

Dunadd. This rock was the centre of Dalriada, a Kingdom founded in the 6c mainly by people from Ireland, from whom the Scots are descended.

TIC Tarbert (01880) 820429
Lochgilphead (01546) 602344
'Sailmakers', Tarbert
Crinan Cycles, Ardrishaig (01546) 60351

Kilmartin - Connel

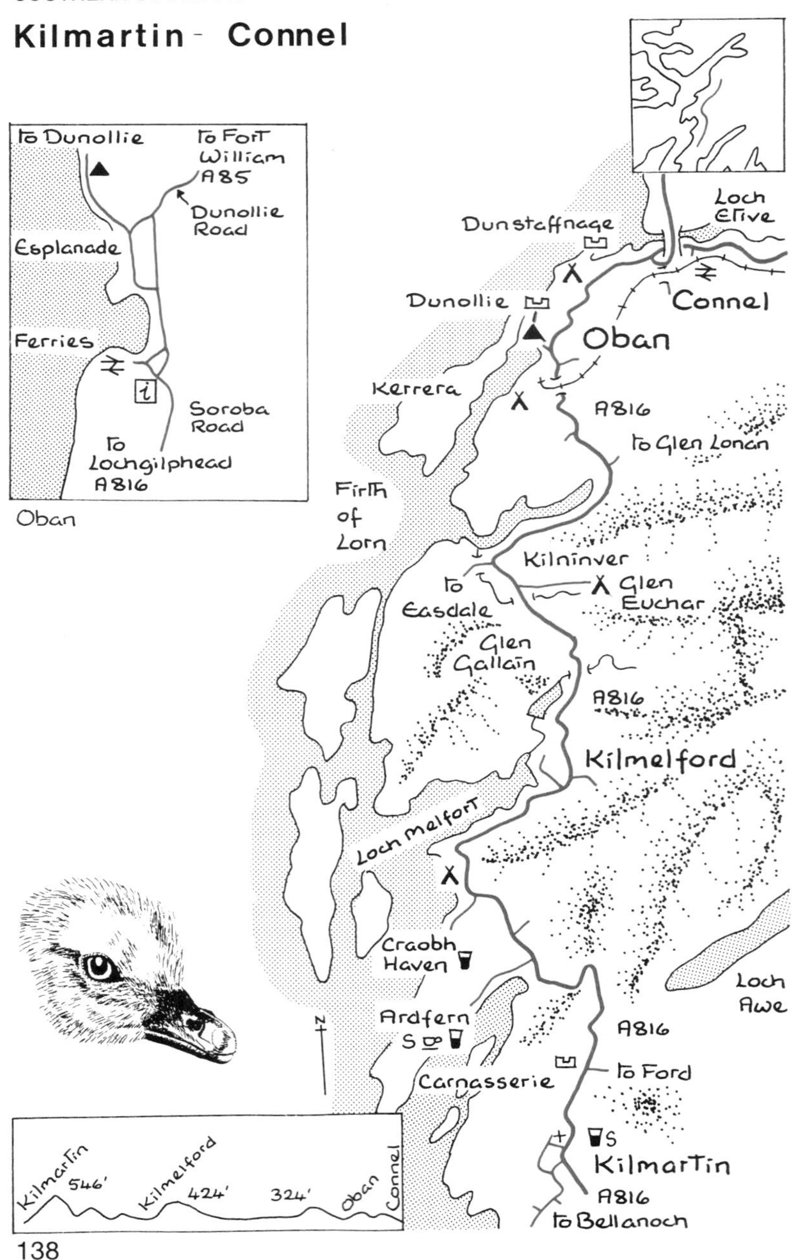

KILMARTIN – CONNEL 3l miles

A land of moods and textures, with islands sitting offshore like dumplings in a stew. It is a pity so much of the run is on 'A' roads, though there is only one real hill.

Kilmartin **S** The location of twelve large megaliths in a circle, and a string of burial cairns and ritual monuments covering two thousand years. The churchyard also contains remarkable 14c/15c pictorial grave slabs.

Carnasserie Castle. A partially ruined late 16c tower house, the home of John Carswell, the first protestant Bishop of the Isles and Rector of Kilmartin.

Kilmelford **S** A gunpowder factory blew up here in 1867.

Glen Euchar Green mounds mark the Sabhal nan Cnamham (Barn of Bones). Alexander Colkitts MacDonald is said to have collected all the Campbells in the glen into the barn, and burned them alive.

Oban **S** Busy tourist resort, and yachting centre, developed by the Victorians when the railway arrived. The town was filmed as 'Glendoran' in the BBC's 'Sutherland Law'. McCaig's Tower was begun in 1897 to provide work for local stonemasons, and to provide a monumental monument to his family. Work was abandoned on McCaig's death in 1902. See also Oban Rare Breeds Farm; 'A World in Miniature Museum'; Highland Discovery Centre; Oban Distillery; Glass Works, and two modern cathedrals.

Dunollie Castle. The stronghold of the Lorn Kings in 7c and 8c north Dalriada. The castle became the seat of the MacDougalls (who once owned a third of Scotland), until it was abandoned in 1715 when the Jacobite MacDougalls had their land confiscated.

Dunstaffnage Castle. First built in the 13c as protection against the Norse.

TIC Oban (01631) 563122
SYHA Oban (01631) 562025
Accomodation – Jeremy Inglis, 21 Airds Crescent (01631) 565065
Oban Backpackers Lodge, Breadalbane St (01631) 562107/563323
D. Graham, Oban (01631) 562069
Oban Cycles (01631) 566996

Loch Awe - Connel - Loch Linnhe

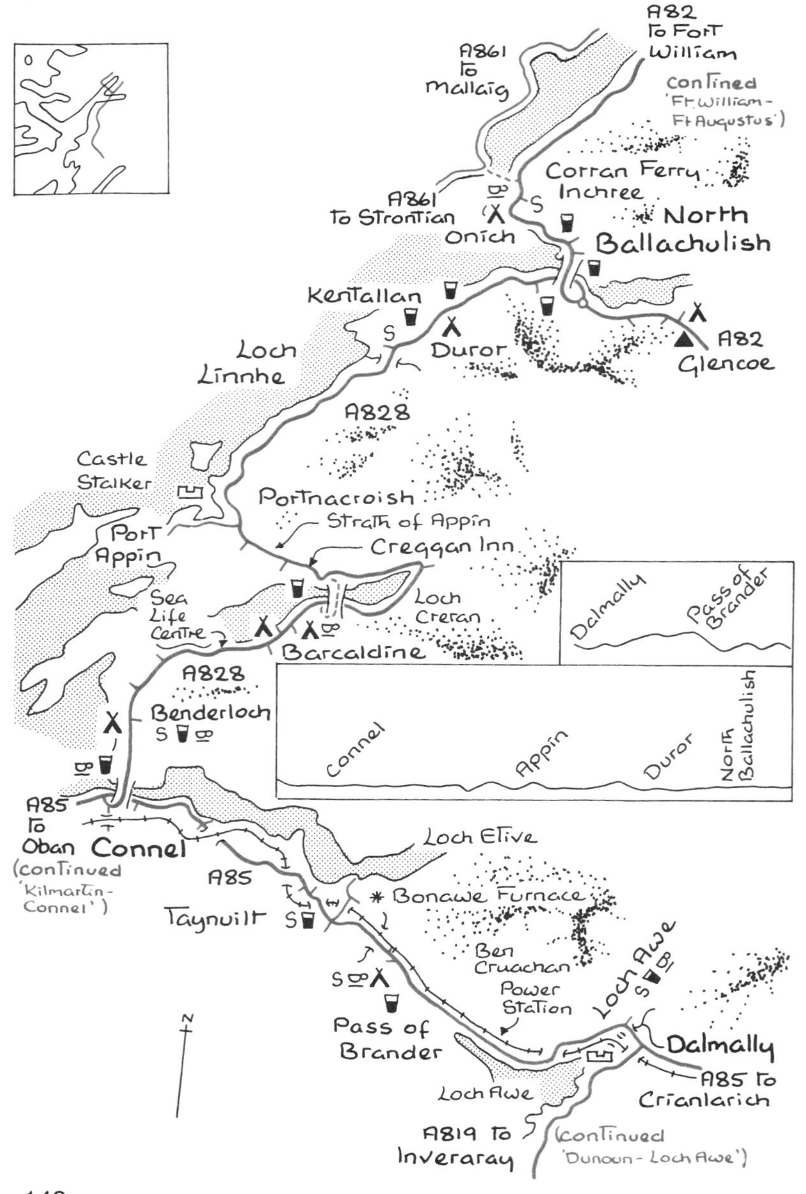

LOCH AWE – CONNEL – LOCH LINNHE 56 miles

Most of the little ferries have disappeared before the onslaught of the car. The A85 and A82 are not too pleasant, but the A828 is a beautiful, shore-lapped ride with islands to the west, and mountains rising inland. Take a short cut at Loch Creran by pushing the bike up and over the old railway bridge, and at Onich, although against the law, there is a rideable footpath. On those fragile mornings when the head is not quite there and the legs ache, Scotland can be quite fearsome; the distances, the views, the traffic, the breakfasts, the midges and the tourists.

Ben Cruachan. Water from Loch Awe is pumped up to a lake on the mountain as a means of storing electrical energy.

Taynuilt **S** In the 18c a number of charcoal burning ironworks were built to utilise the vast Caledonian forests. The most complete is here, at Bonawe. Established in 1753, the furnace could make 700 tons of iron a year, for which it required 3,500 tons of wood. Canon balls used at Trafalgar were made here.

Connel **S** Beneath the bridge are the 'Falls of Lora', powerful tidal currents which were a great hazard to the ferries.

Barcaldine. The grey buildings by Loch Creran are the 'seaweed' factory, for emulsifiers and thickeners in, among other things, ice cream. See also the Sea Life Centre.

Portnacroish. Castle Stalker was the 16c home of the Stewarts of Appin. There is also the Appin Wildlife Museum.

Glencoe. Two monuments bear witness to the Massacre of Feb 13, 1692, when 130 Government troops under the orders of Archibald Campbell, 10th Earl of Argyll, slaughtered 38 MacDonalds for their tardiness in swearing allegiance to King William the Third. There is also a heather-thatched museum.

Corran Ferry takes vehicles across to the A861 on the west side of Loch Linnhe, a much more gentle road than the A82. The return ferry to Fort William is from Camisnagaul, a passenger ferry (cycles carried free) operated by Highland Regional Council. It only sails 5 or 6 times a day; ask for details at Corran Ferry or ring (01463) 702000.

TIC Ballachulish (01855) 811296
Fort William (01397) 703781
SYHA Glencoe (01855) 811219
Glen Nevis (01397) 702336
Accomodation – Inchree Bunkhouse, Onich (018554) 471/402
Mountain Madness, Ballachulish (01855) 811728

ALTERNATIVE

Ardrossan - Largs

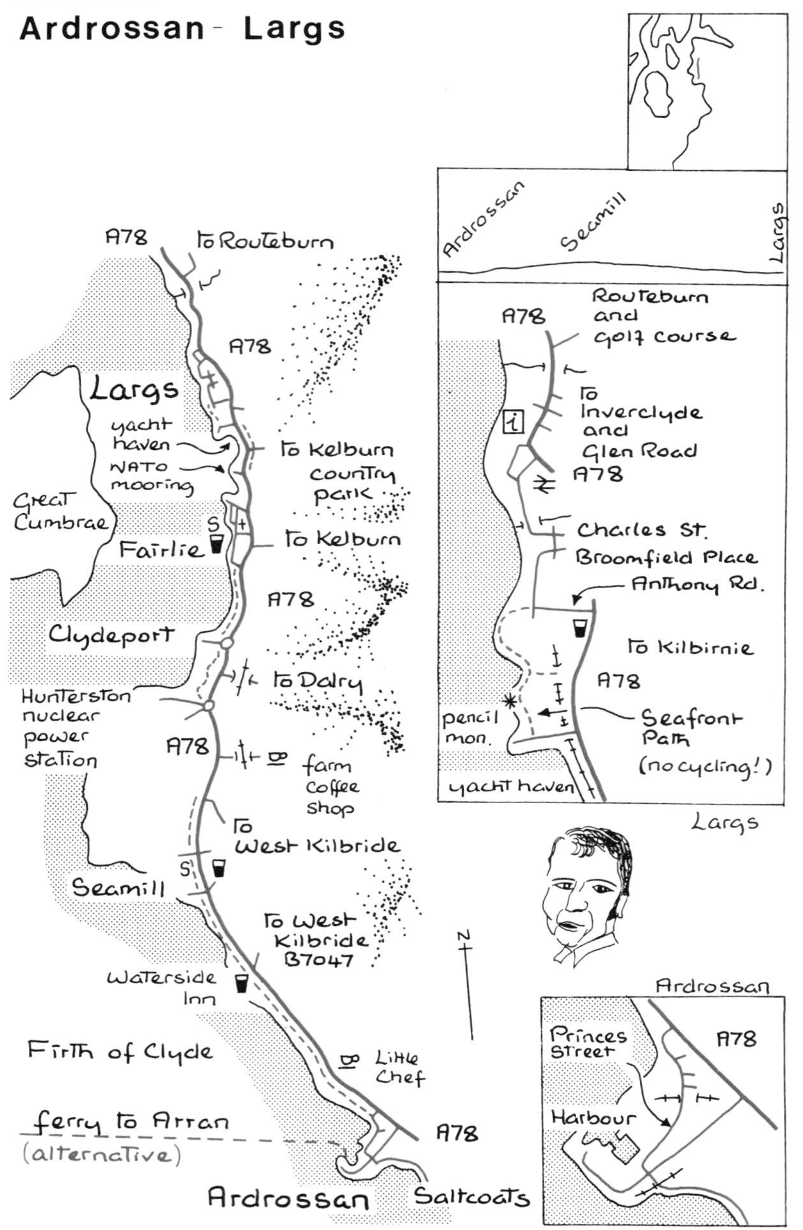

ARDROSSAN - LARGS 12 miles

The coastal route is spectacular with the Firth of Clyde, the islands of Arran, Great and Little Cumbrae and Bute, a multitude of sea lochs wriggling into the big mountains, and boats plying this way and that. Unfortunately the coastline itself is not particularly pleasant, a string of industry, resorts and marinas linked by a major traffic artery.
Cunninghame District Council are building a cycle network along the North Ayrshire coast, and the footpath is presumably meant to be shared with cyclists. However, it disappears for a while north of West Kilbride, at Fairlie and altogether north of Largs.

West Kilbride. Law Castle is a 15c tower house belonging to the Boyd family. Portencross Castle is a 15c keep, used by the early Stuart Kings. There is a costume museum.

Hunterston gas-cooled nuclear power station has a visitor centre.

Kelburn Country Park. The 13c castle is home to the Earls of Glasgow.

Largs **S** The phallic obelisk, the Pencil, celebrates the battle of 1263 when the Scottish King Alexander the Third defeated King Haakon of Norway and freed Scotland from the grip of the Vikings. September sees a Viking Festival. Note the Historical Museum and Christian Heritage Museum.

TIC Ardrossan (01294) 601063
Largs (01475) 673765

Close to the Edge, Largs (01475) 689119
Hastie of Largs (01475) 673989

ALTERNATIVE

Largs - Gourock

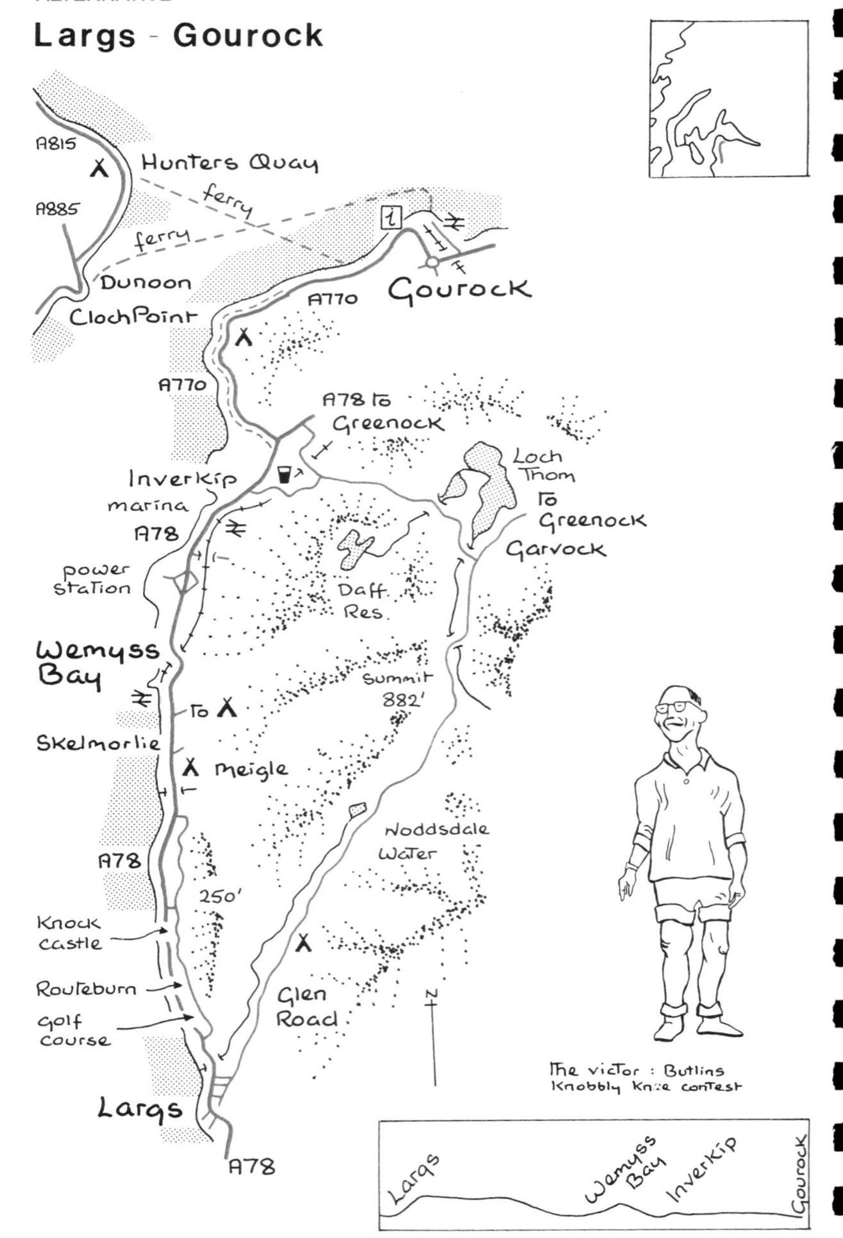

The victor : Butlins Knobbly Knee contest

LARGS – GOUROCK 13.5 miles

The minor road above Largs gives wonderful views over the Clyde estuary, but from Skelmorlie north the A78 becomes progressively more unpleasant and dangerous for the cyclist. Much of the A770 has a rideable footpath. Alternatively, the Glen road climbs steadily to the summit at 882ft, then delivers you down safely to Inverkip.

Skelmorlie S The Aisle is a 1636 mausoleum.

Wemyss Bay **S** A recent town with a 19c mansion called Castle Wemyss, where Trollope wrote Barchester Towers.

Inverkip **S** 'Kip' is a marina village. Originally called 'Auldkirk' because the people of Greenock came here to church before their own was built, it was also an infamous centre of witch mania in the 17c, and smuggling in the 18c.

Cloch Point. The lighthouse was built in 1796, but is now a private house.

The Offshore Islands are Little Cumbrae and Great Cumbrae. Millport boasts the 'Cathedral of the Isles', the smallest in Europe.

The Clyde Estuary is a sea-drowned trough, originally scoured out by glaciers.

TIC Largs (01475) 673765
Gourock (01475) 639467

Kilwinning - Johnstone

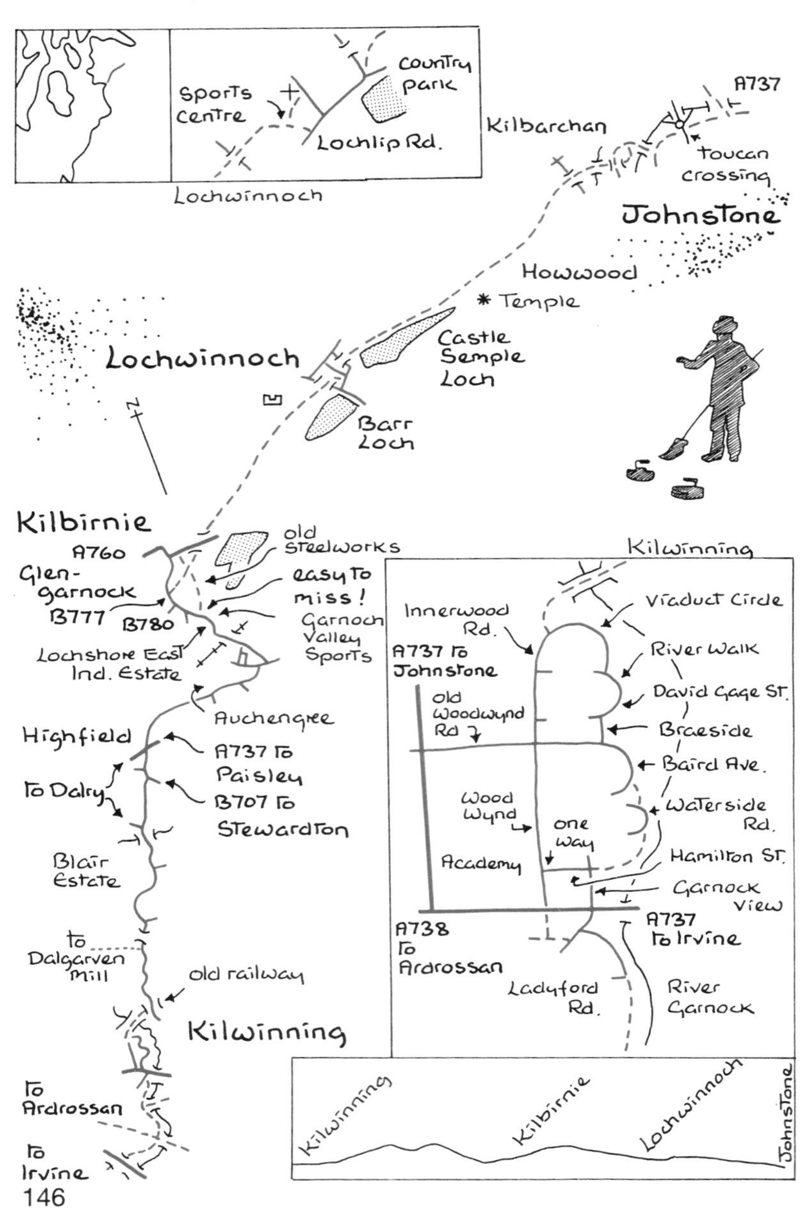

KILWINNING – JOHNSTONE 18 miles

A mixture of railway path and minor roads leads to Glen Garnock, a contradictory, fascinating blend of pleasant, undulating farmland, and people desperately trying to carve out a living on the skeletons of industry past. On areas such as this was the Empire built. The cycle path is confusing in places, notably in Kilwinning and in Glengarnock. Beware of cycle path signs which are missing or have been turned around.

Kilwinning **S** The Abbey ruins date from the 13c. Dalgarven Mill is an early 17c flour mill holding the Ayrshire Museum of Countryside and Costume.
Blair House, with its 15c keep has been in the hands of the Blair family for seven hundred years.

Kilbirnie **S** The town prospered from its large steelworks, now razed to the ground. Remnants of an older past remain with the ruins of Kilbirnie Place (1627), the Barony Church, the old church of St Brendene (dating back to 1275, making it one of the oldest in Scotland still being used), and Glengarnock Castle (the oldest surviving castle in the west of Scotland, home to Hugo de Morville in the 12c.)

Lochwinnock **S** Here you'll find the Castle Semple Loch Country Park, an important bird reserve, and a Community Museum.

Davidson Sports, Dalry (01294) 833332
RT Cycles, Glengarnock (01505) 682191

ALTERNATIVE

Johnstone - Gourock

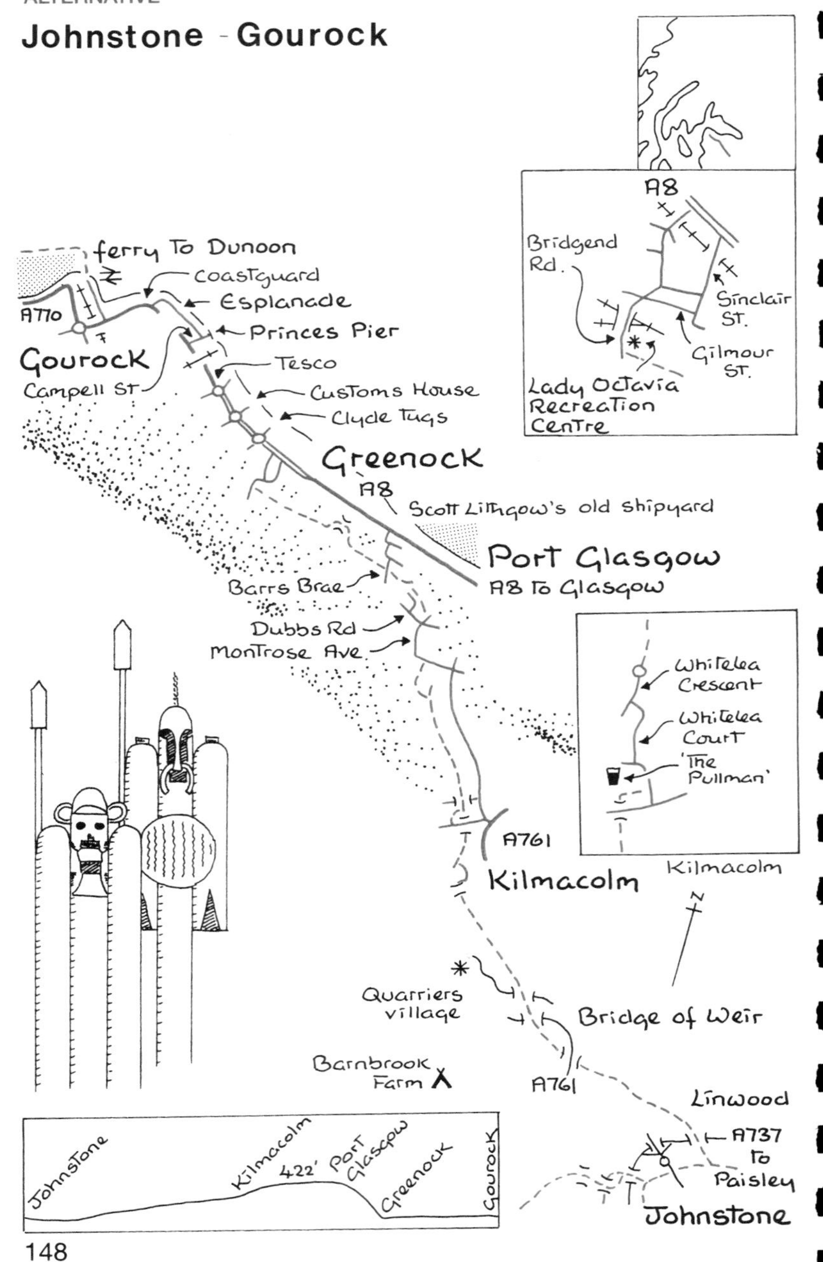

JOHNSTONE - GOUROCK 16 miles

This is a freewheeling cycle route through broken country skirting the Glasgow conurbation. Experience the awesome sight of a pack of day-glo helmeted toddlers just out of stabilisers bearing down at full lick. At Greenock is the swift descent to urban pandemonium, with the all-pervading smell of curry, and a truly amazing backdrop across the Clyde. Two rival ferry companies operate to Dunoon all year round.

Kilbarchan. An 18c handloom weaving centre; a weaver's cottage has been preserved.

Kilmacolm. A well-heeled residential area for the Glasgow conurbation since the 19c.

Greenock **S** In the late 18c/early 19c it became the deep-water port for Glasgow. Badly damaged by German bombs in the 1939-45 War, many fine Victorian buildings survive, including the Municipal Buildings and Customs House. On Lyle Hill, above the town, stands a huge granite Cross of Lorraine, a memorial to the 'Free French', who used Greenock in the same war.

Gourock **S** Half port, half resort and half neither. On Kempock Point is Granny Kempock's Stone, of prehistoric origin. In 1622 a group of witches were burned, including Mary Lamont, a teenage girl who 'confessed' to having wanted to throw the stone into the sea to cause shipwrecks.

TIC Glasgow Airport (0141) 848 4440
Greenock (01475) 724400
Gourock (01475) 639467

Tortoise Cycles, Johnstone (01500) 007533
Aerobikes Cycle Co, Greenock (01475) 888900
Halfords Ltd, Greenock (01475) 781444
JS Phillips, Greenock (01475) 726322

ALTERNATIVE

Dunoon - Loch Awe

(continued 'Loch Awe - Connel - Loch Linnhe')

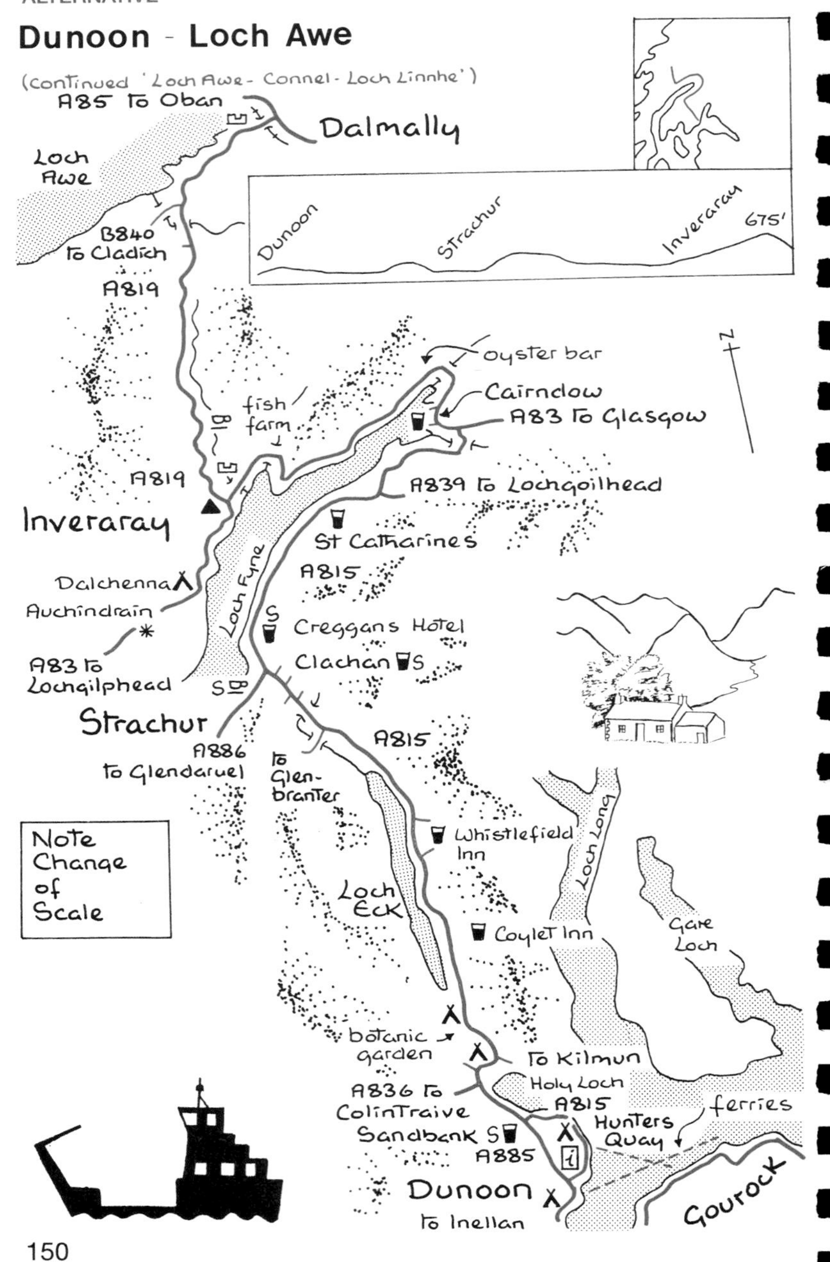

DUNOON – LOCH AWE 46 miles

Suddenly it's a different place; midges, mist and mountains; distances seem to double; and the power of the landscape makes itself felt. The route is relatively flat to Inveraray, though the A83 is not pleasant, then there is a long, gently climb to Loch Awe.

Dunoon **S** A Clyde tourist resort and yachting centre.

Hunters Quay **S** The first Scottish yacht club was formed here in 1856. It boasts the smallest post office in the UK, built for King George the Fifth, a keen sailor, to use when he stayed at the Royal Marine Hotel.

Benmore. Younger Botanic Garden has a famous avenue of redwoods, rhodedendron and azaleas.

Strachur **S** At Creggans Inn is the site of MacPhunn's Cairn. MacPhunn of Drip was a local laird who fell on hard times and took to stealing sheep. For this he was hanged at Inveraray, and his wife, who was nursing a baby at the time, invited to collect his body. This she did by boat, but half way across Loch Fyne she saw the body move, so she mixed up some of her own milk with whisky, and forced it through his lips. He recovered, and, as the law did not allow him to be hanged twice, they lived happily for many years.

Inveraray **S** For centuries the centre of the Campbell clan. In the 18c the old village was burned to make way for the Castle, and the present village built by the third Duke of Argyll.
The Castle, 1770, contains paintings and other treasures; the Jail is a must for all punishment enthusiasts (there is a souvenir shop); the Bell Tower has the World's third heaviest ring of ten bells; Auchindrain Museum is an old West Highland township restored as a museum.

Dalmally. Grew in the 1880's around the West Highland Railway, and now known for its angling, sheep market and shinty pitch.

Kilchurn Castle, built by the Campbells in 1440.

TIC Dunoon (01369) 703785
Inveraray (01499) 302063
SYHA Inveraray (01499) 2454
Tortoise Cycles, Dunoon (01369) 702001/705607

THE HIGHLANDS

THE HIGHLANDS

Negociate the Great Glen with ease to Fort Augustus. The flat route, and the most unpleasant, then takes the A82 to Inverness. The alternative is to climb out of the valley on either side and rejoin the route in either Inverness or Cromarty.
In Caithness the choice is between getting there, and taking the chance to experience the Flow Country.

The Highlander. The Highlands have nothing like such a long history of human habitation as England, and were still under ice when people were colonising the south. In addition, the West Highlands are the wettest part of Europe and land use, as a consequence, is much less flexible.
The Highlander has been much caricatured, from Sir Walter Scott's swash-buckling, tartan-clad Rob Roy, to Harry Lauder's whisky-swiller. Highland history is not one of romance but a blood-stained record of petty rivalries and major horrors, and was finally finished off by patriotism.
Following the Battle of Culloden in 1746, the King forbade the Highlander to carry arms, wear the 'tartan' or the kilt and play the bagpipes, and the lands of all known rebels and sympathisers were confiscated.

The Clearances. The calculated dismemberment of the clan system paradoxically, went hand in hand with farming improvements. Lairds, both local and from the south, acquired vast estates and saw the swift profits to be made from sheep. There followed a century of population clearances, forced evictions and emigration under duress.
The transition from sheep farms to sporting estates began in the 1850's. By 1884 deer forests covered nearly two million acres.
The depopulation of the Highlands has continued into the 20c. Economic decline was arrested in 1965 with the establishment of the Highlands and Islands Development Board. Fish and deer farming have been encouraged, and North Sea Oil has brought wealth to some areas.

Habitat Destruction. Man's greatest impact on the landscape of

the Highlands has been the destruction of the ancient forest. In the early 16c the forests were 'discovered' by Lowland Scots and the English, who had already devastated their own woodlands. Especially after the Jacobite Rebellions the forests sheltered rebels, and business interests purchased forfeited estates. The wood went for charcoal smelting in the iron furnaces (including Bonawe), for bobbins for the cotton mills, for tanning sails and ropes and to satisfy the demands of war.
Habitat destruction caused the disappearance of the brown bear (9/10c), reindeer (12c), elk (13c), beaver (15/16c), wild board, wild ox, wild horses (13 to 15c), wolf (18c), crane, bittern, auk, osprey, goshawk, kite and sea-eagle. The red squirrel was almost extinct by 1800 and the capercaillie became extinct for 67 years in the 18c. Some of these species have been reintroduced, polecats, pine marten and wildcats have survived and the re-establishment of the golden eagle is astonishing. The growth of the deer population, with no natural predator, is a major problem if woodland is ever to be re-established.

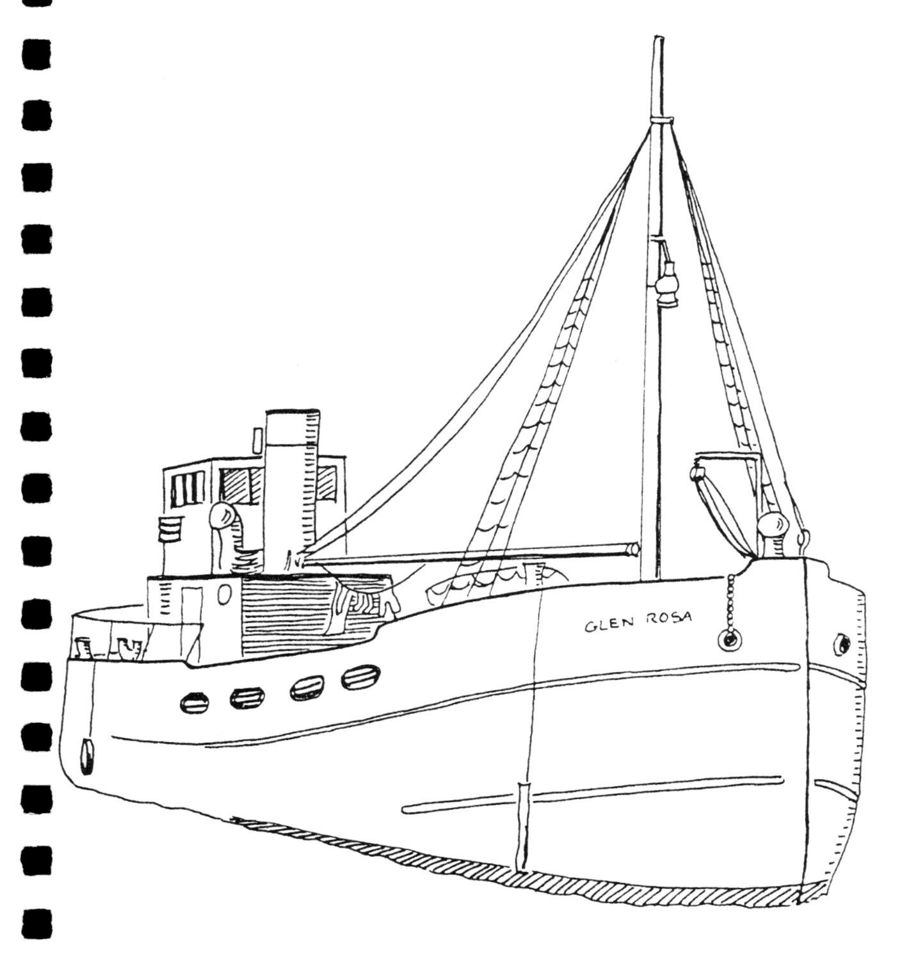
GLEN ROSA

Fort William - Fort Augustus

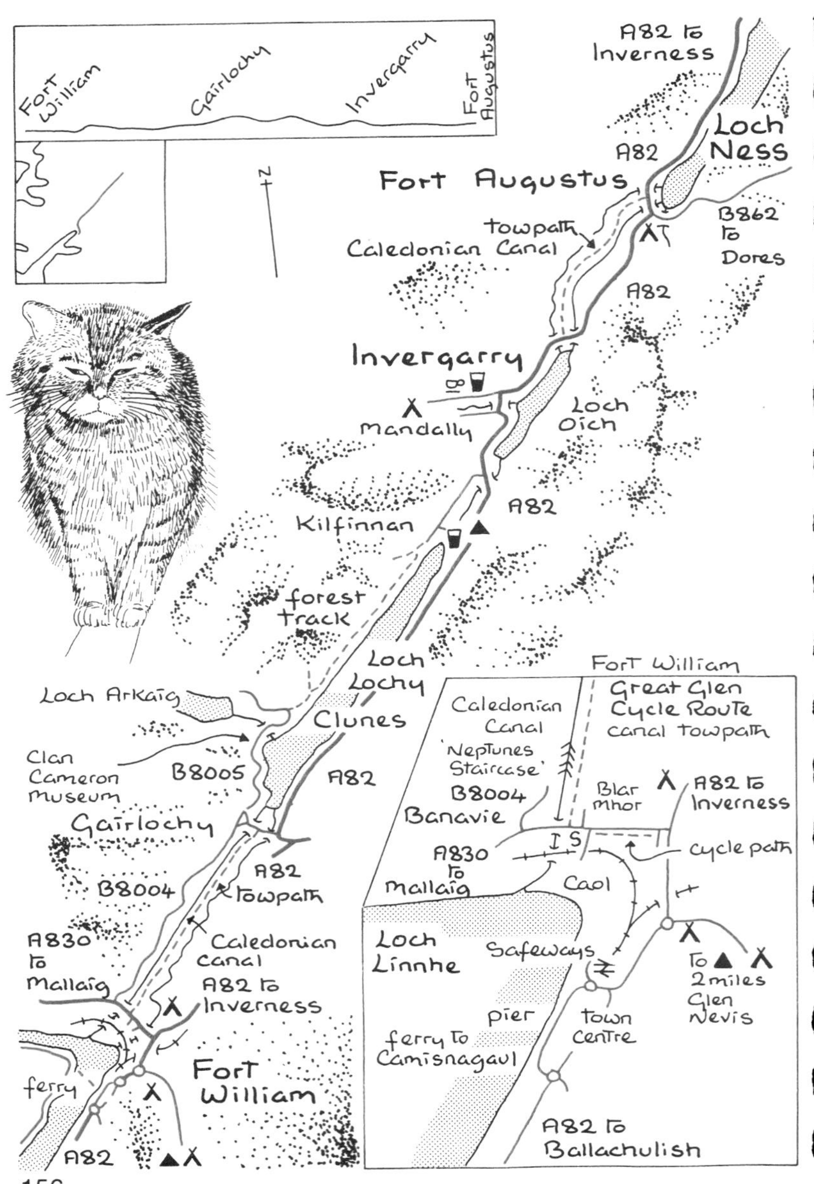

FORT WILLIAM – FORT AUGUSTUS
(The Great Glen) 30 miles

Leaving behind the horrors of Fort William, peace is soon gained on the towpath of the Caledonian Canal, a gentle ride with spectacular views of Ben Nevis and Aonach Mor. From Clunes is a quiet, isolated stretch of forestry road, roughish in parts, with only the sound of the wind for company. The final canal towpath into Fort Augustus is a delight.

Fort William S The original 1655 fort was rebuilt in stone and named Mayburgh after the wife of King William the Third, before being named for the King himself. The fort has since been demolished and the town is a Victorian nightmare. There is the West Highland Museum.

The Great Glen Cycle Route has been waymarked along the Great Glen. The Forestry Commission has exploited this valley for two generations now, and, at minimal cost, have produced a curate's egg of a cycle route. Cyclists deserve better than these mountain-climbing rough roads, eventually dissolving into an apology at the Inverness end.

The Great Glen Road was originally completed in 1727 by General Wade, with garrisons at Fort William, Fort Augustus and Inverness (Fort George), as part of the security measures following the first Jacobite Rebellion in 1715.

The Caledonian Canal was built 1804 to 1822 and financed largely by the government to provide a link between the North Sea and Atlantic for the Royal Navy.

Invergarry Invergarry Castle, seat of the Macdonnells, was burnt by 'Butcher' Cumberland in 1746 for their part in helping Bonnie Prince Charlie.

Fort Augustus S Previously called Kilcumein. After the 1715 Jacobite rising, General Wade made this his HQ, and built the fort in 1729. 'Augustus' was William Augustus, Duke of Cumberland, at that time the fat, eight year old schoolboy son of George the Second, later to become 'Butcher' Cumberland. The ruins became an abbey, then a private school and home to 'The Young Clansman', a 'living' exhibition.

TIC Fort William (01397) 703781
Fort Augustus (01320) 366367
SYHA Loch Lochy (01809) 501239
Accomodation – Fort Augustus Abbey Backpackers Lodge (01320) 366233
Off Beat Bikes, Fort William (01397) 704008

Fort Augustus - Beauly Firth

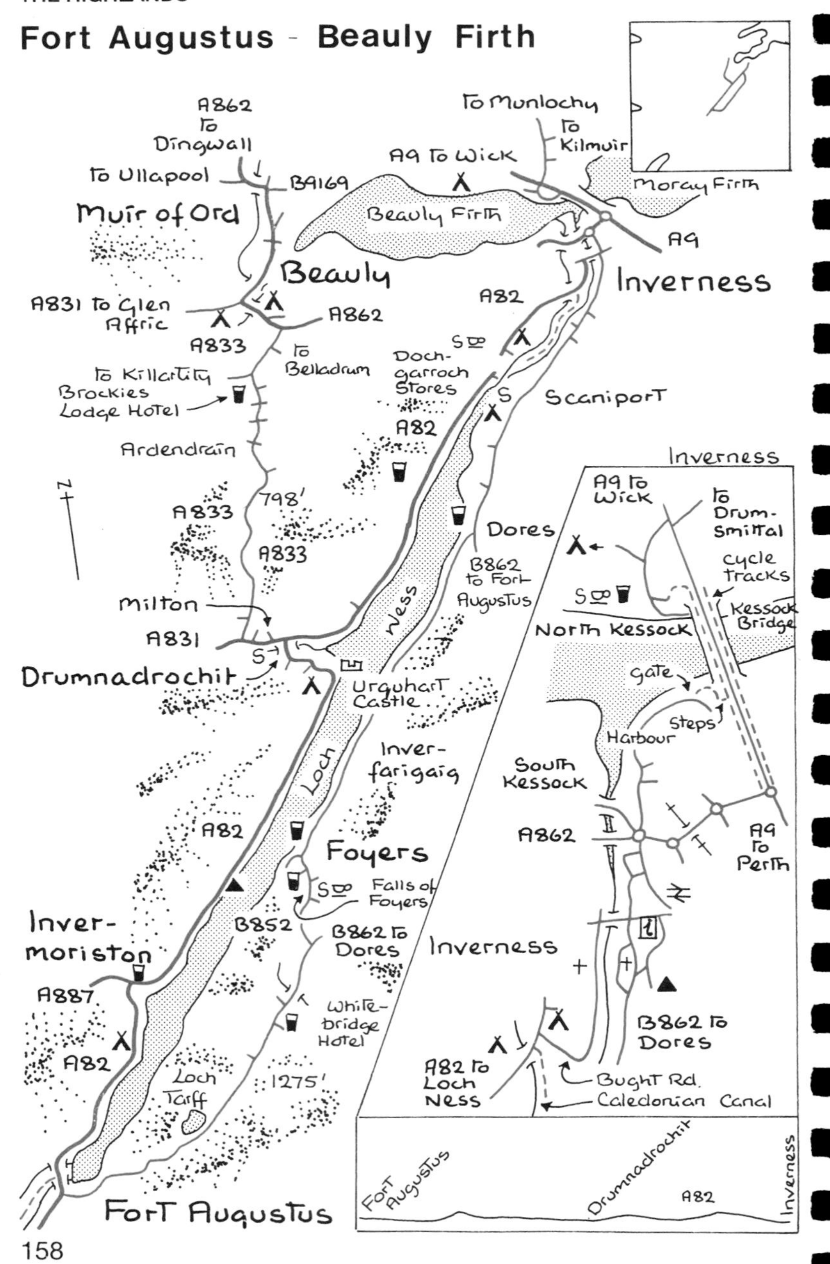

FORT AUGUSTUS – BEAULY FIRTH
(The Great Glen) 33 miles

Having brought you comfortably into the jaws of the Great Glen, you can now choose your poison. The first alternative is the A82 along the length of Loch Ness, relatively flat but humming with overpowered coaches and swaying caravans. The second takes the A82 to Drumnadrochit, then an escape on the A833, a relatively short but very punchy climb. The third disregards the A82 and chooses the excellent minor roads on the eastern side of the loch, but this involves a climb out of Fort Augustus as long as any you've encountered on the whole trip. Car-borne tourists congregate in the valleys. It pays the cyclist to climb to the wonderful country beyond, the wild, open spaces, lovely lochans, bog myrtle and skylarks.

Invermoriston Into these hills fled Bonnie Prince Charlie after his defeat at Culloden in 1746.

Drumnadrochit **S** More than a thousand witnesses have testified to seeing the monster. Check out the Loch Ness Monster Exhibition Centre and Visitor Centre. The loch is the largest freshwater lake, by volume, in Britain.

Urquhart Castle. Built in the 14c, one of the largest in Scotland, but blown up in 1692 to save it from Jacobite hands.

Inverness **S** 'The Capital of the Highlands'. A military stronghold for centuries, though Fort George now lies under Inverness Prison. Inverness Museum and Gallery, the history of the Highlands; St Andrews Cathedral, 1866/69; the Steeple, 1791, formerly the jail steeple; the 'Amazon' Museum Ship, the floating home of Arthur Lowe; Cromwell's Clock Tower, all that remains of his 1652/57 citadel.

TIC Inverness (01463) 234353
North Kessock (01463) 731505
SYHA Loch Ness (01320) 351274
Inverness ()1463) 231771
Accomodation – Foyers House Backpackers Bunkhouse
Loch Ness Backpackers Lodge, Coiltie Farmhouse, East Lewiston, Drumnadrochit (01456) 450807
Inverness Student Hostel, 8 Culduthan Rd (01463) 236556
Glen Cycles (hire) Drumnadrochit (01456) 450554
BI Cycles, Inverness (01463) 715733
Bikes of Inverness (01463) 225965
The Cycle Works (01463) 222522
Wm. Mitchell (01463) 715733
Thornton Cycles (01463) 222810

Beauly Firth - Dornoch

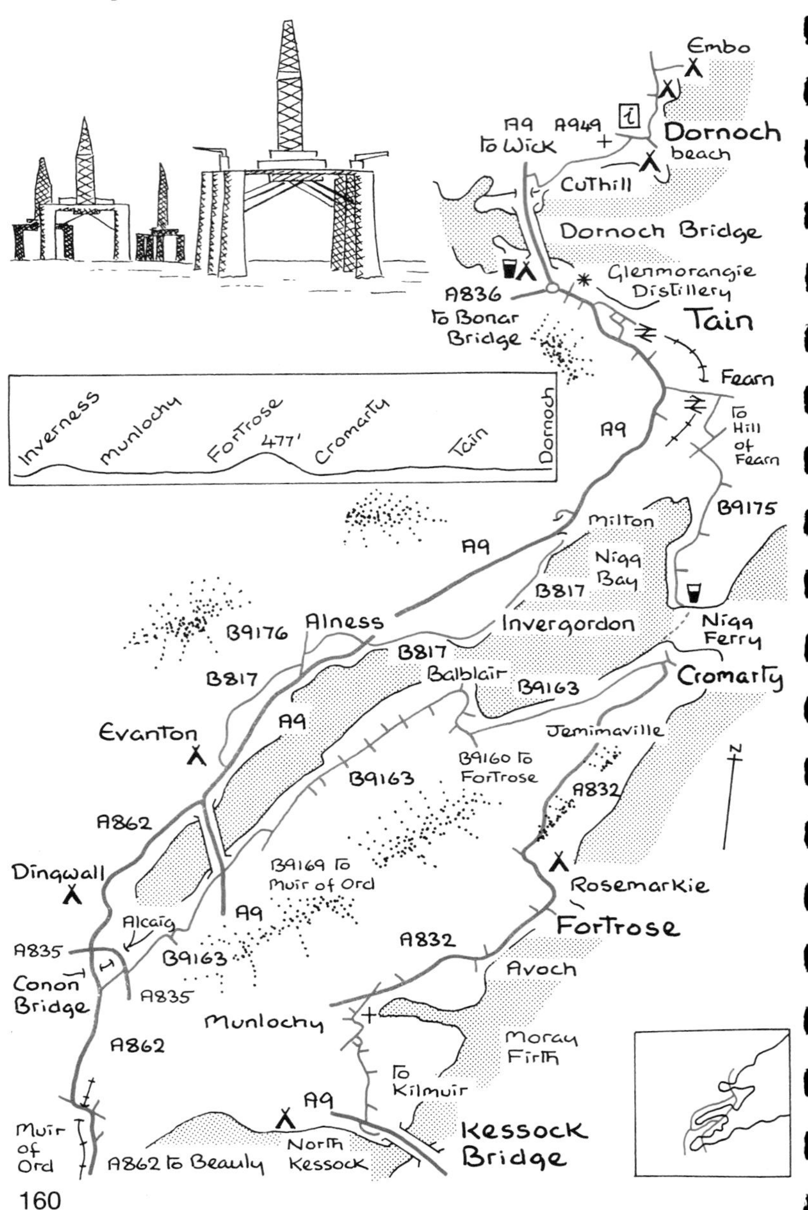

BEAULY FIRTH – DORNOCK

(The Black Isle) 36 miles

Your route choice has already been made. If you're in Inverness, take the eastern coast of the Black Isle to Cromarty. If you're in Beauly take the western coast, the B9163 from Canon Bridge. The one further complication is that both these routes involve the Nigg Ferry. From November to March this ferry doesn't operate, in which case take the busy route via Dingwall, Evanton, Alness and Invergordon.
This is a real change. The brooding Glens are replaced by forestry, 'East Coast' arable farming, oil rigs, gorse and militaristic silo's. It is envigoratingly comfortable cycling.

The Eastern Coast

Munlochy **S** The Clootie Well.

Avoch Heritage Exhibition.

Fortrose **S** A sailors' haven, with Cathedral remains.

Rosemarkie **S** 'The Riviera of the North'. Groam House Museum, an award-winning Pictish Interpretive Centre.

Cromarty **S** A pleasant, friendly little town. The Courthouse is an award-winning museum with animated figures. Hugh Millars Cottage is a small, thatched cottage of 1711, birthplace of the stonemason turned writer. Dolphin Ecosse operate evening, guided, dolphin-watch trips. Beauly, Cromarty and Dornoch Firths have resident populations of seals and otters. The Morary Firth is home to dolphins and whales.

The Western Coast

Beauly **S** Priory ruins.

Muir of Ord **S** Glen Ord Distillery, guided tours.

Balblair Distillery, and Udale Bay a birdwatching mecca.

Nigg Ferry runs every half hour, 9am to 6pm, including Sundays, from 1st April to 31st October.

Tain **S** A smart, well-heeled little town. Scotland's oldest royal burgh has a Tolbooth, Mercat Cross, ecclesiastical ruins, 'Tain through Time' Visitor centre, and the Glenmorangie Distillery.

TIC North Kessock (01463) 731505
Dornoch (01862) 810400

Tain Cycles (01862) 893332
Dryburgh Cycles, Dingwall (01349) 862163
Ken Ross Cycles, Invergordon (01349) 852538

Dornoch - Dunbeath

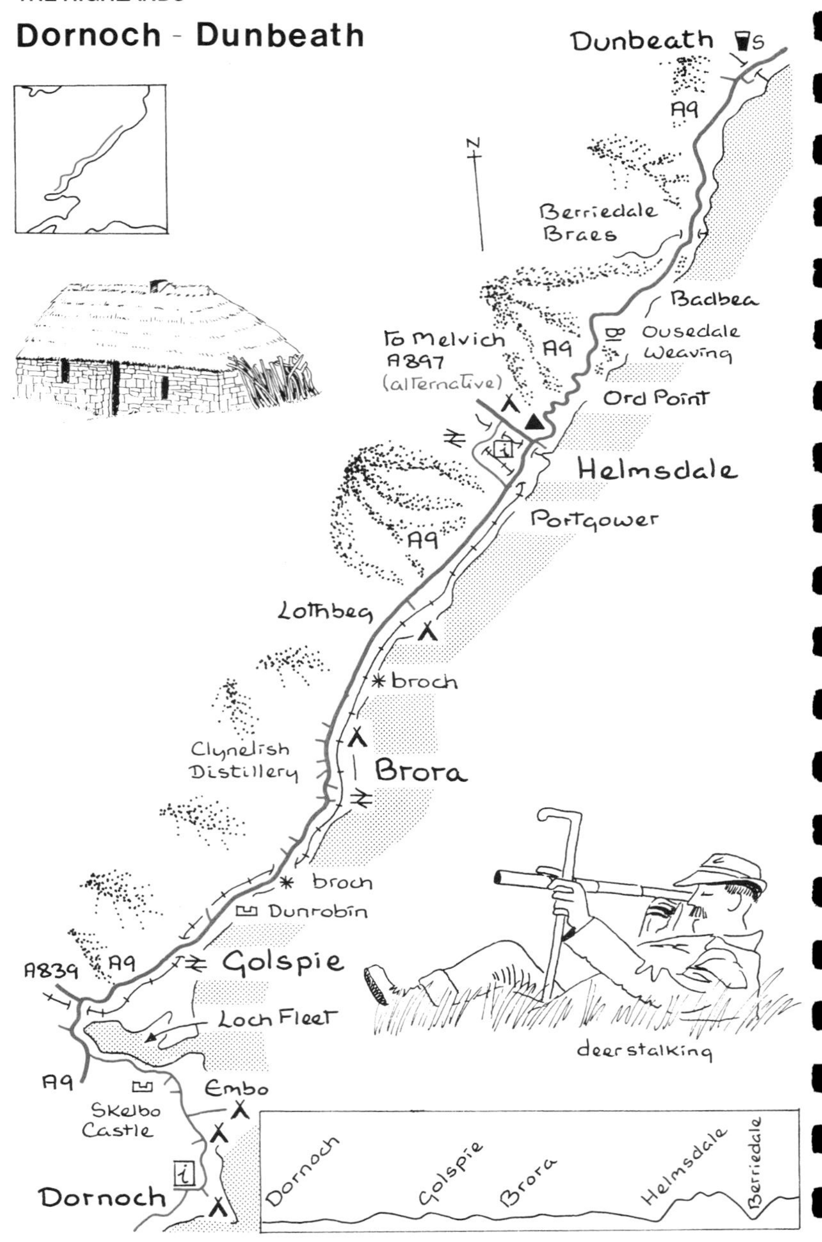

DORNOCK – DUNBEATH 43 miles

The route hugs Loch Fleet for a wonderful few miles, with the mountains of Sutherland ranged to the north, before the A9 is reached. Farms are strewn like boulders in this other-world between sea and mountains. At Helmsdale there is a choice (see pages 166-167).
The reputation of the next section has caused quivering knees among a century of 'End to End' cyclists. The road climbs and twists around the Ord of Caithness, and Berriedale Braes, a wild, high section spattered with stark homes among the derelict cottages, and out in the North Sea, oil rigs.

Dornoch S An unspoiled, charming town with a Cathedral (1224), the Dornoch Craft Centre and Town Jail. A stone marks the site of the burning of the last woman to be judicially executed for witchcraft in Scotland, in 1722.

Skelbo Castle. Emissaries of Edward the First waited here to greet little Princess Margaret, Maid of Norway, whose marriage to Edward's son was to solve the problem of sovereignty in Scotland. She died of sea sickness on the voyage. The present ruins are from the 14c.

Golspie S A planned 19c village. Dunrobin Castle, the turreted, 'over the top', ancestral home of the Earls of Sutherland, is claimed to be Britain's oldest continuously inhabited house.

Carn Liath Broch. A well preserved broch (communal refuge).

Brora S From here the first settlers left for New Zealand following the Clearances. Clynelish Distillery has guided tours. At Lothbeg a stone commemorates the killing of the last known wolf in Sutherland, in 1700.

Helmsdale S A planned fishing settlement built by the Countess of Sutherland. For a while it prospered, with, in 1819, over two thousand inhabitants, but all the commercial ventures failed. The story is told in the Timespan Heritage Centre.

Badbea. Tenants were 'cleared' to this village, which was so steeply situated on the cliff that the children had to be tethered for their own safety.

TIC	Dornoch (01862) 810400
	Helmsdale (01431) 821640
SYHA	Helmsdale (01431) 821577
	Pedal Power, Helmsdale (01431) 821229

Dunbeath - John o'Groats

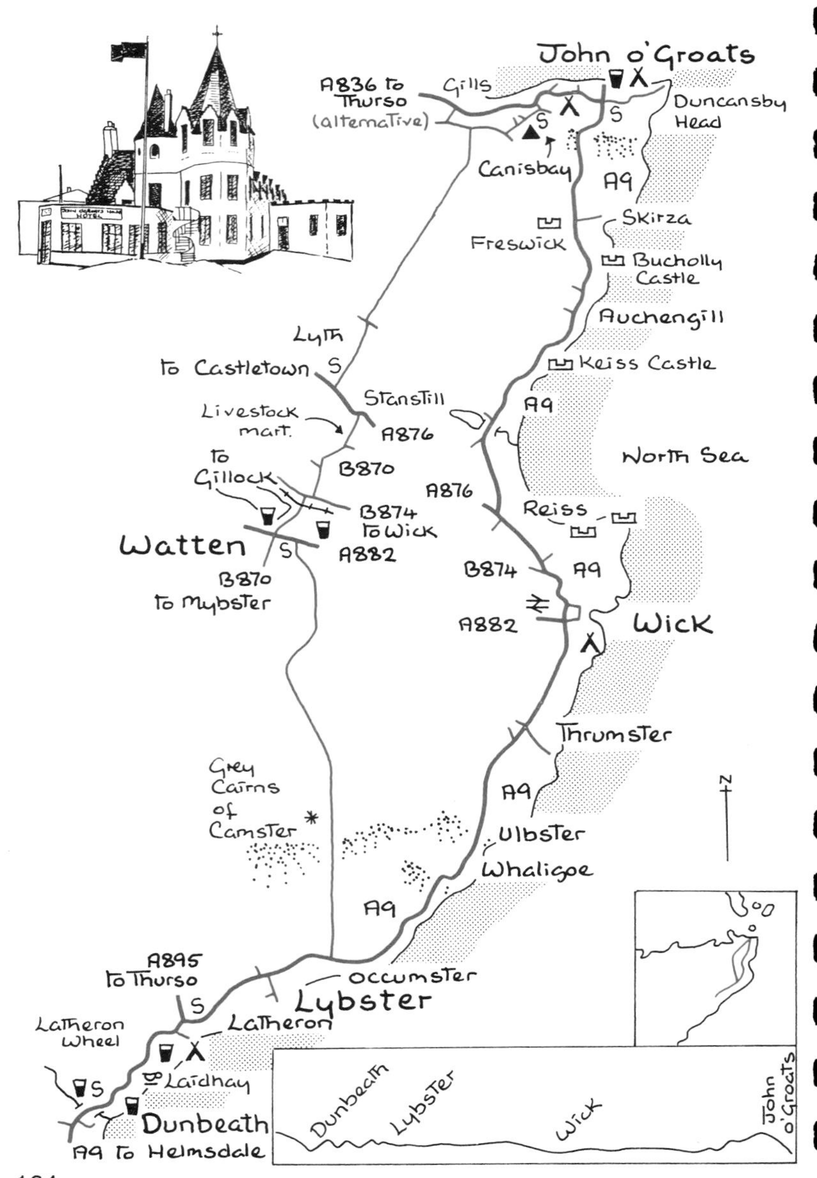

DUNBEATH – JOHN O'GROATS 37 miles

The coastal route continues much as before, with scatterings of spartan, windblasted houses. Enjoyment is tempered by the traffic on the A9, and the temptation to 'get there' is difficult to resist. The 'Watten' route takes the cyclist through blanket bog and sheep country, past smiling, waving people and the atmospheric Grey Cairns. The coast at John O'Groats is splendid, with sea traffic weaving between the offshore islands of Stroma, the Skerries and the Orkneys.

Dunbeath **S** Built 1840/50 to house evicted smallholders. There is a Heritage Centre, and the Lhaidhay Croft Longhouse.

Latheron **S** The Clan Gunn Museum and Heritage Centre

Lybster **S** The harbour and settlement were built by Sir John Sinclair in 1849. The Bayview Hotel contains a pictorial history of the settlement, now much reduced in size and activity.

The Route Choice lies between continued rubber-burning on the A9, via Wick, and very minor roads via Watten.

The Grey Cairns of Camster. Stunning burial chambers, 5,000 years old, in an impressive state of preservation.

Wick **S** The town began as a Viking settlement ('Vik' means 'bay' in Old Norse), but the real boost came in 1824 when Thomas Telford was commissioned by the British Fisheries Society to build Pultneytown Harbour. Wick Heritage Centre tells the whole story.

Auckingill. Northlands Viking Centre covers the Vikings and pre-Viking Caithness.

John O'Groats **S** John O'Groats was Jan de Groot, one of three Dutch brothers who arrived in 1496 at the request of King James the Fourth to run a ferry to the Orkneys. Only a few years before, the Islands had been part of the combined Kingdom of Denmark and Norway, and James was anxious that they should not be so again. Passengers were charged 4d (old pennies), which became known as a 'groat'. The Orkney Islands Ferry and Wildlife Cruises sail from here.

TIC Wick (01955) 602596
John O'Groats (01955) 611373
SYHA John O'Groats (Canisbay) (01955) 611424
Wheels Cycle Shop, Wick (01955) 603636

ALTERNATIVE

Helmsdale - Melvich

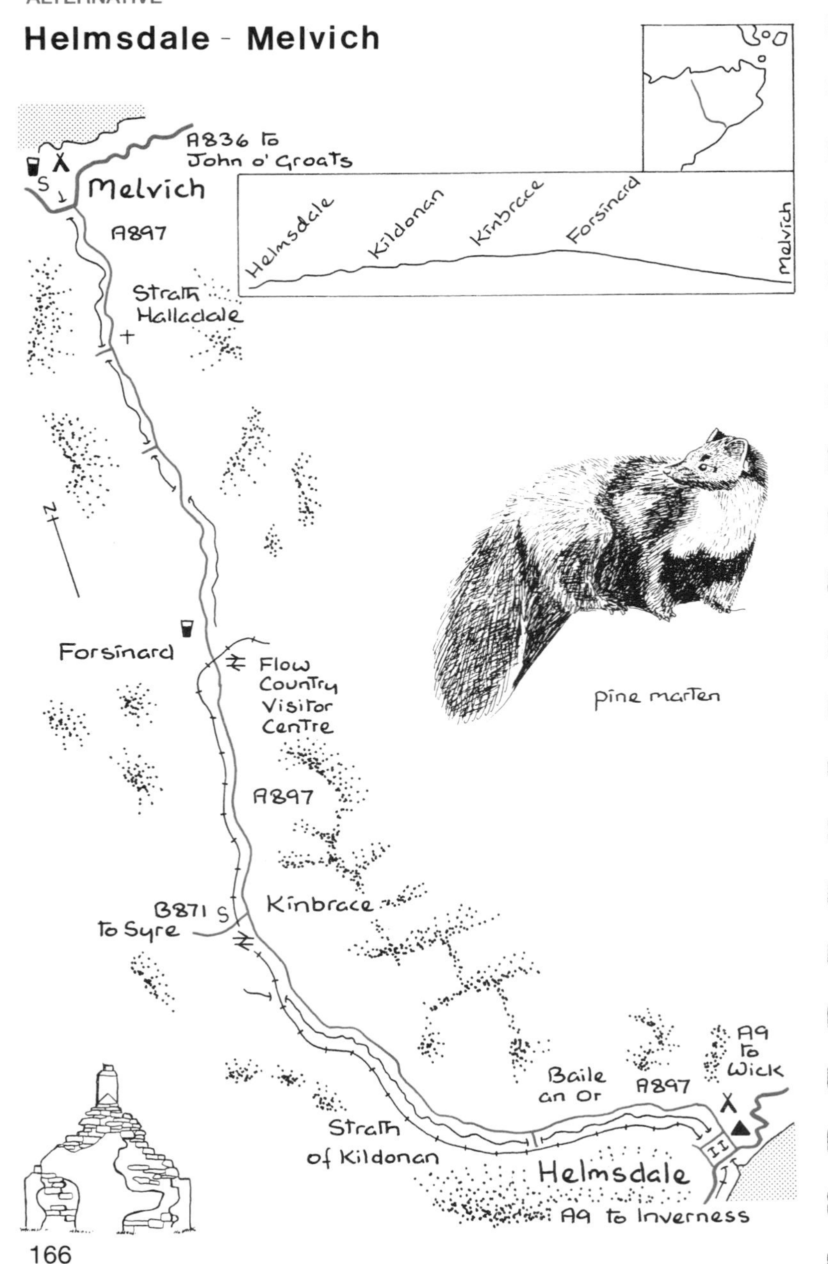

HELMSDALE – MELVICH 40 miles

For the cyclist much depends upon the wind, for this is not an exacting route, but a series of gentle climbs along the full lengths of the Straths of Kildonan and Halladale. Red deer abound and the chances of spotting an eagle good, in possibly, Britain's last remaining, natural landscape.

The Strath of Kildonan. Two thousand years ago this wooded valley was well occupied, and remains can be seen of long cairns, hut circles and brochs.
Two hundred years ago, the eviction of a large number of peasant smallholders to make way for commercial sheep farming is held up as an example of oppression, greed and inhumanity by the landowners. There were mitigating circumstances. By the late 18c the post-1746 peace saw a rising population, but bad weather led to cereal harvest failure and blighted the potato. The Sutherland estate hoped to improve their own income by raising sheep, and that of the tenantry by resettling them along the coast where fish could augment their diet, and they could make textiles. Unfortunately the evictions by the Factor, Patrick Sellar were brutal; the settlements were often not ready; and textiles and fish were in a slump. Many people left for North America and the slums of Glasgow. The parish of Kildonan saw a fall in inhabitants from 1,574 in 1877 to 257 in 1837. The sheep prospered.
1868-70 saw a gold rush, at Baile an Or, with thousands flocking in. Ultimately the landowner, the Duke of Sutherland, made more money than most of the propectors by granting expensive licences, then, when the salmon fishing became disturbed, he called a halt to the panning. Twenty or thirty enthusiasts still pan for gold here each summer, and the river is still one of Scotland's finest for salmon.

The Flow Country. Much of this area is 'flow' or deep, wet peat bog. It is naturally so, having only partially been forested 4,000 years ago during a warm spell (the remains of the Scots pine stumps can still be found). In fact the area is like a giant sponge. Until recently man's influence was limited to cutting peat for fires, stalking, fishing and, during the 1914-18 War the collection of quantities of spagnum for use as wound dressings. The 1970's commercial forestry has had a dramatic effect, and further afforestation is only held at bay by paying landowners not to plant from the public purse. The Flow Country Visitor Centre gives a good account, including information about some of the vast range of Wildlife to watch for. The estate at Forsinard was recently purchased by the RSPB.

ALTERNATIVE

Melvich - John o'Groats

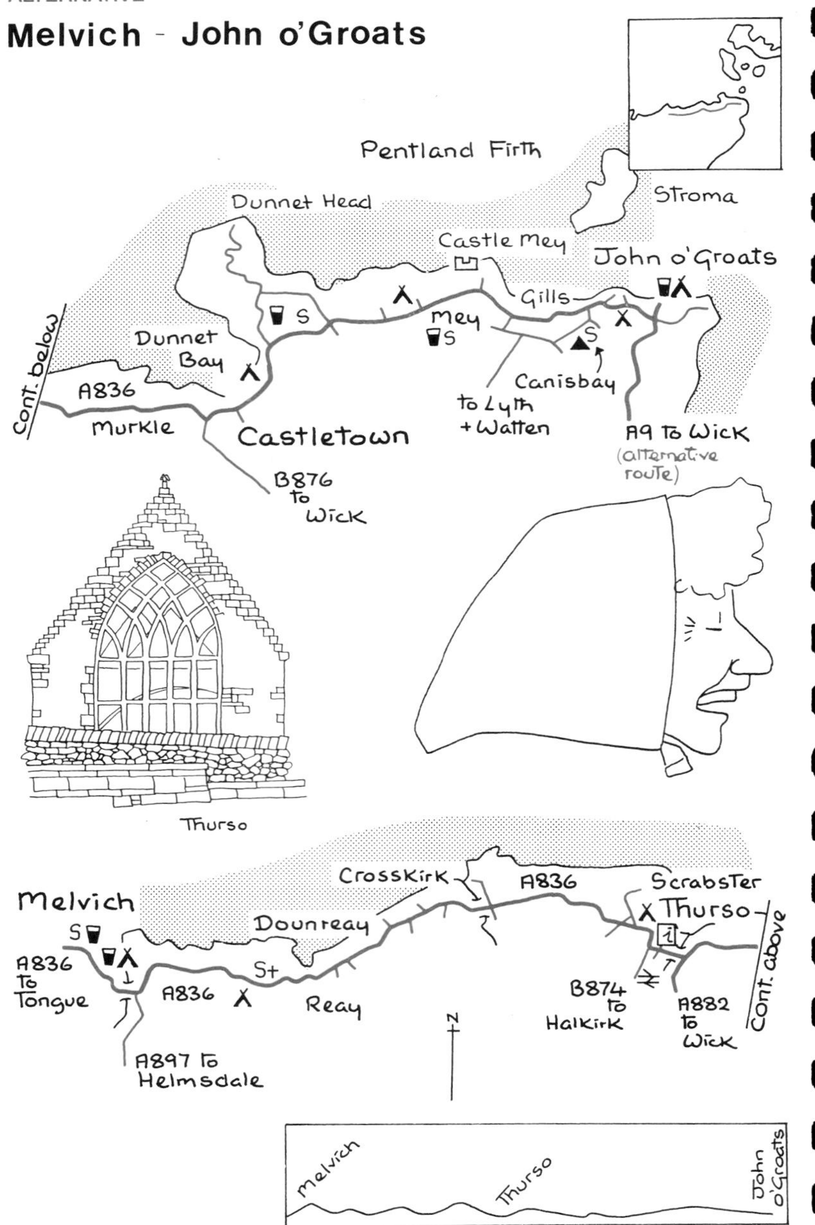

MELVICH – JOHN O'GROATS 39 miles

Straightforward run along the northern coast, through bleak, windlashed farmland, the grey stone, slates and weather setting off the rusting red of generations of farm implements. The people are 'verra verra' friendly, the drifting smell of peat fires delicious, and the accent is a joy to listen to. The prevailing wind is northerly; its precise direction crucial for the cyclist.

Dounreay. The first experimental fast breeder nuclear reactor, built 1954. Still the major local employer though the reactor is being shut down.

Scrabster. The major harbour on this exposed coast. There is also the remnants of the Bishops Castle, 13c home of the Bishops of Caithness.

Thurso **S** From the Middle Ages, an important fishing and trading port to Scandinavia and the Orkneys. Ruins include the 12c/13c church of St Peter, the Victorian castle built on the site of the 17c Castle of the Sinclairs, and Thurso Heritage Museum with its Pictish relics.

Castletown **S** Centre of the flagstone industry. They can be seen forming local walls and roofs, and were also exported all over the world.

Dunnet Head. The lighthouse keepers are the most northerly inhabitants on the British mainland.

Dunnet Hill. Mary Anne's Cottage, owned by the Caithness Heritage Trust, is just as she left it.

Castle of Mey the Queen Mother's private residence.

Stroma. In the 1940's the island had a school with almost fifty pupils, but by 1962 the last permanent family had left. At each ebb tide the great whirlpool, the Swelkie of Stroma, roars off the island.

TIC Thurso (01847) 892371
John O'Groats (01955) 611373
SYHA John O'Groats (Canisbay) (01955) 611424
The Bike and Camping Shop, Thurso (01847) 896124
Leisure Activities, Thurso (01847) 895385

USEFUL ADDRESSES

The Association of Lightweight Campers
11 Grosvenor Place
London SW1 OEY
(0171) 828 1012

British Cycling Federation
16 Upper Woburn Place
London WC1H OQE
(0171) 387 9320

Camping and Caravanning Club Ltd
Greenfields House
Westwood Way
Coventry CV4 8JH
(01203) 694995

Cyclists' Touring Club
Cotterell House
69 Meadrow
Godalming
Surrey GU7 3HS
(01483) 417217

The Lands' End – John O'Groats Association
Sec. Mrs Carol Webb
25 Langdon Way
Corringham
Essex SS17 9DS

Offa's Dyke Association
Offa's Dyke Centre
West Street
Knighton
Powys LD7 1EW
(01547) 528753

Rough Stuff Fellowship
4 Archray Avenue
Callander
Central FK17 8JZ
(01877) 30104

Scottish Youth Hostels Association
National Office
7 Glebe Crescent
Stirling FK8 2JA
(01786) 2821

Youth Hostels Association (England and Wales)
National Office
Trevelyan House
8 St Stephens Hill
St Albans
Herts AL1 2DY
(01727) 55215

Tourist Boards
English Tourist Board
Thames Tower
Black's Road
Hammersmith
London W6 9EL

Scottish Tourist Board
22 Revelston Terrace
Edinburgh EH4 3EU
(0131) 332 2433

Wales Tourist Board
2 Fitzalan Road
Cardiff CF2 1UY
(01222) 227281

West Country Tourist Board
60 St Davids hill
Exeter
Devon EX4 4SY
(01392) 76351

Chepstow Tourist Centre
Bridge Street
Chepstow
Gwent NP6 5EY
(01291) 623772

Heart of England Tourist Board
Woodside
Larkhill
Worcester
WR5 2EF
(01905) 763436

Chester Tourist Centre
Town Hall
Northgate Street
Chester CH1 2HJ
(01244) 317962

North West Tourist Board
Swan House
Swan Meadow Road
Wigan Pier
Wigan
Lancashire WN3 5BB
(01942) 821222

Cumbria Tourist Board
Ashleigh
Holly Road
Windermere
Cumbria LA23 2AQ
(015394) 44444

Dumfries and Galloway Tourist Board
Campbell House
Bankend Road
Dumfries DG1 4TH
(01387) 253862

Ayrshire Tourist Board
Burns House
16 Burns Statue Square
Ayr KA7 1UP
(01292) 288688

Largs Tourist Centre
Promenade
Largs KA30 8BG
(01475) 673765

Isle of Arran Tourist Board
Information Centre
The Pier
Brodick
Isle of Arran KA27 8AU
(01770) 302140

Bute and Cowal Tourist Board
Tourist Information Centre
7 Alexandra Parade
Dunoon
Argyll PA23 8AB
(01369) 703785

Oban, Mull and District Tourist Board
Argyll Square
Oban PA34 4AR
(01631) 563122

Fort William and Lochaber Tourism
Cameron Square
Fort William
Inverness-shire PH33 6AJ
(01397) 703781

Inverness, Loch Ness and Nairn Tourist Board
Castle Wynd
Inverness IV2 3BJ
(01463) 234353

Ross and Cromarty Tourist Board
North Kessock
Black Isle
Ross-shire IV1 1XB
(01463) 731505

Sutherland Tourist Board
The Square
Dornoch
Sutherland IV25 3SD
(01862) 810400

Caithness Tourist Board
Information Centre
Whitechapel Road
Wick
Caithness KW1 4EA
(01955) 602596